The Political Economy
of Russian Oil

The Political Economy of Russian Oil

edited by
David Lane

ROWMAN & LITTLEFIELD PUBLISHERS, INC.
Lanham • Boulder • New York • Toronto • Plymouth, UK

ROWMAN & LITTLEFIELD PUBLISHERS, INC.

Published in the United States of America
by Rowman & Littlefield Publishers, Inc.
A wholly owned subsidiary of The Rowman & Littlefield Publishing Group, Inc.
4501 Forbes Boulevard, Suite 200, Lanham, Maryland 20706
www.rowmanlittlefield.com

Estover Road
Plymouth PL6 7PY
United Kingdom

British Cataloging in Publication Information Available

Library of Congress Cataloging-in-Publication Data

Lane, David Stuart.
    The political economy of Russian oil / edited by David Lane.
        p.   cm.
    Includes bibliographical references and index.
    ISBN 0-8476-9508-5 (alk. paper)—ISBN 0-8476-9509-3 (pbk. :
alk. paper)
    1. Petroleum industry and trade—Political aspects—Russia
(Federation)   2. Petroleum industry and trade—Russia (Federation)
I. Title.
HD9575.R82L36   1999
338.2'7282'0947—dc21   99-15556
                                                        CIP

Printed in the United States of America

♾™ The paper used in this publication meets the minimum requirements of
American National Standard for Information Sciences—Permanence of Paper for
Printed Library Materials, ANSI Z.39.48–1992.

Contents

Acknowledgments

We acknowledge the assistance of the British Economic and Social Research Council, which supported the research of David Lane (Grant no. R 000221716) and also provided support for a conference held at the University of Cambridge on the topic of Russian oil. The following, in addition to those included in this collection, are thanked for their participation in the activities of the conference: Duncan Allan, Gregory Krasnov, Bulent Gokay, Kevin Rosner, Jonathan Stern, Jon Stern, Roy Allison, Marcia Levy, Mario Nuti, Neil Malcolm, Julian Cooper, and Bob Graham.

We acknowledge permission from the Royal Institute for International Affairs (Chatham House, London) to publish a revised version of chapter 2 by Arild Moe and Valery Kryukov, which first appeared as a paper in 1998 under their imprint.

Oil and Gas Regions

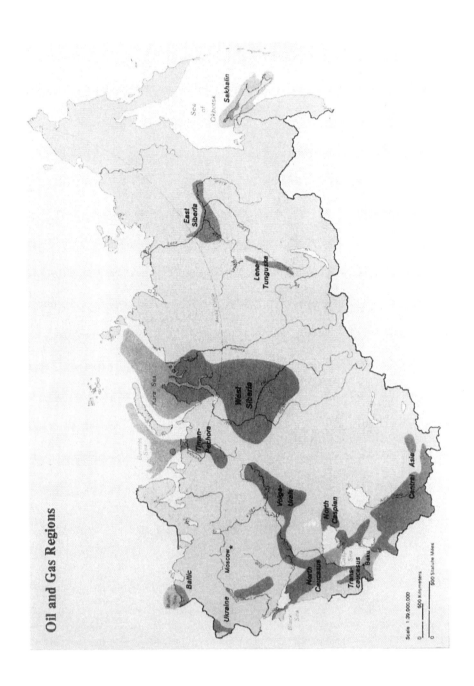

Introduction

David Lane

By 1998 the major changes in the transformation of the Russian economy from state ownership and administrative control to private ownership and market relations had been completed. Unlike many other industries, the oil and gas interests were well placed to benefit from the transition to world market conditions. They were an important industrial asset under Brezhnev and, by the 1970s, centralized state control of industry and pricing led the profits and rents from energy exports to be utilized to maintain economic growth and consumer satisfaction. Oil and gas had become the main source of foreign currency earnings for the country, earnings which were used to finance the increasing import of machinery, equipment, and consumer goods. Within the USSR, prices of fuel and power were as little as 5 percent of world prices, and its COMECON partners received imports at considerably less than the world price level. This low price policy had the effect of subsidizing manufacturing industry as well as domestic consumers, and its imprint is still important. It was (and still is) an important component in maintaining political and social stability. International trade in oil also has important implications for the world role of Russia and its relations with other countries. It may be used as a tool to promote Russian interests as well as a means for foreign interests to exert influence on Russian economic and political policy.

The newly founded companies of the energy complex dominate the economy. In 1997, eight energy-complex companies were among the top ten, in terms of capitalization: Gazprom was first, followed by LUKoil (third), then YuKOS, Surgutneftegaz, Sidanko, Surgutneftegaz (subsidiary), Sibneft, and Slavneft (ninth).[1] Compared to Western companies, in terms of output, Gazprom is the world's largest single energy company, three times the size of Royal Dutch Shell. The other oil companies, however, are smaller than Shell, Exxon, Mobil, BP, Chevron, and Amoco.[2] In terms of earnings, of the

1

top twenty Russian companies, thirteen are in the oil/gas complex, including five of the top six.[3]

The fuel and energy complex is a key sector in the Russian economy. It accounts for 25 percent of the industrial output, 38 percent of the federal budget revenues, and more than 50 percent of the overall value of exports. It absorbs more than a fifth of the total internal investments. As basic industrial inputs, the companies of the fuel and energy complex influence the production costs of other sectors of the economy, and the dynamics of energy prices are an important component in determining price levels and inflation rates.[4] Russia has the second largest proved recoverable oil reserves in the world, second only to Saudi Arabia. Western oil companies and financial institutions seek a way to profit from one of the world's most abundant reserves of oil, and Western governments also have a strategic interest in the price and supply of this major source of energy. Since the move to a market economy, and since privatization of the oil industry in 1993, production of oil has seriously declined: crude oil production fell from 11.3 million barrels per day in 1986 to 7.12 million barrels per day (b/d) in 1993 and to 5.04 in 1996, and refinery output from 3.58 million b/d to 2.62 million b/d between 1993 and 1996. Net oil exports, however, have risen from 3.14 million b/d to 3.43 million b/d between the last two dates.[5] This is an attempt to maintain foreign earnings in the face of the cumulative and steady decline in the late 1990s of the price of oil on the world market: the international price of crude oil fell from $156.7 per metric ton in March 1996 to $98.7 in March 1998.[6]

The fall in the world price of oil was reversed in 1999, in the first quarter of which oil prices rose on average by 15 percent. This was partly a consequence of the world recovery from the Asian financial crisis, but also due to the reduction of supply taken by the OPEC countries. Russia attended meetings of OPEC from March 1998 and in June promised a reduction in output of 4 percent. This did not materialize by August 1998 when Russian oil exports reached their highest ever. The objective of Russian exporters was to compensate for the fall in the world price of oil, which had fallen 30 percent between January and August 1998. In March 1999, OPEC cut production by 7 percent. As part of this policy, Russia reduced production by 5 percent (1998 over 1997 output). In May 1999, the world price of oil recovered and reached $16 per barrel; this peak is unlikely to be sustained and it is expected that the price will fall later in 1999 to $13.3. Even this, however, is a considerable rise compared to the January 1999 price of $9.55.

The oil and gas companies have been the most successful Russian companies in the process of the transformation to capitalism. Oil and gas is an export-oriented industry and is able to compete relatively successfully in the global economy. What runs behind the political claims for the free market advocated by the companies of the oil and gas sector, and for greater government intervention and protection by manufacturing and agriculture, is that oil and gas is able to profit from international free trade whereas manufacturing and agriculture suffer from it. Because oil is a natural resource capable of earning considerable economic rents, control of Russian oil is contested. On the world stage, the resources of Russia make foreigners important actors in Russia as investors and purchasers of energy.

In this book, an attempt is made to provide a scholarly account of the development of the Russian oil industry under the Yeltsin administration. In the first chapter, David Lane and Iskander Seifulmulukov consider the ways in which the oil industry has relatively successfully adapted to a world market economy. In chapter 2, Valery Kryukov and Arild Moe outline the growing importance of the role of the banks and financial institutions in the context of world markets. In the third chapter, David Lane examines the social and economic origins of the oil industry's leaders; he highlights divisions within the industry between management and financial interests and disagreements within the ruling political apparatus about the extent and type of regulation and control.

As oil is a natural resource capable of earning considerable economic rents, the quest for control of Russian oil is a site of contest, not only between senior oil management in place since the Soviet period and the reformist liberal government (which itself has internal divisions), but also between the regions and republics of the Russian Federation, the federal government, and political interests represented in the Russian Parliament. (See chapters 5 and 6.)

The resources of Russia make foreigners important actors there, as well as providing the country with important economic assets in its own foreign policy. (See chapters 7 and 8.) As Peter Rutland puts it in chapter 7, Russia faces challenges at three points of the compass: to the west, there is the challenge of securing transport routes through unstable and potentially hostile states; to the south, there is the challenge of the new oil states of the Caspian basin; and to the east, the proximity of Russia's oil deposits to East Asia provides an incentive for development. Russian oil, therefore, has to be analyzed in a global perspective as well as a domestic one. This position is stressed in the chapter by Jean-Christophe Peuch, who emphasizes the way in which oil is utilized as a strategic weapon of foreign policy.

While the structures and process of state socialism have left an imprint, the principal political contest is between different interests over the type of market economy and the relative role of different political and economic institutions—the state, investors, management, and financial (including foreign) interests. The Russian oil industry has to be analyzed in the context of the international, regional, and sectoral interests that seek to influence the government.

Compared to other industries, oil has made a relatively successful transition to a market economy. However, it is confronted with serious internal problems of price and investment policy with respect to the wider economy. There are significant differences of interest between management, financial interests, and political interests, and these provide the themes for the chapter by Valery Kryukov and Arild Moe. They consider the role of the banking sector and its intrusion into the oil industry, and the linkages and strategic alliances between oil and banking companies and the implications for foreign trade and investment. They, together with other authors, point to the declining role of the state as a regulator and to the rise of bank-finance capital, which they contend will lead to greater foreign investment. David Lane's study of the social composition of the banking and oil elites (chapter 3) indicates a considerable difference in origin, education, and probable orientation between the two groups. The traditional oil elite is more a reproduction of the (middle) industrial executives of the former oil industry, whereas the banking elite contains more people from the Soviet administration and new people—probably with more market orientation—from outside the apparatuses of power.

A theme that surfaces in many chapters is that internal political interests have their roots in the structures and values inherited from state socialism. The evolution of the contemporary Russian oil industry has been, in current political science terms, "path dependent." But it is more than that, as market and international forces bring their own influence to bear on the formation of the economy.

The internal components of change are highlighted in chapter 4 by Heiko Pleines, who emphasizes the inheritance of various forms of corruption from the Soviet economy. In the early stages of the transition to capitalism, the great difference between the price of internally marketed oil and the world price led to great opportunities for individual profit by oil executives. These developments have to be analyzed in the context of the chaotic fashion in which the Russian economy rushed into capitalism and the insecure nature of the transfer of ownership in the early period. In the more mature form of capitalism, profits may be made legally and enforced by law, and corruption and criminality decline. The criminalization and corruption of the economy was not only due to the opportunities to extract rents in the oil industry, but also to the instability of property ownership and to the lack of confidence of the possessing classes in the political order. These views are made explicit in the interviews with oil executives outlined by David Lane in chapter 3.

The contributors bring out the conflicting interests of the center and the periphery. With the dissolution of the Soviet ministries in 1990–91 and the shift of control from the USSR to the republics and regions, a spontaneous process of privatization began. Enterprises and organs of local administration together began to form independent companies. The management of the local enterprises, as well as leaders of the local administrations, took over assets in the oil industry. The new political structures, however, were weak, and management, being in control of productive assets, was strongly positioned to act in its own interests in production, refining, and sales. In 1991, the All-Union ministries of the USSR were liquidated and a single Ministry of Fuel and Energy of the Russian Federation was formed (Mintop: Ministerstvo topliva i energetiki RF). But its activity was confined to the legal and general regulation of the fuel and power complex, and it had no direct control over production activities. It became a channel between government and industry. Perhaps even more important is the fact that institutional reforms were not imposed from the top, but developed with participation from the executives of the oil industry including those in the local enterprises themselves. This was the basis on which the corruption described by Heiko Pleines occurred.

This situation is also the cause of a major structural conflict between the center and the localities where the oil is located. (See map.) Bruce Kellison in chapter 5 emphasizes the role of Moscow versus the provinces. The interests of the center are articulated by the Ministry of Fuel and Energy (Mintop) and the presidential administration. Mintop performs two roles: as an organ of state supervision, and as an advocate of the interests of the complex. At different stages of Mintop's existence the relative importance of these two roles has varied. Its advocacy role, however, has often overshadowed its supervisory one. Its first head, Vladimir Lopukhin, acted largely as an agent of the reform strategy of the government. An economist by education and a supporter of radical reforms in the oil/gas industry, he failed to transform the oil sector to his policy preferences. In January 1993, Yuri Shafranik became the head of Mintop. Unlike Lopukhin's, Shafranik's whole career had been tied to the oil industry. In the 1980s, he was a general director of Langepasneftegaz, then chairman of the Tiumen Regional Council and the head of Tiumen Region. In the first two years of his leadership, Shafranik and his office acted in the interests of the fuel and power complex and especially in those of the oil industry. It was largely due to Shafranik's efforts that almost all the Russian oil companies in 1993–94 received considerable advantages in terms of exporting oil. Shafranik became an active supporter of a reduction of the tax burden on the complex. He consistently defended the peculiarities of restructuring and privatization in the fuel and power industries against attacks by Goskomimushchestvo (GKI—Gosudarstvenny komitet po upravleniyu gosudarstvennym imushchestom RF) and the Anti-Monopoly Committee (GKAP—Gosudarstvenny komitet po antimonopol'noy politike RF). The Ministry of Fuel and Energy had its own agenda—to maintain its supervisory functions—and should not be considered simply a conduit for the oil and gas companies. It is in this respect that the Ministry, as well as the companies, has come into conflict with interests in the localities as detailed in the chapters by Bruce Kellison and Peter Glatter.

However, as Kellison points out, the "center" is not a unitary bloc. We can distinguish ten major areas of influence which may impact on decision-making on the oil industry.[7] Decision-making is "pluralistic." There are five areas internal to the state apparatus and five external clusters. First, within the government apparatus, is the Ministry of Fuel and Energy (Mintop); second we have the processing and manufacturing groupings—consumers of energy—consisting of industrial ministers (often headed by one of the first vice prime ministers). Third is the "macro-economic bloc": this involves the liberal reform ministries and committees that steer the economy to a market economy—consisting principally of the Ministries of Economics and Finance, GKI (the privatization committee) and GKAP (the anti-monopoly committee). Fourth, there are other ministries whose policies are affected by issues of energy: important here are the Ministry of Foreign Affairs and the ministries of the armed forces. Fifth we have President Yeltsin and his *apparat*; they play a key role in interest aggregation.

Constituencies external to the formal governing apparatus include the following: first, committees of the Duma and leaders of the republics and regions (governors); second, the Duma itself as a forum for deputies; third, financial and economic interests; fourth, international financial institutions and companies, particularly the IMF; and fifth, other Russian companies and political parties. The policy of the state in relation to the energy complex is formed as a result of the interaction of these political forces.

One might generalize that the policy of Mintop is to maximize output of oil and to seek greater control for itself of prices, investors, and investments. It has sought to obtain a greater share of state ownership, and here it comes into conflict with other parts of the government and the president's apparatus. It distances itself from the oil companies over free market pricing and is prone to support policies that it sees as being in the general interest of the economy—such as subsidies for other industries and penalties for non-payment of taxes by oil producers. The role of the oil companies in using Mintop to express their views depends on the issue and has changed over time. As privatization matures and the companies become stronger, the trend is for them to become more independent: they conduct business with financial interests and foreign companies, and they affect political policy directly through contact with the president's office or indirectly through political groups.

Because the fuel and power sector is a major resource affecting tax income, cost of living, and manufacturing, many government departments and ministries have an interest in the sector. There is a powerful Fuel Administration of the Ministry of Economy. Overseeing the development of different industrial sectors is the Ministry of Industry (dealing mostly with the processing industry, including chemical engineering and the manufacture of equipment for the fuel and power industries). Financial issues relating to different industries are dealt with in special sections of the Industrial Department of the Ministry of Finance. Departments in the Ministry of Science deal with the coordination of scientific and technological progress.[8]

The ministries and committees seeking a free market policy include Finance, Economy, the State Committee for the Administration of State Property (Goskomimushchestvo—GKI), and the State Committee on Anti-Monopoly Policy (GKAP). Generally, these interests support an anti-inflationary monetary policy and their views usually coincide with those of the IMF: they support a minimal state role in the economy, open market pricing, and priority for financial stabilization, competition and privatization of assets, free movement of capital, and Western involvement. In some respects, these policies coincide with the interests of the oil elites, but in others they do not. These ministries have certainly been more influential than the industrial ministries.

On the other side seeking protection for particular interests that are consumers of fuel are ministries and committees associated with production and consumers. Ministries associated with the military industrial complex are important here, as are those concerned with social welfare. These ministries seek low-priced fuel to keep down costs. The Foreign and Defence Ministries are also concerned with the strategic aspects of fuel. Price levels, the enforcement (or non-enforcement) of debt repayments by foreigners, the threat to national security of foreign ownership and company alliances, and financial dependence probably influence these ministries to support "protectionalism" and oppose a free market policy. Apparatuses concerned with state security also have an interest with respect to financial dependency and crime—particularly money laundering, illicit sales of products and assets,[9] and private ("mafia") policing of such processes. The energy complex itself needs investment in order to function and develop and favors a high-price policy and foreign investment.

The president is a crucial determinant in the aggregation of interests. His task is to reconcile a number of contradictory policies: to balance the interests of the energy-producing and the consuming industries, to provide sufficient tax income from the energy sector in order to finance the public sector, to hold levels of inflation, to stimulate competition through the market, to utilize oil as a strategic resource in foreign policy, and to take account of foreign political and economic interests. Yeltsin has often been inconsistent, though generally he has sided with the liberal reformers and has conformed to the free market policy of the IMF. The president is also confronted by internal political interests, particularly in the Duma. It is here that the interests of the localities where the oil is located are articulated. Pete Glatter in chapter 6 discusses the formation of local elites and their relative weakness against the dominant powers located at the center.

However, in conditions of the collapse of the national economy, the demands of the localities themselves are increasingly pronounced, and they call for greater power to be ceded to them. This point is discussed in chapter 5 by Bruce Kellison. Regional oil interests may come into conflict not only with the banking groups, described by Moe and Kryukov in chapter 2, but also with other regional interests. The members of the Russian Parliament (the Duma) generally advocate strengthening of state control of the oil and gas sector, and a massive redistribution of resources from these industries to those unable to withstand competition (processing and agriculture) and to support social welfare. Their programs include the restoration of the state monopoly of the export of oil, plus gas and oil derivatives, and the maintenance of state property through government ownership of shares in the energy complex. In the past the left-wing opposition opposed privatization and insisted on annulling the loans-for-shares auctions. There are also calls for the renationalization of the oil companies and the formation of a national state-led oil company.

The nationalist-communist-agrarian faction advocates the regulation of prices for energy and their maintenance at levels much lower than world ones. It supports the transfer of the tax burden to the energy complex, and the use of rents and profits from the oil/gas industries to support domestic industries. It seeks to limit the access of foreign investors to the strategic sectors of the economy, particularly in the energy sector (the left opposition has blocked the introduction of a production-sharing law in a form that would have been acceptable both to foreign investors and to the Russian oil companies)—though in 1999 the Duma agreed to the proposals of Premier Primakov. This type of opposition helps explain why the oil/gas elite has unequivocally supported Yeltsin and his administration.

In the upper house of the Russian Parliament, the Council of the Federation, where representatives of the regions sit, the interests of the fuel and power complex are again in the minority. Most of the Russian regions lack energy resources, and their enterprises and community services as a rule are not able to pay the rising prices of fuel and power. They therefore support regulation of fuel prices. They oppose any movement to independence or secession by the oil-rich regions.

In the final section of the book, we turn to consider the international dimension of the Russian oil industry. In postcommunist Russia, industries vary greatly in their capacity to adapt to market conditions, particularly when exposure to global competition is taken into account. As a consequence of marketization, the industries dealing with energy and raw materials (metals) on the whole have adapted to the world market whereas manufacturing and agriculture have not. The adoption of a free market policy by the oil and gas industries, for instance, by raising internal prices to the world level, would be detrimental (at least in the short run) to manufacturing and agriculture, and would severely depress production serving the home market and domestic consumers. Russia is not Kuwait: it is a major world power with a comprehensive industrial economy, a major military capacity, and a highly educated and urban population. The weakness of the Russian economy impacts on the politics of Russian oil; should it adopt a market policy internally, there would be unacceptable political and social costs.

Both Jean-Christophe Peuch and Peter Rutland consider the international dimension. Peter Rutland provides an analysis of the countries of the former USSR that have oil deposits: the Caspian countries and those in central Asia, as well as those through which oil passes en route to international markets. He points not only to the dependence of Russia on countries to the west to export its oil, but also to these countries' reliance on Russia for energy supplies. He also suggests that the landlocked central Asian and Caspian countries (at least at present) are dependent on Russia for the export of their oil. He argues that Russian policy toward Kazakhstan is driven by Russia's dominant oil companies: LUKoil, Sidanko, and Transneft. In the context of the complex tangle of pipeline politics, he shows, with the example of Chechnya, how neighboring countries may have a veto effect over Russian interests. Pipeline politics, through, for example, the Azeri-Turkish partnership, also directly involve NATO and American interests. Some Western groups seek, through strategic alliances, to strengthen the Caspian states as a bulwark against Russian (and Iranian) influence. The United States' policy of sanctions against Iran also impacts on Russian deals with Iran—an alliance between Russia and Iran would contest American hegemony in the region.

The study of the oil industry illustrates the nature of the Russian economy and polity in transition. As a prerequisite to the understanding of this transition, one needs to conceptualize the phenomenon. Peter Rutland in his chapter suggests paradigms by which geopolitical commitments may be analyzed: Kuwaitization, liberalization, rent-seeking, a "Russian bear" paradigm, and a pluralistic school. He suggests that policy toward the "near abroad" is opportunistic and negative rather than strategic and positive, but that there is a strong "*potential* for the emergence of a neoimperialist strategy that suits both the oil companies and the 'power ministries.'" He considers that the oil companies and the central interests have a common interest here. Jean-Christophe Peuch develops this view but goes further by arguing that the oil companies are the government's foreign-policy agents.

My own view is an extension of the pluralist model described by Rutland. The picture he describes as "pluralistic" is one of "fragmentation and confusion," characterized by a "chaotic free-for-all." This view is substantiated in the interviews reported in chapter 3 by David Lane, in which he asks oil executives and politicians who has influence over economic policy. As a social system, however, I would define the Russian form of transition as one of "chaotic capitalism." This I define as a social and economic system in which private ownership and production for the market is dominant but one that lacks coordination: goals, law, governing institutions, and economic life lack cohesion. Its characteristics are elite disunity, the absence of a mediating class system, criminalization and corruption, inadequate political interest articulation, and an economy characterized by decline, inflation, and unemployment.[10] There is no clear compact between the elites concerning the extent of state regulation and market competition. But in the wider context of political and economic interests we may yet see a revival and strengthening of the state. Even a deregulated, privatized oil industry is subject to political intervention—as the history of the Middle East bears witness. It seems unlikely that the federal government will retake a controlling interest in the major oil companies. Not only is the Russian "state" divided between federal and regional bodies, but also external interests—Western governments and international agencies—are likely to be influential players and, at least in the foreseeable future, will demand a privatized and open economy. An alternative scenario is that outlined by Jean-Christophe Peuch in the final chapter: essentially he envisages a revitalized hegemonic Russian state pursuing a more traditional policy. Internally, this would involve a constellation of political interests of the dominant groups in the Duma, allied with industries and their ministries operating principally for the domestic market. Such an alliance would also work against secessionist tendencies in the oil regions, highlighted by Kellison and Glatter. But in opposition to any such alliance are the currently relatively successful export industries, such as oil, which are associated with radical market reformers and external powers, such as the IMF. I agree with Peter Rutland that at the macro level there is a *potential* for politicians in control of ministries and the economy, and particularly the president, to gain greater control and probably to move toward a self-generating form of capitalism with energy industries at its center. Such a scenario would not fit the interests of the dominant export-oriented Russian oil corporations, whose interests are more in line with a Kuwaitization policy. Clearly, the economic and political elites are far from achieving a consensus or pact about the kind of policy that Russia should follow. Until that is achieved, instability will characterize policy. A key factor is the presidency because the political sphere is a major determinant of economic policy. Further internal dislocation and a new nationalist or Communist president could well turn the country in the direction of a more corporate state capitalism.

NOTES

1. In spring 1998, the merger of YuKOS and Sibneft into Yuksi was announced; this would have been a larger company than LUKoil. However, in May 1998, no agreement was reached between the firms, and the merger did not take place.

2. A quarter of the output of Shell. *Economist*, 24 January 1998, p. 68.

3. *Ekspert*, no. 38, 6 October 1997.

4. *Sotsial'no-ekonomicheskoe polozhenie Rossii*, no. 12 (Moscow: Goskomstat RF, 1995).

5. World Energy Analysis and Forecasting Group, cited by Eugene M. Khartukov, *Oil and Gas Journal*, 18 August 1997. p. 39.

6. Kortes Information Agency, cited by Eugene M. Khartukov, "Low Oil Prices, Economic Woes Threaten Russian Oil Exports," *Oil and Gas Journal*, 8 June 1998, p. 25.

7. This section draws on my article, "The Political Economy of Russian Oil," in Peter Rutland, ed., "The Political Economy of Post-Communist Russia: From 'Chaotic' to Cooperative Capitalism?" To be published in Peter Rutland, ed., *Economic Change in Post-Soviet Russia* (Westview Press, 1999).

8. The development of contacts with the countries of the Commonwealth of Independent States (SNG) is undertaken by the Ministry of Foreign Economic Contacts (MVES). The collection and use of geological information and the granting of licenses for deep extraction are carried out by the Ministry of Natural Resources.

9. Capital flight has been estimated to total $10–15 billion per annum. *Finansovye izvestiia*, 22 April 1997. Cited by Peter Rutland, "Lost Opportunities: Energy and Politics in Russia," in *National Bureau of Asian Research*, vol. 8, no. 5, Washington, D.C., 1997.

10. David Lane, "Poltical Economy of Russian Oil," in Peter Rutland, *Economic Change*.

Part 1

The Evolution of the Post-Soviet Russian Oil Industry

1

Structure and Ownership

David Lane and Iskander Seifulmulukov

The transition from state socialism to capitalism has led to much speculation concerning the structure and process of the emerging countries in central and eastern Europe. Corporatism, "wild capitalism," "crony capitalism," state capitalism, "Latin American capitalism," authoritarian statism, and even reformed state socialism are terms which have been used to describe the evolving economic formation or to predict its future course. Many generalizations are based on secondhand, anecdotal, and even speculative evidence. In this chapter, we outline the evolution of the structure of the postcommunist Russian oil industry from the administrative units of the USSR, then we describe the different types of oil companies and the emerging forms of ownership and control. The chapter is based on published data on the structure of companies and on interviews with sixty-five oil executives. In the conclusions, we make some generalizations about the implications for the political economy of transition and about the development of Russian capitalism. Appended to part 1 is a profile of four major vertically integrated companies.

THE STRUCTURE OF THE OIL INDUSTRY UNDER STATE SOCIALISM

Under state socialism, the fuel and energy complex, like other branches of the economy, was characterized by state ownership and formal control of production, processing, transportation, and distribution of energy; there was a state monopoly of exports, with administered prices and centralized investments. While many accounts of state socialism assume a monolithic, centrally administered form of administration, there was no single hub controlling the oil and gas industries, which were horizontally organized with extraction, production, refining, and distribution of oil products coming under different ministries. Extraction came under Minnefteprom, refineries

15

under Minneftekhimprom, distribution under Gossnab, and export was controlled by Soyuzneft ekhsport—a division of the Ministry of Foreign Trade. Exploration and exploitation of mineral resources came under three ministries (Geology, Minnefteprom, and Mingazprom). Also linked to the oil and gas complex were ministries of oil and gas equipment and building.

The strategic decisions were made centrally by the appropriate ministry, and production and regional institutions had little control over investment, prices, exports, and output. In the early 1980s, a Bureau for Fuel and Energy was formed within the Soviet government, which coordinated the policies of the various ministries. At the level of oil production, moreover, production associations (PAs) were formed, into which were brought extraction units and other associated production plants, such as oil exploration and transport. Refineries were independent of oil production associations and were subordinate to the Ministry of Petrochemical Industry (Minneftekhimprom). The domestic oil products distribution network was organized on a regional basis and included oil storage facilities and filling stations.

One might conceive of the industrial structure being made up of a heterogeneous set of units each with its own economic (and political) interests—all with different outlooks and agendas. The Soviet bureaucratic structure, then, was not a simple, centrally arranged hierarchy but a number of different hierarchies in which horizontally linked economic units, with considerable administrative control over production at the enterprise level, were formed in the regions.

THE OIL INDUSTRY AFTER THE COLLAPSE OF THE USSR

Following the collapse of the USSR, a radical restructuring of the oil and gas industry took place. Given the strategic and dominant role of the fuel and energy complex, a shift to a market type economy involved a considerable number of problems: the sale of its assets, the control and liberalization of its price structure, the receipt of tax revenues, and the international effects of its exports, as well as the internal impact of the global financial system. In 1991, the All-Union ministries of the USSR were liquidated and a single Ministry of Fuel and Energy of the Russian Federation was formed (Mintop—Ministerstvo topliva i energetiki RF). Its activity was confined to the legal and general regulation of the fuel and energy complex, and it had no direct control over production activities. As in the economy as a whole, firms, corporations, and associations took over the administrative functions of the previous ministries. The production associations in the fuel and energy sector (PAs) became important actors in this process.[1]

The Rosneftegaz association was constituted in 1991. From the outset, however, Rosneftegaz did not have a structure or powers analogous to the unitary hierarchy of Gazprom. Rosneftegaz was an amorphous and ineffective association (*ob'edinenie*) formed by voluntary agreement between forty-seven regional oil extraction units. Its administration was not formed from the top, as was the case with Gazprom, but was elected by the regional production units.

The component parts of Rosneftegaz also sought their own economic independence. Of great political and economic importance was that with the breakdown of the USSR and its forms of central control, the various parts of the oil industry asserted their own narrowly conceived autonomy. From the autumn of 1991, a spontaneous process of privatization began. Enterprises and organs of local administration together began to form independent companies. The management of the local companies, as well as leaders of the local administrations, took over assets in the oil industry. This was a time when, to assure political legitimacy, the old administrative institutions associated with state socialism were being destroyed, and the regions and localities were asserting their own sovereignty. The regions' and localities' political power, however, was weak, and management, being in control of productive assets, was strongly positioned to act in its own interest over production, refining, and sale. As prices were administratively controlled, companies sought to sell on the world market where prices were considerably higher; this structure (of local devolution, inadequate financial control, and market opportunity) provided the basis for speculation, fraud, and corruption, which is considered in chapter 4 by Heiko Pleines.

Concurrently, to maintain state control, the government of the Russian Federation formulated plans to form several holding companies from parts of the oil complex. Here the intention was to create vertically integrated oil companies on the model of the leading Western oil companies. By the middle of 1992, the government proposed to organize the oil industry into ten to twelve large, vertically integrated companies able to compete, it was thought, on Russian and world markets. Unlike Middle Eastern governments who, in the post–World War II era, sought control through nationalization, for reasons of political legitimacy in the world order, the Russian government had to privatize the companies and adopt a market strategy. As in the oil-dependent Middle East countries, however, the industry was crucial to the well-being of the economy, and it was conceded that some form of government control was essential.

In the gas industry, a single company (Gazprom), effectively under state ownership and control, prevailed. In oil, the government faced a large number of conflicting interests and the plan was to form two types of company: holding companies and subsidiaries. There are some similarities here with the form of nationalization taken under Carlos Perez in Venezuela. There the government, when considering nationalization plans, was confronted with a strong indigenous management structure. It set up a state holding company

(Petroleos de Venezuela) and proposed three or four integrated oil companies based on previous units. Competition between them, it was thought,
would enhance efficiency. The holding company would ensure that rents
and taxes accrued to the state. In Russia, because of the size and geographical distribution of oil, many more holding companies were formed, and
government control was to be ensured by at least 38 percent of total shares
(51 percent of voting shares) remaining under government ownership. The
government of the Russian Federation was also to retain from 45 percent to
51 percent of the shares in the holding companies for a period of at least
three years. This would ensure not only a flow of earned profits to the central treasury but also would secure the new companies under the jurisdiction
of the federal government, safeguarding its right to taxation revenues.

Intuitively, one sees here the basis of division of interest between the
regions, in which the oil (and gas) is located, and the center, which is controlled by the federal government. (See chapters 5 and 6.) Tiumen, for
example, produces about two-thirds of oil output (90 percent of natural
gas): of this some two-thirds are in Khanty-Mansi Autonomous Okrug, and
10 percent in Yamal-Nenets; the republics of Tatarstan account for 7 percent,
Bashkortostan 5 percent, and Samara and Perm 3 percent. Regions in which
oil is located would obviously be richer if they had ownership and control
of these resources, and, if they had some form of sovereignty, they could
claim tax receipts (as well as profits from ownership). In the postcommunist
settlement in Russia, the central government asserted its rights to the tax
income from this major export industry, which also has significant international implications. This right (analogous to the claims of Iraq over Kuwait)
is questioned by many of the regional republics and is one of the main
causes of the secession movement in Chechnya. (In Chechnya, the material
interest is in royalties from the pipeline running through its territory, as well
as a small amount of extraction and refining. This issue is dealt with by Peter
Rutland in chapter 7.)

By 1996, a major reconstruction of the oil industry had taken place. Unlike
the gas industry, in which Gazprom is a united, centralized structure, with
all the structural subdivisions coming under the strict control of a single
management, the oil industry has been severely deregulated. In 1998, there
were thirteen large, integrated (or partially integrated) oil companies, several small Russian-owned oil extracting companies, joint ventures (*sovmest-
nye predpriiatiia*) and a large number of private firms, as well as local government institutions, involved in oil retailing and export. Large scale
privatization has taken place, and government ownership in the largest oil
groups has declined considerably—it is no longer the majority owner in
many holding companies. Moreover, deregulation of the oil sector has
occurred, involving the dropping of export quotas and licenses and the freeing of prices for oil and oil products. Gradually, the difference between

Russian internal prices and world prices has narrowed. For example, Russian crude oil sold internally for only 0.9 percent of the world market price in 1990, but this figure rose to 47.9 percent in 1997. For gasoline and diesel fuel the figures are, respectively, 1.5 percent and 81.5 percent; and 1.4 percent and 96 percent.[2]

The government, through Mintop, still exerts various forms of control, particularly over access to the export pipelines. In June 1998, it decreed that—following the decision of OPEC—oil exports would be reduced by eighty thousand barrels per day; and in May 1998, following the recommendation of the IMF, it ensured a greater tax take from export earnings by maintaining scrutiny of income.

The Russian financial crisis of autumn 1998 had a generally positive effect on the finances of the oil industry. Since it is an export industry with commodities priced in dollars, the devaluation of the ruble by 70 percent led to an immediate appreciation of stocks in ruble prices. As more than 90 percent of their costs are ruble denominated and approximately half of earnings are dollar denominated, the oil companies were significant beneficiaries of devaluation. Devaluation has also reduced the burden of ruble-denominated, revenue-based taxes, which are only partially compensated for by new export duties on crude oil and refined products. The average costs of production dropped from $9.50 to $5.50 per barrel. This has made Russian oil much more price competitive in world markets. Since in the near future domestic inflation is not likely significantly to outpace the ruble depreciation, the Russian oil and gas sector will continue to enjoy a favorable cost-revenue structure.

TYPES OF COMPANIES IN THE OIL INDUSTRY

By 1997, six different sectors of the oil industry were in place. First, the backbone of the industry comprising large, vertically integrated or partially integrated companies, formed by governmental decree. These companies are the successors of the former state enterprises organized in production associations. In this sector are thirteen oil companies, which include enterprises of oil production, processing, and supply: LUKoil, YuKOS, Surgutneftegaz, Sidanko, Slavneft, Rosneft, Sibneft, Tiumenskaia Neftianaia Kompaniia, Vostochaia Neftianaia Kompaniia, ONAKO, Komitek, and Tatneft.

There are also a number of established companies that are not entirely integrated. The principal ones are: NORSI-oil (no oil extraction), Bashneft (no market outlets), Bashneftekhim (no oil extraction), Vostochno-Sibirskaia Neftianaia Kompaniia and Poliarnaia Geologodobyvaiushchaia Kompaniia (enterprises in geology and geological extraction), and Sibirsko-Ural'skaia Neftegazokhimicheskaia Kompaniia (SIBUR). Several of these companies have a regional character: ONAKO (Orenburg Region), NORSI-oil (Nizhnii Novgorod Region), KomiTEK (Komi Republic), Tatneftekhiminvestholding (Tatarstan), Bashneft and Bashneftekhim (Bashkortostan), and to a slightly lesser extent Vostochnaia NK and Sibneft, linked to Tiumen. The regional administrative bodies in turn seek profits and taxes from the companies.

This sector accounts for the overwhelming share of oil extraction: in 1995, 284 million tons of oil and gas condensate, or 92.6 percent of the total extraction in Russia.The companies here are also responsible for almost all oil processing.

Table 1.1 indicates the major assets of the companies: four majors, six minors, four independents, and two pipeline companies. The assets in column 7 include only those parts of the holding companies on which data are available. The amount of oil extracted and the reserves, of course, vary from year to year depending not only on output but also on revisions of reserve estimates. However, the data show the dominant role of four major companies. Each of these companies has a particular history, and brief accounts of the companies are given in the appendix at the end of part 1 of this book.

The second category is composed of nonspecialized oil production companies—the ones for which oil extraction is not a profile branch of activity. In this category are enterprises of Gazprom, which in 1995 extracted 8.8 million tons of oil and gas condensate (2.9 percent of the all-Russia total), as well as enterprises of Rostoprom and Roskomnedr, which in 1995–96 together extracted 1.6 million tons (about 0.5 percent of the country's total). The share of other Russian producers is another 1.5 million tons, or about 0.5 percent of total oil extraction. This category includes fifteen small Russian joint-stock companies (which extract from several thousand to 0.5 million tons a year). Most of these companies originated as small state geological or experimental enterprises and exploit small oil fields of regional importance. Many are now owned by local government authorities.

A third sector includes joint ventures or other enterprises with foreign investment. According to data in *Neft i kapital* (the leading Russian journal on Russian oil), in 1995 there were thirty such firms concerned with oil extraction. Among these, the most important, in terms of total extraction, were Polar Lights (Poliarnoie Siianiie), Van'eganneft, White Nights (Belye Nochi), Nobel' Oil, KomiArktikOil, and AIK. In 1995 this sector extracted 10.8 million tons of oil and gas condensate (3.5 percent of the total amount in Russia), and their cumulative exports (taking their own oil and bought oil into account) in 1996 constituted 11.6 million tons, or 12.7 percent of all Russian exports.[3] In 1997, these companies accounted for 6.3 percent of Russian oil production, and they recorded the highest rise of growth of output (113 percent).[4]

Fourth, the most strictly regulated part of the Russian oil complex is the oil pipeline network. Companies here have effective control over the firms

Table 1.1 Russian Oil Companies, Key Data

1 Company type	2 Company name	3 No. of employees (1995)	4 Level of vertical integration	5 Retail outlets (1995) $m	6 Revenue (1995) $m	7 Market capitalization (June 1997) $m	8 Oil extraction (1998) million tons	9 Reserves (1996) 1,000 bbl
Integrated majors	LUKoil	107	High	712	6,470	13,386	54	13,460
	YuKOS	110	Medium	940	4,785	5,553	34	14,875
	Surgut	81	High	700	4,550	6,081	36	8,500
	Sidanko	101	Medium	766	4,836	1,313	20	13,465
Integrated minors	Slavneft	n.a.	Medium	177	2,894	415	12	2,800
	Sibneft	n.a.	High	200	—	2,553	18	4,850
	Tiumen	59	Low	333	2,983	14	19	13,220
	Vostochnaia (VNK)	41	Medium	300	1,773	—	11	3,000
Autonomous republic companies	ONAKO	32	High	132	1,297	318	8	2,175
	Rosneft	75	Medium	1,580	2,894	274	12.5	10,825
	KomiTEK	n.a.	Medium	—	547	540	3.26*	2,540
	Tatneft	73	—	—	2,494	2,431	23.5	5,595
	Bashneft	38	—	—	852	—	12.5	2,665
	Yunko	n.a.	—	—	—			
Independents	Nefteotducha	n.a.		—	—			
	Sibur	n.a.		—	—			
	NORSI-Oil	n.a.		—	—			
	East Siberian	n.a.		—	—			
Pipelines	Transneft	n.a.		—	—			
Crude products	Transneft produkt	n.a.		—	—			

*1996

Source and notes: Column 4: This is an indication of the extent to which the holding company has control over the subsidiaries based on qualitative data. See examples in the appendix to part 1. Column 5: Ekspert no. 33, September 2, 1995, 14–20. Column 6: ibid 8–9, 14–20. Column 7. S. O. Sullivan, Russian Oil: Financial Analysis, London: MC Securities, 1997. In some cases, this column refers only to companies within the holding companies for which data are available and may undervalue some of the holding companies. Column 9: E. M. Khartunov, Oil and Gas Journal, 18 August 1997, 37. Note: this column is used for comparative purposes; the measure is in billion barrels, whereas in the text below the unit is tons. The second category is comprised of nonspecialized oil production companies, i.e., the ones for which oil extraction is not a profile branch of activity. Here are enterprises of Gazprom, which in 1995 extracted 8.8 million tons of oil and gas.

extracting and exporting oil. All the main crude oil conduits in the country are controlled and operated by the Transneft company, and by the pipeline system for oil products—the Transnefteprodukt company. Both were established in 1993 as joint-stock companies with a 100 percent state holding (i.e., government institutions bought the shares and appointed the directors rather than, as under state socialism, having formally responsible ministries controlling state assets). Privatization of the pipelines began in 1997 (discussed below). Taxes for transportation along the pipelines as well as the amount of oil for each manufacturer are established by the Federal Energy Commission and Mintop respectively. Ownership of the oil pipelines gives strategic control over the export of oil to the government, which, though the barriers to oil export have been lifted, still regulates the quotas of oil flowing through the pipelines. This also makes the pipelines a cause of political contest between the localities in which the pipes are located (e.g., Chechnya) and the legal owners, effectively the government of the Russian Republic.

Fifth, unlike oil extraction, processing, and transportation, in which companies created on the basis of the former state enterprises are dominant, in wholesale and retail distribution of oil products on the home market there is active competition between private commercial firms. As early as the beginning of the 1990s, before privatization really was underway, oil extraction enterprises and refineries (NPZ) were allowed to trade some of their production, thereby undermining the old centralized system of supply.

By the late 1990s, the role of private firms, of which there is a large number, has become dominant. Some of the firms trade only on the wholesale market, others on the retail market, and a third group carry out the whole cycle: buying crude oil, processing it through refineries, and then selling oil products on the wholesale and retail markets. Most of these oil traders are small companies, which rent oil storage facilities, petrol stations, and other assets from the former state enterprises. During the mid-1990s, however, large oil trading firms appeared, possessing their own market infrastructure and covering wholesale and retail markets in several regions of the country. One of the most important of these is the Central Fuel Company, which dominates oil refining and distribution in Moscow. Its sources of oil are LUKoil and Tatneft, it is partially owned by Moscow City Council (38 percent), and LUKoil (13 percent) and the Tatarstan government (also 13 percent) are major shareholders.[5]

The sixth sector is composed of oil exporting firms, most of them private. These firms were greatly assisted in their development by the deregulation and privatization strategy of the government, particularly the abolition of the state export and import monopoly. In the conditions of the early 1990s, the great difference between internal and external prices made the export of oil and oil products very profitable. The export of liquid fuel as well as other resources quickly turned into one of the most important spheres of Russian foreign currency earnings. Moreover, it was subject to corruption and is inextricably connected to large-scale crime in the form of illegal procurement and sale of oil products.

The fifth and sixth sectors, defined above, provide a major site for "mafia" control of legally and illegally sold products. Money for sales abroad is often not repatriated to the company at home but illegally banked abroad—defrauding the government to the advantage of company executives and others. Alternatively, sales of oil have been recorded at internal prices when sold at export ones, the difference being illegally appropriated. The severe financial crisis of the Russian government in 1998 has led to greater government control of revenues remitted to Russia.

OWNERSHIP AND CONTROL

The privatization of the Russian oil industry began in 1993, following a presidential decree of November 1992. As noted above, the companies are layered on two levels: "subsidiaries" (*dochernye predpriyatiya*) and "holding" companies to which the subsidiaries are subordinated. Initially, the holding companies and subsidiaries had (and sometimes they still have) a different spread of owners. Crucially, however, the government, according to the decree, would have majority ownership rights in the holding company, which in turn would have a majority interest in the subsidiary. The government's intention was to privatize assets and form competing companies while giving the state a significant level of control over these companies.

The division of ownership and the level of control of the holding companies, moreover, varies not only with the extent of ownership but also with the management and ownership structure of the subsidiaries. In some cases, also, the subsidiaries and the holding company have entered into share exchanges ("share swaps") in which the holding company acquires shares in the subsidiary—thereby increasing its potential or actual control. An unintended consequence of the Russian government's precarious financial position is that its shares have been "swapped" for loans ("shares-for-loans"), either from the oil companies themselves or from financial institutions giving ownership rights to the latter until the shares are redeemed. An important economic and political consequence here is that the federal government is losing control to private financial institutions. (See chapter 2.) An interesting comparison might be made with the progression of government-oil company relations in other (Third World) countries, where the trend has been for governments to increase their ownership and control of (foreign) oil companies within their boundaries.

THE PROCESS AND RESULTS OF PRIVATIZATION 1990–1998

With the collapse of the Soviet ministries in 1990–91 and the shift of control from the USSR to the republics and regions, a "free-for-all" process took place, in which the management of enterprises took control of the assets of their enterprises and operated as independent units. This process is sometimes referred to as "spontaneous" privatization. The privatization that followed this involved the distribution of the assets of these production enterprises and concurrently the organization of vertically integrated holding companies.

The more "official" privatization in the period from 1993 to 1999 has involved the consolidation of this process. As we describe in the studies of the four companies in the appendix to part 1, in some cases the holding company has a strong position with financial and managerial control over the subsidiaries, in others the "subsidiaries" maintain effective control over physical assets. Divisions within and between holding and subsidiary companies reflect differences in the ownership and control of assets. The principal actors are the government of the Russian Republic, the governments of regions and localities, financial institutions (such as banks), and managerial executives working in the industry. The forms of political contestation for control are not unlike those in the post–World War II period between the governments of the Third World oil states, the Western governments, and the oil companies, except that the Western oil companies were established powers whereas the Russian ones are only in the process of formation.

The general laws for privatization of the oil complex were laid down in Presidential Decree no. 1403, issued on 17 November 1992. This decree envisaged the division of assets between subsidiaries and holding companies in the following way. For the subsidiaries, the stock was divided into two parts: the smaller (25 percent) was composed of preference (non-voting) shares. These were to be distributed free of charge among the employees (management and workers) of the enterprises. The remainder, the ordinary voting shares, were to be divided as follows. Thirty-eight percent was placed with an oil holding company, or in some cases transferred for temporary management to the state enterprise, Rosneft—the objective here was to give a controlling stake of 50.7 percent of voting shares to the holding company. Ten percent was to be offered for sale on advantageous terms to the enterprise's workers, 5 percent was for sale on advantageous terms to the enterprise's management, and 3.75 percent was for sale by "check auction" (described below) to small nationalities of the north and employees of joint stock companies (JSCs) of oil pipeline transport enterprises. Finally, 18.25 percent was for sale through check and/or cash auctions to other (local and foreign) buyers.

These regulations have to be seen in the context of the first stage of the Russian privatization procedure (1992–June 1994) in which "vouchers" (or "checks") were distributed (free of charge) to Russian citizens (one per person). These checks represented a share of the "people's property." There were three main ways of realizing the value of these cheques: first, to buy shares of a given person's own enterprise; second, to take part in "check auctions," where packages of shares of enterprises were sold; and third, to buy shares of "check investment funds," which in turn bought shares in privatized enterprises. These "check investment funds" are a specifically Russian type of mutual investment funds dealing with privatization checks (vouchers). Since 1 July 1994, such vouchers have not been valid and state enterprises' shares are sold only for cash in cash auctions or investment tenders. Check investment funds have been transformed into mutual investment funds or investment companies.

Turning to the actual settlement of the oil complex, in addition to the distribution of vouchers, initially the ownership of assets of the holding oil companies was also divided between government and financial institutions with the former having a major share. There were differences, however, between the various companies. For LUKoil, YuKOS and Surgutneftegaz, during the first three years, 45 percent of the stock was owned by the federal government; 40 percent was to be sold on investment tenders to financial institutions such as banks, and the remainder was to be tendered for privatization checks (*privatizatsionnye chekhi*). For companies established in 1994 and 1995, the share retained for three years as federal property was increased to 51 percent, while 49 percent was to be sold. Overall, a limit of 15 percent of total assets was placed at this time on ownership by foreign investors. (This limit was later lifted.) Schematically, the planned form of ownership (based on LUKoil) is shown in table 1.2.

The scheme of privatization in the fuel and energy complex has been slower and more cautious than in other sectors of the economy. For three years, control of the stock of the established companies belonged to the

Table 1.2 The Planned Form of Ownership for Russian Oil and Gas Companies

Holding company	Percentage share	Subsidiaries	Percentage share
Government	45	Preference (no vote)	25
Investment institutions	40	Employees, management, auctions	37
Open sale	15	Holding	38

state, whose representatives became directors of oil companies. Initially, when the oil holding companies were created, the government retained 100 percent of their shares, giving it the right to appoint all the directors, as well as top management. As privatization progressed, of course, these government appointed directors were gradually replaced by others. By 1997, there were usually two or three nominees from ministries and other government bodies on the oil companies' boards. However, in companies which are totally privatized, with no government stake, there may be no representatives from the government.

The strictest governmental control was in the sphere of transportation of oil and oil products. Fifty-one percent of shares in the companies of this industry became share capital in the Transneft and Transnefteprodukt companies, and 49 percent for three years remained federal property. In this way, the total ownership of shares in Transneft and Transnefteprodukt themselves remained in federal government hands. The aim of this measure was to regulate the activity of the monopolists in the transport of fuel and also to keep an additional lever of governmental influence over the oil companies. Also, this control ensured that the fuel companies continued to function without interruption during the transitionary period. Another argument in favor of a relatively slow pace of privatization was financial. The market value of the assets of the Russian oil industry is at least 200 billion dollars. Neither Russian citizens nor private financial institutions could raise such sums, and even potential Western investors would find such amounts difficult to raise. Rapid privatization in such a context would lead to the undervaluation of state assets.

Against this background, to illustrate the process of change we consider the structure of ownership of the four major companies (LUKoil, YuKOS, Surgutneftegaz, and Sidanko), then outline the trends from 1994 to 1999.

LUKOIL

LUKoil's strategy in the distribution of its shares was a gradual sale of comparatively small or medium-sized stock packages. The management of the company had three aims: first, to attract maximum available investment resources; second, to prevent a fall in the price of its shares on the stock market; and third, to keep in its own hands full control over the company.The sale of LUKoil's stock began in 1994 when 7.42 percent of the stock fund of the company was sold at check auctions (for vouchers), about 2 percent was distributed to employees and administration, 7 percent was transferred to the company for subsequent sale on the stock market, and 3.19 percent of preference shares was released in "closed check auctions.[6] There were no limitations on the size of bids in open check auctions, except a 15 percent limit for foreign investors.

In April 1995 (when the state still owned 80.44 percent of LUKoil's stock) the capital stock of the company was increased more than 1.5 times, from 11.9 to 17.9 billion rubles. The additional shares reflected the inclusion in LUKoil of new oil enterprises and also the conversion of shares of subsidiaries into shares of the holding company. LUKoil was the first Russian oil company to move to possess subsidiaries' stock, thereby forming a commonly owned company. This was part of the general strategy involved in the creation of vertically integrated companies.

In 1995, LUKoil started to issue convertible bonds and in September the first tranche of 320 thousand bonds was put up for sale. Of these, 241 thousand (at an overall cost of 250 million dollars) were bought by Atlantic Richfield Company (ARCO). In March 1996, a second sale took place, in which 140 thousand of LUKoil's convertible bonds were on offer. ARCO acquired another 94.8 thousand bonds, and the Russian bank, Imperial, itself owned by LUKoil, bought the rest. On 5 April 1996, convertible bonds were exchanged for ordinary (voting) shares of LUKoil.[7]

In the international stock markets, LUKoil was the first Russian oil company to have rights to release American Depositary Receipts (ADRs), which allow non-American companies to sell their securities, denominated in dollars, to American (and other) investors. LUKoil was also the first to deliver the new type of securities, that is convertible bonds released with deposit of stock packages, fixed for a certain term as state property.

The transition to a single stock and active advertising on the Russian and international stages have helped to increase the value of LUKoil's stock from $5.5 per share on average in 1995 to $10–12 in summer 1996 and $15 in 1997. Thus, the company is unquestionably the leader among Russian companies in terms of market capitalization. A rating in *Ekspert* magazine estimated that by 1 July 1996, LUKoil's capital totaled 7.6 billion dollars, whereas Gazprom's was only 2.6 billion.[8] LUKoil's shares are among the Russian "blue chips" with the company being the unquestionable leader in terms of its share price.

LUKoil made an offer of 5 percent of its stock in a "loans-for-shares" auction in December 1995. This had the effect of diluting the government's holding, in exchange for income to bridge its serious budget deficit. The shares were taken up by a group consisting of LUKoil itself and Imperial bank, which is closely associated with LUKoil (see also chapter 2).[9] At the same time, another 16.07 percent of LUKoil's stock was purchased by the Nikoil investment company. The government has benefited financially: in 1995 alone, from the three sources (issue of convertible bonds, loans-for-shares sales, and share offers) of LUKoil's privatization it received about 390 million dollars, which is more than from any other company.

Among all the Russian oil holdings, only LUKoil's shares are unconditionally liquid and widely quoted on the Russian stock market. (In other companies, shares of a holding are either partially liquid, as in Surgutneftegaz and

YuKOS, or are not quoted at all; and their trade on the stock market is led mostly by the shares of subsidiary extracting subdivisions.)

OWNERSHIP OF LUKOIL 1996

Table 1.3 illustrates the profile of ownership in July of 1996. The state nominally remains the largest shareholder of LUKoil with 33 percent of shares being federal property. However, of these, 5 percent is in the form of a deposit with Imperial bank (owned by LUKoil). A further 15 percent of shares from the state package was sold in 1997 in a share offer, and 1.52 percent in a cash auction. The result of these sales is that only 11.57 percent of shares remain state property. Though it owns much less than originally intended, the state will nevertheless continue to be a major shareholder with leverage in internal and international oil politics.

The company itself, its workers and administration, and associated financial institutions own more than 31 percent of LUKoil's stock, and together with the depository package this comes to more than 36 percent. A total of 10.85 percent of the shares in the company is owned by the LUKoil-Garant Pension Fund, where the shares of united LUKoil's employees share fund are held. The second largest shareholder is the Nikoil investment company, which owns 16.2 percent of LUKoil's share capital. The Nikoil company is formally independent of LUKoil but is closely associated with it. Nikoil's head (in 1996), Nikolai Alelsandrovich Tsvetkov, was previously a vice president of LUKoil, and Nikoil also owns stock in some of LUKoil's subsidiaries.

LUKoil-Fund was established and is controlled by the management of the LUKoil company, as well as by representatives of local administrations. LUKoil's vice president, Leonid Fedun, is on its board of directors. At present, LUKoil-Fund comes under the administration of Nikoil, and this company plans to make it into a mutual investment fund.[10] LUKoil-Fund is among the five largest check investment funds in Russia. The value of its assets is estimated as being 120 million dollars; of which more than two-thirds is concentrated in subsidiaries of oil production companies mostly belonging to the LUKoil group. The fund has bought the shares of the twenty-six largest companies of the oil industry, including 3.3 percent of LUKoil's shares, and packages from 1 to 6 percent of a number of its large subsidiaries. The share of LUKoil-Fund in the company has been reduced to 1.13 percent.

Other Russian investors own about 15.5 percent of LUKoil's shares, of which about 10 percent is owned by legal entities and 5.5 percent by individuals. Among this group of shareholders, the investment companies Olma and Troika-Dialog are important. However, no Russian investor outside of LUKoil possesses a large stock holding, and some part of this 15.5 percent

Table 1.3 Ownership Structure of LUKoil (percentage of outstanding shares as of 11 July 1996)

Owner	Total percentage	Breakdown of shares	Percentage
Formally state property	33.09	For sale in special auction	1.52
		For sale in investment tender to foreign investors	15.00
		Secured as federal property	11.57
		Loans-for-shares sale (LUKoil-Imperial)	5.00
LUKoil employees, management, and related investors	31.15	Nikoil	16.20
		LUKoil-Garant pension fund	10.85
		LUKoil-Fund	1.13
		LUKoil (share-swap–subsidiaries)	1.68
		Transferred to LUKoil for sale in security market	1.29
Other Russian investors	15.38	Legal entities	9.89
		Individuals	5.49
		Foreign investors (ARCO)	20.38
			7.99
Other institutional investors	11.12	Individuals	1.27

Sources: Neft Rossii (monthly magazine edited by LUKoil), no. 8, 1996; *Neft i kapital*, nos. 7–8, 1996, p. 26.

of shares presumably belongs to the company's own workers as well as to institutional investors associated with LUKoil. As a consequence of the distribution of the second tranche of convertible bonds, a small package of LUKoil's stock was bought by Imperial bank, whose main shareholder is LUKoil itself. Hence LUKoil's management is strongly positioned against other shareholders' interests.

Since Russian commercial structures do not possess substantial financial funds, LUKoil's management has sought foreign investors. In 1997, foreign investors owned more than 20 percent of the share capital of the company, and a further 15 percent sale to foreigners in an investment tender was planned. In 1995–96 ARCO became a large shareholder in LUKoil. It owns a total of 7.99 percent of LUKoil's share capital. This figure is not arbitrary: according to LUKoil company's statutes an investor with 8 percent of its stock would qualify for a place on the board of directors. ARCO's acquisition of a large stock package of LUKoil is a consequence of a strategic partnership between these two companies. In September 1996 ARCO and LUKoil agreed to establish a joint-venture, LUKARKO, with the aim of exploration and development of oil fields in Russia and the Commonwealth of Independent States (CIS), as well as exploitation of Western technology in LUKoil's activities.

Virtually all LUKoil's shares belonging to foreign investors (including ARCO) are converted into ADRs traded on the New York, London, and Berlin stock markets. Further development of its market (both in Russia and in the West) and of sales of stock are seen by LUKoil as an effective way of attracting investments.

OWNERSHIP OF YUKOS

Unlike LUKoil, in the course of privatization the management of YuKOS has not managed to keep full control over the company's assets. YuKOS has had a weak financial basis, and its subsidiaries have not been brought under its control. The administration of the company has been forced to allow the acquisition of a considerable part of its stock by a strategic investor, the Menatep bank group.

In December 1995 Menatep acquired 33 percent of YuKOS's shares in an investment tender, and simultaneously won a loan-for-shares auction for a 45 percent state stock holding in the company. In May 1996 a cash auction took place in which 7.96 percent of YuKOS's charter capital was sold. Of this, Menatep acquired 7.06 percent. The upshot of these transactions is that by the beginning of 1997 more than 85 percent of the stock of the YuKOS oil company was controlled by the Rosprom-Menatep group (40 percent of the charter fund belongs to the group, and 45 percent is mortgaged to it).

The second biggest YuKOS shareholder is the Renessans-Kapital company, which, during the May 1996 cash auction of shares, bought about 0.3 percent of YuKOS's charter fund. The rest of the package in the May auction was purchased by the Prospekt investment company.[11] Roughly 14 percent of YuKOS's initial charter fund was sold on advantageous terms to its workers and its administration, or transferred to the company for distribution on the fund market. Some of these shares were then sold to outside shareholders.

In October 1995, the charter fund of the YuKOS oil company was increased from 5.13 billion to 6.63 billion rubles because a number of new subsidiary subdivisions were included in the company, and packages of 38 percent of their shares were transferred to YuKOS's charter fund. In September 1996, YuKOS's charter capital was increased by about a third, up to 8.95 billion rubles. The profit from the additional issue of shares (about 500 billion rubles, or approximately 80 million dollars) was spent on covering salary debts in its subsidiary subdivisions. Shareholders in the company were offered a rights issue of new shares, proportional to the packages they already possessed, at 90 percent of the market price. The state did not use this right, whereas virtually all the other stockholders purchased additional shares and kept their part in the company. The remaining part was bought by a company called Russian Investors, which held 12.79 percent of the new YuKOS charter fund.

Thus the state's ownership was again diluted. The part owned by the state (through the mortgaging to Menatep) decreased from 45 percent to 33.3 percent. Three subsidiary firms kept their shares totaling 38.57 percent of YuKOS's charter fund. Moreover, Menatep has strengthened its position, and Russian Investors is very closely linked to the bank. By 1996 the Menatep group owned 51.5 percent of YuKOS's charter capital and, in addition, controlled a depositary package of 33.3 percent of shares.[12] For the ownership of YuKOS in November 1996, see table 1.4.

Table 1.4 Ownership Structure of YuKOS (percentage of outstanding shares as of 1 November 1996)

Shareholders	Percentage
State property pledged to Menatep through loans-for-shares	33.30
Menatep group, including	38.57
Astarta	18.00
Tonus	15.00
Makhaon	5.57
Russian Investors	12.79
YuKOS-Invest	7.05
Others (mostly individuals, including YuKOS employees and management)	8.29

Source: Kommersant-Daily, 21 November 1996.

Furthermore during 1996–97, Menatep acquired the government's stock, effectively giving it control of the company (the regulations of any Russian shareholding company can be adopted or changed by 75 percent of the votes).

In January 1998, it was announced that YuKOS had a protcol of understanding with Sibneft, which would have led to a merger and the formation of a new company, Yuksi, making it the largest Russian oil company in terms of oil and gas output. However, the increasingly difficult trading conditions (the fall in oil prices, financial uncertainty, and forceful government demands for the payment of tax arrears) exacerbated tensions between the two companies, and in July 1998 the merger was called off.

OWNERSHIP OF SURGUTNEFTEGAZ

The management of Surgutneftegaz originally intended to make the company a "people's company" by distributing the shares of the company and its subdivisions among the largest possible number of small investors, thus precluding control by outside investors (see table 1.5). Surgutneftegaz's regulations initially contained the strictest of all Russian oil companies' limitations to the acquisition of its shares by large outside, especially foreign, investors. Purchase of more than 1 percent of charter capital required the approval of the board of directors. The share of foreign investors was limited to 5 percent of the charter capital.

The company's strategy of independence from foreign investors was successfully realized in the course of its privatization. At the first stage, 8 percent of the company's shares were sold in check and cash auctions in 1993. However, both these auctions were held by the local property fund, and as a result of some infringements, a considerable fraction of shares was bought back, through nominees, by the company itself. A further 7 percent of the stock was acquired by the company for a nominal price in return for vouchers with the aim of subsequent realization for cash on a fund market. The package of 40 percent was purchased in summer 1994 in an investment competition by the Neftinvest oil company, which is under the control of Surgutneftegaz.

In November 1995 a loans-for-shares auction for 42.12 percent of Surgutneftegaz's stock took place; it was won by the Surgutneftegaz Pension Fund. The successful bidder was obliged to give the state a credit of 300 billion rubles ($66.4 million), as well as to pay more than a trillion rubles ($227 million) worth of the company's debts to the state budget. The Surgutneftegaz Pension Fund is fully controlled by the company's management: of its funds 50.6 percent belongs to the Surgutneftegaz holding company, and 43.3 percent to its subsidiary, the Surgutneftegaz extracting shareholding company.[13]

After privatization, the Surgutneftegaz oil company bought with its own means or received as pledges 90–95 percent of its shares. This became possible due to the stable financial state of the company, as well as to the benevolent attitude of the Russian government, which closed its eyes to a number of procedural infringements.

"Self-purchase" has allowed the management of Surgutneftegaz to maintain absolute control over the company. However, this strategy has had some negative consequences. The idea of the transformation of Surgutneftegaz into a "people's company" has turned out to be impractical, since attracting any considerable resources from personal investors by selling shares proved unrealistic. Surgutneftegaz's inaccessibility to large investors seriously limited the input of outside financial resources. Also the opaqueness of the company (the difficulty of finding out about its assets and liabilities) had a negative influence on quotation of its shares.

The management of the company has therefore altered its policies on the fund market. At the general meeting of shareholders of the Surgutneftegaz stockholding company in June 1996, amendments were made to its regulations, eliminating the majority of limitations on the participation of outside investors in its stock holdings. The approval of the board of directors is no longer necessary when a package of more than 1 percent of shares is acquired. Also the 5 percent limit for foreign investors has been rescinded (Surgutneftegaz's regulations no longer contain any restrictions on foreign investors, whereas in many companies the 15 percent limits are retained). Finally, the company intends to attract foreign firms to carry out financial and resources audits, which will be made public.[14]

Table 1.5 Ownership Structure of Surgutneftegaz Holding (percentage of shares as of 1 July 1996)

Shares	Percentage
Secured as state property (of which 40.12% is pledged under loans-for-shares scheme to the Surgutneftegaz Pension Fund, which is controlled by the company)	45.0
Sold through the investment tender to Neftinvest, which is controlled by the company	40.0
Sold in specialized check auction	7.8
Sold in cash auction	0.2
Sold to the company for subsequent sale on securities market	7.0

Sources: United City Bank, ed., *Surgutneftegaz Oil Company* (Moscow: 1996), p. 3; *Finansovoe Delo* (Moscow), no. 12, 1995, p. 10.

OWNERSHIP OF SIDANKO

Although the Sidanko company was established as early as 1994, unresolved discussion about the composition of the company (the place of Purneftegaz) precluded its privatization. Only after the government's decision defining the structure of companies had been announced in September 1995 did the State Property Committee approve a plan of privatization. Accordingly, the state package of 51 percent of the company's shares was put to a loans-for-shares auction (including up to 15 percent for foreign investors), which took place in 1995. The purchaser was an alliance of the International Financial Company and Oneksimbank.

In September 1996, an investment tender for another 34 percent of Sidanko's shares was held. The minimal price of the package was 435.1 billion rubles, including 110 billion as a price for shares and 325.1 billion as the minimal amount of investments. The main part of these resources (more than 300 billion) was to be directed at covering the debts of Sidanko and its subsidiary divisions. A peculiarity of this investment competition was a requirement that the competitors should hold either a 13 percent package of shares in the Chernogorneft stockholding company (Sidanko's subsidiary enterprise) or an agreement to acquire such shares, which would then be transferred to the company.

Sidanko's motives were to acquire a majority holding in Chernogorneft. Sidanko had received 37.73 percent of the shares of this stockholding company, but lacked control. The introduction of this condition greatly narrowed the circle of competitors, since the necessary package of Chernogorneft shares was owned only by the MFK-Oneksimbank group, who had bought more than 15 percent of the shares of this enterprise on the secondary market in February 1996.

The shares finally went to Interros-oil, a participant in a financial-industrial group, Interros, established by Oneksimbank. Here again we see the decline of state ownership and the growing ascendancy of the banking-financial interests.

TRENDS IN OWNERSHIP AND CONTROL

The outline history of privatization in the four top companies illustrates the fundamental shift in the ownership of assets away from the government to the private sector, in which the banks and financial companies, often working through nominees, had, by 1997, secured large holdings. Table 1.6 shows the precipitous decline of the state sector against the holding companies in the industry.

Table 1.6 Government Share in Russian Oil Companies, 1994–1997

Company	Percentage of government holding			
	1994	1995	1996	1997
Sidanko	100	85*	51*	0
Vostsibneftegaz	100	85	38	0
Sibneft	--	100*	51*	0
YuKOS	86	53*	0.1	0.1
Surgutneftegaz	40.1	40.1*	40.1*	0
KomiTEK	100	100	92	0-22
LUKoil	42.1	26*	16.6*	6.6
NORSI-Oil	--	100	85.4	45
Tatneft	46.6	46.6	35.1	20-25
Transneft	100	100	75	51
Rosneft	--	100	100	100
Tiumen oil	--	100	91	51
Sibur	100	85	85	51
Vostochnaya oil	100	85	85	51
Slavneft	93.5	92	90.1	56-68
ONAKO	100	85	85	85

*Wholly or partly in the hands of "pledgeholder."
Source: Eugene M. Khartukov, *Oil and Gas Journal*, 18 August 1997, p. 38.

In 1997, the government relinquished ownership rights in a large number of companies. Pipeline operators Transneft and Rosneft were privatized through a 25 percent offer of stock to present and former employees and another 25 percent were to be offered to the investment market. Despite political pressure from the Duma and from regional authorities, President Yeltsin—confronted with serious budget deficits—lifted restrictions on the sale of oil assets in 1997, and an unprecedented rate of destatization has taken place.

The last major energy asset to be sold is Rosneft. The tender for 75 percent of the company's shares was set for May 1998, and the minimum price was fixed at 2.1 billion dollars. The successful bidder was also required to invest 400 million dollars in the following three years. The price was regarded as too high for potential purchasers: Mikhail Khodorkovski (on behalf of Yuksi), Gazprom (with Shell) and LUKoil, and Oneksimbank (with British Petroleum) all withdrew from the auction. The crisis in international markets, the precipitous fall in the value of the ruble, and the decline in the price of oil led to the auction being called off in the summer of 1998.

The major players in the privatization stakes have been Russian banks, particularly Alfa-Bank (40 percent of Tiumen Oil), Oneksimbank (85 percent of Sidanko), Menatep (85 percent of YuKOS), and SBS/Berezovsky (99 percent of Sibneft) acting through intermediaries such as Laguna, NFK, Interrosoil, Sins, Rifainoil, Monblan, and FNK.[15] (For a detailed discussion see chapter 4.)

Due to the uncertain legal status of capital, the difficulty of repatriating profits, the extent of crime and corruption, and the hostility of sections of the government and the oil industry and the Russian Parliament, direct foreign investment in the oil industry has been small—in 1996 joint ventures accounted for 7 percent of oil production and 12.5 percent of exports.[16] Shareholdings of foreigners in oil companies have been limited by law, and foreign shareholders have effectively been excluded from the boards of companies. In 1997, however, President Yeltsin lifted the legal limit of 15 percent of shares that could be owned by foreigners—though of course companies themselves could fix such a ceiling.

WHO CONTROLS THE COMPANIES?
VIEWS OF ELITES: DIRECTORS AND POLITICIANS

Ownership is one important aspect of the organization of companies, but the extent to which it affects control is problematic. As the decision-making process is often secret and internal to the "inner circle" of company directors, it is usually very difficult to discover who controls companies and to determine whether ownership rights are transferred into control. Western industrial sociology has a vast literature on the subject. Ideally, one would like a number of case studies of decision-making in various oil companies to determine the extent of control of different interests. Another method is to interview directors and management to ask their views about control over strategic decisions.

The first author of this chapter organized sixty-five interviews with Russian oil executives.[17] Respondents were asked their opinions on the weight of various interests on the board of their company with respect to the making of "strategic decisions" in the company. They were asked to estimate the importance of management, financial institutions, other companies, the labor collective, large personal shareholders, foreign shareholders, and government representatives. Table 1.7 illustrates the responses with respect to the various interests within the board of directors (*soviet direktorov*). In columns 1 to 5 are shown the percentages of persons giving an answer. Column 6 is an index of the importance of the item—the higher the number the greater the importance. Column 7 gives the number of respondents not answering the question.

The relative ranking of the importance of the different interests is shown in column 6: of greatest importance are the representatives of management, government delegates, and financial interests. Labor collectives can clearly

Table 1.7 Influence on Strategic Decisions: Role of Interests on the Board of Directors

Interests	1	2	3	4	5	6	7
Management	1.9	3.8	5.7	15.1	73.6	4.55	12
Financial interests	17.9	3.6	21.4	25.0	32.1	3.5	37
Other (nonfinancial companies)	24.1	27.6	24.1	6.9	17.2	2.66	36
Labor collective	41.9	22.6	25.8	9.7	0	2.03	34
Large personal shareholders	31.6	5.3	21.1	26.3	15.8	2.89	46
Foreign shareholders	33.3	14.3	19.0	9.5	23.8	2.76	44
Government representatives	8.8	17.6	5.9	20.6	47.1	3.79	36
N=65	%	%	%	%	%	index	N

Key:
Columns 1–5. Five point scale: 1–not important; 5–very important. Percentages of those answering the question.
Column 6. Average scale.
Column 7. No response (number of respondents).

be ruled out as an important interest, and large individual shareholders also seem to be very unimportant. To some of the questions there was a high level of non-response: this is because many of the companies had not been fully privatized, other categories (foreign owners) were absent, and in some cases the respondents had insufficient knowledge to answer the question.

A number of questions were devised concerning the role of external interests not on the board of directors. These included: the Russian government, federal Russian institutions, regional powers, other Russian oil companies, and foreign oil companies. (See table 1.8.) Of these, the political groups—the Russian government, and federal and regional powers—were of greatest importance, foreign and other oil companies playing a minor role in the strategic decisions of the companies.

While the government has sold assets in oil companies, one may not conclude that the government exerts only a minor influence over the economy.

To probe further the differences between executives and politicians, the first author interviewed thirty politicians with an interest in the energy field[18] and compared their attitudes. The results are shown in tables 1.9 and 1.10. Here there is considerable agreement on the part of both oil executives and politicians that the government of the Russian Federation, followed by the president, have the most influence over the economy. (See column 6 where these two groups receive the highest rankings—in Table 1.9 of 3.8 and 3.6, and in Table 1.10 of 3.7 and 3.5.)

Table 1.8 Influence on Strategic Decisions: Interests External to the Company

Interests	1	2	3	4	5	6	7
Government (president/ *apparat*/ministers)	14.3	17.9	25	19.6	23.2	3.2	9
Federal authorities	15.3	16.9	28.8	15.3	23.7	3.15	6
Regional authorities (governors/local interests)	19.4	21	22.6	19.4	17.7	2.95	3
Russian oil companies	23.3	25	21.7	26.7	3.3	2.62	5
Foreign oil companies	44.3	34.4	16.4	1.6	3.3	1.85	4
N=65	%	%	%	%	%	index	N

Key:
Columns 1–5. Five point scale: 1–not important; 5–very important. Percentages of those answering the question.
Column 6–Scale (average)
Column 7–No response (N)

Table 1.9 The Influence of Russian Institutions on the Russian Federation's Economy: Oil Executives' Views

	1	2	3	4	5	6	7
Parliament	18	23	39	18	3	2.6	3
President	3	10	32	34	21	3.6	3
Government RF	2	7	27	44	21	3.8	3
Regional authorities	5	18	44	18	16	3.2	3
State companies and enterprises	13	36	34	15	3	2.6	3
Private companies	7	23	38	24	8	3	5
N=65	%	%	%	%	%	index	N

Key:
Columns 1–5. Five point scale: 1–no influence; 5–very much influence. Percentages of those answering the question.
Column 6–Scale (average)
Column 7–No response (N)

Question: What is the extent of the influence on the economic structure of the Russian Federaton of the following?

Table 1.10 The Influence of Russian Institutions on the Russian Federation's Economy: Politicians' Views

	1	2	3	4	5	6	7
Parliament	17	53	20	10	0	2.2	0
President	3	17	27	37	17	3.5	0
Government RF	0	0	47	37	17	3.7	0
Regional authorities	0	20	47	33	0	3.1	0
State companies and enterprises	10	47	27	13	3	2.5	0
Private companies	13	47	7	30	3	2.6	0
N=30	%	%	%	%	%	index	N

Key:
Columns 1–5. Five point scale: 1–no influence; 5–very much influence. Percentages of those answering the question.
Column 6–Scale (average)
Column 7–No response (N)

Question: see table 1.9.

Tables 1.11 and 1.12 illustrate the perceived role of foreign bodies. Here, for both the politicians and the oil executives, international organizations (such as the IMF and the World Bank) were regarded as having considerable influence (for the oil executives a rank of 3.4 and for the politicians 3.7—see column 6 in both tables). An interesting difference here is the higher ranking given to foreign oil companies by politicians.

CONCLUSIONS

From this overview of the Russian oil industry one might generalize about the structure of evolving capitalism in Russia. The intention of the Yeltsin government was to maintain a large stake in the ownership of strategic industrial assets. Such state ownership provided the basis for the idea that the system would evolve into some form of state capitalism operating within a market society. This policy, however, has been undermined by the serious budget deficits that have led to the sale of assets and, by 1997, a destatization of the oil industry had occurred. Another important determinant has

Table 1.11 The Influence of Foreign Institutions on the Russian Federation's Economy: Oil Executives' Views

	1	2	3	4	5	6	7
International organizations (IMF, World Bank)	5	20	30	33	13	3.4	4
Foreign oil companies	13	27	50	10	0	2.6	5
Governments of Western countries	9	23	47	16	5	2.9	8
N=65	%	%	%	%	%	index	N

Key:
Columns 1–5. Five point scale: 1–no influence; 5–very much influence. Percentages of those answering the question.
Column 6–Scale (average)
Column 7–No response (N)

Question: Estimate the degree of influence on the economy of the Russian Federation by the following (five-point scale).

Table 1.12 The Influence of Foreign Institutions on the Russian Federaton's Economy: Politicians' Views

	1	2	3	4	5	6	7
International organizations (IMF, World Bank)	10	0	27	40	23	3.7	0
Foreign oil companies	10	23	20	30	17	3.2	0
Governments of Western countries	7	47	27	20	0	2.6	0
N=65	%	%	%	%	%	index	N

Key:
Columns 1–5. Five point scale: 1–no influence; 5–very much influence. Percentages of those answering the question.
Column 6–Scale (average)
Column 7–No response (N)

Question: See table 1.11.

been the need for capital investment by the large oil companies. In attempting to strengthen their market position and to enter the world market, they have had to turn not only to Russian banks and financial institutions, whose resources are limited, but also to foreigners. Ownership has not been diversified to a large number of private individuals (as was the case initially with the privatization of British Gas, though this company also had a large number of corporate owners). Russian banks and financial institutions during the period 1994–1999 clearly became, with a residue of government control, the leading institutional owners. The aspiration of "people's ownership" trumpeted during the issue of vouchers can clearly be written off. Foreign ownership is relatively small, but significantly, the disposition toward foreign ownership within the industry has become more positive. This has not been the case, however, in the political sphere where opposition to the sale of state property, particularly to foreigners, has been great. In 1999, Prime Minister Primakov succeeded in securing the support of the Duma to pass legislation in favor of profit-sharing schemes for foreign participants: 30 percent of production could come under such agreements.

The problem facing the formal owners, even those with a controlling block of shares, is that ownership may be difficult to transform into control. The attempts to buy into the industry by banks and financial interests have led to protests by management in the form of Vladimir Medvedev, the president of the Union of Oil and Gas Industry, and also by regional government—the governors of the Sakhalin, Khabarovsk, and Yamal-Nenets Autonomous Okrugs. These issues are the subject of further chapters. However, ownership does not automatically give control. While financial institutions may replace members of the boards of directors with their own nominations—in the context of the absence of well-defined and enforced company law, this in itself is not straightforward, and in attempting market type reforms (such as labor reduction and closure of unprofitable enterprises)—they are still confronted with top and middle management which overwhelmingly considers itself to be sovereign. The practices and outlook of an "administrative command" economy do not change overnight. The evidence we have from interviews with oil executives indicates that management is regarded as a major influence on strategic decisions. Managerial groups have operational control of the companies, and many of the subsidiaries are only 51 percent owned by the holding companies—the remaining blocks being owned by the administration, other investors, and local authorities—making it difficult to assert control. Management not only owns considerable numbers of shares but is strategically positioned in the companies to provide leadership. Again, the interviews with oil executives confirmed the important role of the government—both central and local. The political context of state control and the crucial role played by the energy industries in the economic development process of the country will significantly limit the power of the banking and financial interests. Unlike Anglo-American capitalism, in Russia the stock exchange as a medium of control is extremely weak. Ownership is not clearly defined, and the liquidity of shareholdings is low. The stock exchange, therefore, is unlikely to be an important factor determining the ownership, control, and takeover of individual firms. It seems that developments will be more likely to follow the German model of ownership, with financial institutions and other companies having considerable stakes in the holding companies, and management having substantial power over strategic decisions. The institutional framework is not conducive to hostile takeovers, and the stock exchange is unlikely to be an important institution in the regulation of the economy.

The Russian oil companies, moreover, are confronted with a political reality rather different from that of Western companies with extraction rights in the Third World. In countries such as Iran, Iraq, and Kuwait, economic and political boundaries were congruent in a unitary state and the well-established Western companies were threatened with taxes at the well-head and the threat (and reality) of nationalization. In Russia, the oil companies are weak and newly established; they have been formed "from the top" from numerous companies that initially, following the seizure of Soviet assets, had been under management control. The management structure, inherited from the state socialist system,[19] is far more confident in pursuing a hegemonic role than is usual in the oil industry in the West—though a similar situation has occurred in Venezuela. The political sovereignty of Russia as a state is questioned by many of its constituent parts, and the central bodies are confronted with demands for a tax-take from the rents earned from the natural endowments of the republics and regions. (See chapters 5 and 6.) Also within the republics, the oil rich regions (such as Khanty-Mansi and Yamal-Nenets) contest the rights of their republics and insist on fixing their own fees. The ownership profile is unlike that of the Third World oil producing nations: in Russia, directed by the ideology of liberal market capitalism as well as severe budget deficits, state ownership is being replaced by privatization. The local and national governments in turn confront the management of the oil companies who, to realize the potential of the mineral assets under their command, begin to realize their dependence on Western capital as well as the potential of Western export markets. We have noted the abolition by President Yeltsin of the original limit of 15 percent ownership by foreigners, a change reflected by the top companies, which have gradually relaxed their own regulations (see company studies in the appendix to part 1). A major contrast within the political economy of Russia is between firms, such as oil and gas, which have great export potential and see themselves as global companies, and most other Russian industries, whose trade is on the home market. The oil companies favor exposure to the world market, and an export orientation, and a limit to state regulation, whereas other Russian industries, geared to the home market, seek a subsidy from cheap controlled oil prices on the internal market and regulation of imports.

To a greater extent even than in the military industrial complex, the oil companies bring an international dimension to Russian industry and politics, one which is absent from the other major industrial complexes. Ironically perhaps, the feudal sheikdoms of Kuwait, the Muslim traditionalists of Iran, and the military dictatorship of Iraq provide a stronger political shell for the preservation of their respective national oil industries than does the weak, fragmented government of Yeltsin's Russia. Russia's economy is also much more advanced and (like the American economy) comprehensive in scope; hence what is "good for Russian oil" (raising internal prices to the world level) is bad for industrial and domestic consumers. Not only does raising prices lead to a high level of internal debt on the part of consumers but it also severely depresses the production levels of Russian industry, which in turn reduces demand still further and stimulates the export orientation of the oil producers. Hence the weakness of the Russian economy impacts on the politics of Russian oil. In this context, as noted in the interviews conducted with politicians and oil executives, external international agencies, such as the IMF, play an important role in structuring the economy. Under present conditions, the leading foreign actors, the G7 states and the IMF, favor strengthening the market and weakening the role of state regulation. This is a policy position that brings them into conflict with many internal Russian actors.

Finally, the evolving Russian polity and economy is contradictory. There is no clear compact among the elites concerning the extent of state regulation and market competition. The wider context of political and economic interests may yet see a revival of state interest. The absence of buyers in August 1998 for the state company, Rosneft, and the pressure of the fall in the world price for oil led the Primakov government in April 1999 to put forward a plan for the formation of a a National Oil Company (Gosneft). This would be composed of three companies in which the state still had a high level of ownership: Rosneft (100 percent), ONAKO (75 percent) and Slavneft (75 percent). (Other units of Sidanko, such as Chernogorneft, Kondpetroleum, and Angarsk were also proposed for membership.) Such a company would control 10.6 percent of national production of oil, making it the fifth largest oil company with 8.8 billion barrels of oil reserves, and it would include three refineries and over 2,000 service stations. A change in government policy may be observed here, and numerous leading politicians have called for the assertion of state interests over the oil industry. This has been opposed by the "oil oligarchs" (Boris Berezovski, Vladimir Potanin, Mikhail Khodorkovski, Vagit Alekperov) who had secured, through banking interests, control over some of the oil companies. This proposed merger had positive advantages for the governmen: it would secure economies of scale and a source of supply under its own control to fuel Russian domestic consumers (particularly the army, agriculture, and impoverished areas of north Russia). It would however conflict with the economic policy of President Yeltsin and international backers such as the IMF.

Even a deregulated, privatized oil industry is subject to political intervention—as the history of the Middle East oil industry reveals. Present government policies threaten debtor companies with takeovers and renationalization if their debts are not paid. The internal politics of oil as a supplier to the domestic market was exacerbated following the financial crisis and the more conciliatory policy of the Primakov government. The rise in world prices in 1999, coupled with the continual inability of home industries to pay for fuel, led the government to instruct the oil companies to deliver to agricultural producers. In April 1999, the government threatened to restrict oil exports if agriculture was not supplied. The minister of Fuel and Energy, Sergei Generalov, stopped access to the pipelines for one day—more a symbolic gesture, but one which had the desired effect on agricultural supply.However, it is unlikely that a call for greater state involvement through consolidation of the industry into a state-owned company (on the early model of British Petroleum) will occur. Not only is the Russian state divided between federal and regional bodies but also external interests—Western governments and international agencies—are likely to be influential players and, at least in the foreseeable future, will demand a privatized and open economy.

NOTES

1. Changes took place in the gas industry as early as 1989, when its minister, Viktor Chernomyrdin, turned the ministry into a *kontsern*, then into a joint-stock company, Gazprom. It is important to note, however, that he maintained the gas industry as a single unitary body, and it has remained an effective (relatively closed) monopoly up to the present. Analogous structures developed in other branches of the fuel and energy industry: in coal, the *kontsern* Rosugol', in electrical supply, Edinye Energosistemy Rossii (EES Rossii).

2. Data cited in Eugene M. Khartukov, "Low Prices, Economic Woes Threaten Russian Oil Exports," *Oil and Gas Journal*, 8 June 1998, p. 26.

3. *Neft i kapital*, no. 2, 1995, pp. 78–80.

4. State Statistics Committee of Russian Federation, Interfax, 22 October 1997.

5. Reported in *Financial Times*, 9 April 1998.

6. There were three categories of possible participants in closed check auctions of Russian oil companies: (1) the company's employees/managers, (2) representatives of small nationalities of the north, and (3) employees and managers of oil pipeline enterprises.

7. *Neft i kapital*, no. 5, 1996, p. 28.

8. *Ekspert*, no. 33, 1996, pp. 40–41.

9. The conditions of this loan were that they offered the government a credit of 35 million dollars and promised to cover the debts amounting to 108 million dollars of LUKoil's subsidiaries before the budget was announced.

10. *Kommersant-Daily*, 18 August 1993; *Delovoi Mir*, 17 September 1994; *Segodnia*, 4 July 1995; *Delovoi Ekspres*, Moscow, no. 39, 27 October 1996.

11. *Neft i kapital*, no. 6, 1996, p. 28.

12. *Kommersant-Daily*, 17 September 1996, 6 November 1996, 21 November 1996, *Ekspert*, no. 43, 11 November 1996.

13. Brunswick Brokerage, *Oil Industry Update*, May 1996, p. 15.

14. The secondary fund market immediately responded to these decisions. In the first ten days after the Meeting of Shareholders, Surgutneftegaz's shares increased in price more than twice. *Neft i kapital*, no. 7/8, 1996, p. 34.

15. Eugene M. Khartukov, *Oil and Gas Journal*, 18 August 1997, p. 38.

16. *Finansovye izvestiia*, 27 March 1997, p. 1. Cited in P. Rutland, "Lost Opportunities: The Political Economy of Russia's Oil and Gas Sector." In *National Bureau of Asian Research*, vol. 8, no. 5, Washington, D.C., 1997, p. 23.

17. Forty interviews were carried out in Moscow by VTsIOM (a Russian polling company) with directors, presidents, vice presidents, and board members of the following companies: Moscow local companies (4), Tiumenneftegaz, Transnefteprodukt (2), Rostneft (5), Sidanko, YUKos (2) Vostochnaya (2), Slavneft (2), Ritek (2), Uralneft, Nefteresursy (2), Tyumenimpeks, Intol, Rosa Mira, Nakhodka, Komiartiol, Bi-Gaz-Si, Rial, RRK, ZAO, Surgutnefteaz, Mostransnefteprodukt (2), Mezh. Ekon. Sotrudnichestvo, ONAKO, Vitolneft, and Sibur. Five interviews were carried out in Bashkiriia with directors of Bashneft, and another five with directors of Tatneft in Tatarstan. A further fifteen interviews were conducted, independently of VTsIOM, in Moscow with seven directors or vice presidents of LUKoil, two from Transneft, two from Rosneft, two from Octan Plus, and two from Alfa EO joint stock company. Interviews were carried out between June and October 1997.

18. The politicians' group included eight members of the government of the Russian Republic, and twenty-two members of the Russian Duma selected from committees or areas with an interest in energy. They included representatives from Tiumen Oblast, Komi Republic, Orenburg Oblast, Krasnodar Krai, Khanty-Mansi Okrug, Bashkiriia Republic (4), Samara Oblast, Irkutsk Oblast, Ivanovsk Oblast, Perm Oblast, Iakutiia, Kuban-Don, Krasnoiask Krai, Irkutsk Oblast, Koriakski avton. okruk (Kamkhatsk Oblast). Others were directly elected on Party lists.

19. This statement is based on David Lane's study of the boards of directors (*soviet direktorov*) of the twelve oil companies in post in 1996.

2

Banks and the Financial Sector

Valery Kryukov and Arild Moe

Before 1991 almost all economic activity was carried out by state organs working within a planned economy, in which transactions were merely the fulfillment of plans and quotas and banks performed very basic bookkeeping and cashier services. This changed completely within a few years, with approximately two thousand banks emerging by 1995. Many of the new banks have already disappeared, but several have become key players in the oil sector in Russia. There have been multiple stages in the short life of the Russian banking system—a system that grew out of the financial departments of major enterprises in 1991, into the Financial-Industrial Groups (FIGs) that emerged in 1995–96.

In this chapter we trace the evolution of the relationship between the banks and the oil sector, and the banks' continued close relationship with the state. We examine the functions performed by the banks; the kinds of strategies they are implementing with respect to the oil sector; and the prospects for long-term lending and structural investment in the oil and gas sector. We also look closely at the new alliances that have emerged between banks and the oil companies. Although the transfer of ownership from state to private hands has not been an open process, its results herald a new era in the transformation of previously state-controlled industry, with major implications for foreign investors and oil companies.

GENESIS OF THE RUSSIAN BANKING SYSTEM

In the Soviet period, financial management amounted to a method of bookkeeping within the framework of the centralized planning and management system. The fundamental units in this system were physical. The banks carried out a control and distribution role: they distributed planned amounts of financial resources for the achievement of specific plan targets, and they made sure that expenditures were made according to plan instructions and that the proper accounts were debited and credited. Until 1987 the Soviet banking system was organized as a "monobank" system with Gosbank (the State Bank) as the agent of the government, which in turn controlled sectoral banks. The following banks managed the financial affairs of the oil and gas industry:

- *Gosbank SSSR* managed current transactions and channeled revenues from the sales of oil products and gas into the state budget;
- *Stroibank SSSR* distributed investment funds for capital construction and for the modernization of existing plants;
- *Vneshtorgbank SSSR* managed income from exports and the use of these revenues for the purchase of imported materials and equipment for the oil and gas sector.

But this banking system played a very subordinate role in the overall economic system. It serviced the stream of material flows, including hydrocarbons, on the basis of state priorities. Economic considerations had little significance.

The period 1987–1989 saw a limited reform of the Soviet banking system, and several specialized banks were established at the Union level, notably Zhilsotsbank SSSR (USSR Housing and Social Services Bank), Promstroibank SSSR (USSR Bank for Construction and Industry), and Agroprombank SSSR (USSR Agroindustrial Bank). At the same time many regional offices of the state banks became independent, a tendency that continued after the collapse of the USSR. By the mid-1990s there were about six hundred banks that could be seen as descendants of the state banks of the Soviet era. Among the banks descended from Zhilsotsbank, for instance, were Mosbiznesbank and Unikombank, both of which are very significant today.

Other banks that emerged were based on branch ministries and other branch agencies, as well as on individual enterprises, including production associations in the oil and gas industry. Banks in this category included Avtovazbank and Elektrobank. The "branch banks"—*otraslevye banki*—stood out by virtue of their relatively narrow specialization, the clear profile of their client base, and, most importantly, their very strong linkage to the interests of their founders. "Branch banks" were compelled to provide credit to their owners and founders at low interest rates—a fact that goes a long way toward explaining their relatively low profitability.

But their orientation toward industrial production also gave them access to subsidized state credits, which they could then distribute to their clients. They also profited from the general inertia in the system. The transfer of money took an exceedingly long time. In a period of rapid inflation, the bank "holding" a payment gained, since the recipient was not compensated for the inflation that occurred in the interim. This allowed the banks to issue short-term credits and to engage in currency speculation. This was hardly in the interest of the founders of the banks, but it could sometimes serve the private interests of personnel in the founding organizations.

Some branch banks were established as specialized banks for the export of strategic products. The foremost of these in the oil and gas sector were Neftekhimbank, Oneksimbank, Tokobank, and Alfa-Bank. The banks received very good earnings and a very high cash flow from this role, which allowed them to make large profits and to avoid risky operations involving credits to external clients. Banks with this orientation were less likely to be dominated by their industrial founders than other industry branch banks.

The most dynamic and rapidly growing banks, based mainly in Moscow, were established by individuals or came out of firms in the nascent market economy. Banks such as Mezhdunarodnyi Moskovskii bank, Inkombank, Kredobank, and Stolichnyi were notable from the very beginning for their attention to their clients' accounts. Banks like Inkombank and Most Bank flourished. The banks in this category showed less interest, however, in issuing credits to industry and trade, and most of their own capital was simply placed in accounts with the Central Bank. The new banks preferred simple accounting operations, especially in hard currency, to engaging in risky operations.

The rapid growth of many new banks in Russia was boosted by the very high prices they could charge for their services and by the high rates obtained on foreign exchange operations. The shortage of banking services in relation to the increasing numbers of economic actors in Russia resulted in an absence of competition, which allowed credit institutions to pay low interest rates on deposits. Nevertheless, the banks' clients, which were mainly enterprises, remained satisfied provided that the banks could protect their money from inflation. In general, the structure of working assets in Russian banks has meant that they have been far less exposed to risk than is the case with their Western counterparts. Russian credit institutions grant loans to the non-financial sector rather infrequently, whereas they often place their capital in state securities. The reluctance of the banks to lend to, for instance, the oil industry, is in part responsible for the lack of investment in the oil sector.

NEW LINKS BETWEEN BANKS AND OIL

The links between banks and the oil sector changed as enterprises became more economically independent and banks became more commercial:

- In 1991 oil industry enterprises were permitted to sell a fraction of their crude oil and refined oil products on the free market, although the bulk of production was still sold at artificially low prices;
- In 1992 prices for oil and oil products were allowed to rise drastically. Later price controls were removed;
- In 1992–1994, deliveries of oil and oil products at specially low prices were reduced and eventually totally abolished (although some mandatory deliveries for state needs continued).

The increase in market-based transactions necessitated improvements in the accounting system and financial links between the banks and the oil sector. Although in the beginning the proportion of free sales was very small—in 1991 a mere 5 percent of total production—many organizational problems emerged and the inefficiency of the existing banking system became evident:

- Financial accounting in most cases was extremely inefficient, outmoded and unwieldy;
- Bank personnel lacked financial expertise;
- There was a severe scarcity of finance and credit institutions.

For example, the Tiumen division of Promstroibank was the only bank serving the oil and gas sector in the vast territory of Tiumen Oblast, where the bulk of Russian and Soviet oil and gas production took place and which has an area of 554,100 square miles. It had only thirty-two branch offices in the entire territory, and their lack of modern communications equipment meant they were unable to execute swift transfers and operations with clients in other parts of the country. Several types of banks started to emerge against this backdrop as relations between specific banks and specific groups within the oil sector gradually developed.

PROPRIETARY BANKS:
THE TRANSFORMATION OF ACCOUNTING DEPARTMENTS

In the course of 1991 many enterprises in the oil sector transformed their departments of financial services and accounting into banks. Several banks were formed in this way, including the following:

- *Sibneftebank*, formerly the financial department of the Tiumen Main Directorate (*glavk*) of the Soviet Oil Ministry—Glavtiumenneftegaz;
- *Langepasbank*, which grew out of the production association (PO) Langepasneftegaz, itself now part of LUKoil;
- *Kapital*, which was created by Chernogorneft, Tomskneft, Varegan-neftegaz, and the private oil company, Magma; and
- *Yugorskii aktsionernyi bank*, which was established by the oil produc-tion association, Sibneftegazpererabotka (a refinery), and the oil pro-duction enterprises, Megionneftegaz and Nizhnevartovskneft.

Other banks to emerge in this period included Surgutneftegazbank (Surgutneftegaz, Surgutgazprom, Tiumenenergo, Severtrans), Noiabrsknefte-bank (Noiabrsknefteqaz), Yuganskneftebank (Yuganskneftegaz), and Uren-goibank (Urengoigazprom).

The creation of "proprietary banks," also referred to as "pocket banks" (*karmannye banki*), which had close links to their founding enterprises, reduced to some extent the liquidity problem of the oil enterprises involved and facilitated payment for equipment and materials. These new "banks" also took care of payment of salaries and wages as well as taxes. Although they were clearly different from the accounting departments on which most of them had been built, they were not full-fledged banks, as they were capable of executing only an extremely narrow range of financial operations and services and played almost no role in the investment processes in the oil industry.

The second development was the establishment of the first commercial banks, including "new" banks, which sought to act as agents of the state, per-forming various operations required by the state that many of the "old" banks were incapable of conducting under market conditions (e.g., Vneshekonom-bank, which had conducted foreign trade operations). The state itself was active in establishing these commercial banks, as it sought not only to build efficient financial institutions, but also to retain influence over them.

The alliance created between MFK and Oneksimbank illustrates the desire of the state to retain influence over the banking sector. Oneksimbank was registered in April 1993. Its shareholders comprised more than thirty of the largest Russian foreign trade associations with a total turnover of more than $10 billion, including the three oil exporting companies Nafta-Moskva, Ros-neftimpeks, and Sovbunker. Among the shareholders were also Norilsk nikel (the giant metals producer); and MFK bank (Mezhdunarodnaiia finansovaia kompaniia, or International Financial Company). MFK in turn had taken over personnel and functions from Vneshekonombank (Bank for Foreign Trade) and the International Bank for Economic Cooperation, which had previously handled trade within the Council for Mutual Eco-nomic Assistance (CMEA).

The Ministry of Finance and the Russian Central Bank played an active part in the creation of the new Oneksimbank. In the summer of 1994 the bank became an agent for the Russian government in serving centralized foreign trade activity. Thus from the very beginning special links with the government were forged, while the Oneksimbank-MFK group was connected to very solid clients among oil traders as well as companies in the raw materials sector.

Banks with a diversified profile were established not so much with the support and participation of the state as with the participation of various business conglomerates, especially trading companies and middlemen. Such banks include Menatep, Inkombank, Alfa-Bank, and many others. The strength of these banks in the first stage of development lay in their capacity for innovation, flexibility, and provision of several functions that had emerged as important under market conditions. These banks also created and supported trading companies and understood which banking operations were the most profitable and which the least risky. The new multi-profile banks participated in the oil sector primarily in connection with foreign trade operations, including the sales of oil and oil products and purchases of foreign equipment, replacing the role of the old Vneshekonombank.

Menatep was the bank with the highest profile in this group, with no single shareholder holding more than a 5 percent ownership interest. More than twenty organizations were among its initial shareholders, including the oil trader Nafta-Moskva. Menatep grew out of the Center for Interbranch Scientific-Technological Programs (the acronym Menatep comes from its Russian initials). This center, which was a scientific cooperative in Moscow, was a co-founder of an association called Menatep. In 1988 the "Commercial Innovation Bank for Scientific Technological Progress"—AKIB—was formed, and the enterprises belonging to the Menatep Association were amalgamated with this new bank, which soon took the name Menatep. Its initial equity capital was a mere 5 million rubles. Neftekhimbank, in contrast, started with 200 million rubles, but within two years the newcomer had overtaken it. The growth of Menatep was linked to a number of factors. Several foreign trade associations and other foreign trade structures—precisely the sector in which initial capital accumulation took place—were among its clients. The bank worked actively in the currency market and was one of the first commercial banks in Russia to receive a license for this kind of activity. It also worked a great deal with trading companies inside Russia. Finally it approached government circles, and became one of the first banks to serve trade operations with Belarus and the Ukraine at the end of 1991.

The period 1993–94 was marked by many radical developments, which had a major impact on relations between banks and enterprises in the oil sector. These included:

- The abolition of the system of state financing for capital investments in the oil industry;
- Changes in the property structure in the oil sector, including the conversion of oil production associations into joint-stock companies, followed by their partial privatization;
- A deterioration in the domestic economic situation, with steadily falling economic activity and increased taxation on the oil sector.

The narrowly focused oil banks—typically found in the provinces—could not raise sufficient capital to finance investment in the oil industry. Furthermore, they were unable to defend the interests of the new joint-stock companies in the oil sector by fending off unwanted purchasers of shares. Their lack of political capital in Moscow also hindered them in finding attractive strategic partners for their clients, in conducting a dialogue with people in power on an equal footing, and in being heard by the government as well as by Parliament. What is more, in many cases their hands were tied by founders and principal clients who constantly made decisions that ran counter to the commercial agenda of the bank but were in concert with their own short-term needs.

A clear example of such dependence by a bank on an oil company was the relationship between Nizhnevartovskneftegaz and Yugorskii, a bank which in 1992 and 1993 was among the more dynamic in Russia. In early 1994 this bank, together with Imperial bank, worked out a plan to create a bank union with the express task of financing the oil sector in Russia with capital from domestic as well as foreign sources with government guarantees. However, after a conflict with the Yugorskii bank, Nizhnevartovskneftegaz decided to quit this bank as founder and to transfer its accounts to other banks. The clash was purportedly over delayed payments through the bank, but it probably had much to do with attempts by the bank to develop a more independent policy. Another oil producer, Megionneftegaz, followed suit, creating its own proprietary bank, Yugrabank. Very rapidly Yugorskii lost its position, and by mid-1995 it ranked far below the hundred largest Russian banks. These developments clearly showed how vulnerable the "proprietary banks" were.

Thus, during a period of just over eighteen months, the roles of the different types of banks changed substantially. The so-called universal banks (located mainly in Moscow) gained in significance, while the branch banks became less influential. An indication of the change that took place can be found in table 2.1. Though the methodology is far from perfect (a ranking by size of assets, based on information supplied by the banks themselves), the general trend seems fairly clear. We see that the position of the branch banks was drastically reduced, while the universal banks improved or at least maintained their ranking.

Table 2.1 Russian Banks Working with the Oil Sector (Ranking among all Russian banks, According to Size of Assets)

Bank	Main shareholders*	July 1992	July 1993	July 1994	July 1995	July 1996	July 1997	Jan 1999
Inkombank		7	6	4	5	3	2	40
Oneksimbank	Surgutneftegaz, Nafta-Moskva			12	4	4	5	4
Imperial	LUKoil, Gazprom, Zarubezhneft	3	8	6	8	12	14	
MFK				10	11	9	24	15
Stolichnyi Bank Sberezhenii		9	18	19	15	8	4	11
Menatep	Nafta-Moskva	16	14	13	10	10	10	10
Nats. reservnyi bank	Gazprom					13	13	6
Tokobank	Yuganskneftegaz	1	9	11	21	19	23	
Alfa-Bank			98	22	23	17	11	8
Neftekhimbank	60 oil refineries & petrochemical cos.	11	22	17	28	30	43	38
Gazprombank	Gazprom	47	53	76	41	27	18	3
Promradtekhbank	YuKOS			55	62	46	47	35
Yugorskii	Nizhnevartovskneftegaz		19	40	113	n.a.		
Neftegazstroibank	Neftegazstroi	45	36	54	93	n.a.		
InterTekBank	Ministry of Fuel and Energy				49	44	50	150
ZapSibKomBank		15	16	20	53	45	51	64
Kapital	Chernogorneft		60		107	112	86	100
Sibneftebank	Tiumenneftegaz	55			148	96	112	
Urengoibank	Urengoigazprom					192	199	
Yugra	Megnionneftegaz					99	81	116
Yuganskneftebank	Yuganskneftegaz					141	135	132
Yunibest	Nafta-Moskva					135	61	
Kogalymneftekom-bank	LUKoil-Kogalymneftegaz					150	10	
Nefteprombank	Rosneft, Moscow oil exchange					154	115	85

*From the oil and gas sector. Based on various sources, including founders who may have since sold their shares.

Source for rankings: Information Center *Reiting*; rankings published in, respectively, *Ekonomika i zhizn*, no. 31, 1992; no. 41, 1993; no. 45, 1994; *Finansovye izvestiia*, 10 August 1995; *Delovoy mir*, March 1996; *Finansovye izvestiia*, no. 79, 1996; no. 60, 1997; *Den'gi*, 19 March 1999.

CREATION OF THE RUSSIAN
"MAJORS" HERALDS FURTHER CHANGES

The core of the Russian government's policy with regard to reorganization in the oil industry was the amalgamation of industry enterprises into large, vertically integrated companies, which were organized as joint-stock oil companies (as detailed in chapter 1). The creation of a series of such companies during 1993–1995 had a profound effect on the links between the oil sector and the banks. The establishment of holding companies such as LUKoil, YuKOS, and Surgutneftegaz required the presence of more powerful banking institutions that corresponded more closely to the size and activities of the new companies. As the share of exports in total oil output increased, stronger links were required with the universal banks in Moscow, not only to serve the companies' hard currency operations, but to lobby for improved conditions for exports of oil and imports of equipment.

LUKoil-Imperial-Nikoil

In October 1993 LUKoil, the largest Russian oil company, decided to consolidate all the financial assets in Imperial bank belonging to the holding company. These assets had until then been spread over twelve banks. The reorganization of the company as a joint-stock company required a new policy toward the banks that were going to service its operations as a vertically integrated company. For this reason LUKoil also decided to take a significant interest in the bank. In addition to LUKoil, Gazprom and the foreign trade association Zarubezhneft featured among the shareholders of Imperial. They each held approximately equal interests, of about 12 percent. The connection between Imperial and LUKoil was not new, however, as LUKoil's trading house had previously been served by the bank.

In the same year, 1993, LUKoil took part in the establishment of the investment company, Nikoil. The idea came from a group of economists who had already worked out the plan for the privatization of LUKoil. In the spring of 1994 a Russian presidential decree was issued, prohibiting brokers from keeping share registries and shareholder lists, to avoid conflicting interests. For this reason a new company was formed, the independent Nikoil (which held LUKoil's share register). Nikoil became the exclusive representative of LUKoil in the securities market in Russia and abroad and thereupon became the second largest shareholder in LUKoil, after the Russian state.

The alliance among banks, investment institutions, and LUKoil stands out because of the active part played by the leadership of the oil company from the very beginning of the relationship. Banks and investment institutions served to consolidate the oil company, but it was the company itself that decided which institutions and which services to avail itself of, and what it wanted to use them for.

The plans for a vertically integrated state oil concern—LUKoil—were developed as early as 1989 or 1990, spearheaded by Vagit Alekperov, who was then deputy oil and gas minister of the USSR. This put LUKoil clearly ahead of the others when the development of such companies became official Russian policy in 1992. Also, in the ensuing period, Alekperov was a key figure in attracting external investment and solving internal financial structural problems ahead of LUKoil's competitors. From the outset, the leadership took steps to establish a separate, strong holding company over and above the co-founders of the company, the oil producers, refineries, and distributors that were to become its subsidiaries. The holding company was clearly superior to the subsidiaries in both personnel and competence.

YuKOS-Menatep

Initially, YuKOS chose Promradtekhbank as its main banking partner. The investment department of this bank drafted the first schemes for management and consolidation of the oil company in 1992–1993. This alliance did not, however, lead to long-term cooperation: Promradtekhbank was only a medium-sized bank and, more importantly, it was in no way capable of bringing about a change in the internal balance of power in YuKOS—which was a vital precondition for the consolidation of the company. Promradtekhbank was rapidly marginalized, and eventually demoted to the role of depository for the shares of the oil company.

Political, regional, and personal interests played a more important role than commercial and economic considerations when elements of the old state oil industry were regrouped as vertically integrated oil companies, and internal cohesion in the new companies varied significantly. The first years of YuKOS, 1993–1995, were characterized by the often antagonistic relationship between the holding company, YuKOS, and its main production unit, Yuganskneftegaz. The latter, which was itself organized as a joint-stock company, became one of the main founders of a leading Russian bank, Tokobank, with over 20 percent of its shares. Even though the general director of YuKOS, Sergei Muravlenko, was the former general director of the production association, Yuganskneftegaz, the leadership of the holding company could not prevent resistance from Yuganskneftegaz to its policies; nor was the holding company able to control the main material and financial flows within the larger integrated organization. The leadership of YuKOS even turned to the government, as the largest shareholder, for help in solving its internal consolidation problems[1]—but without success.

In fact it took a new owner to remedy the situation. An alliance with the new potential owner had started as early as 1992, when a subsidiary of the French bank, Lazard Frères, served as a consultant to YuKOS. The head of Lazard's Russian affiliate was Vladimir Lopukhin, who had been minister of fuel and energy in Yegor Gaidar's government. Mikhail Khodorkovski, the head of Menatep, had been his adviser at this time and was the architect of one of the first investment programs of the fuel and energy ministry.[2] Cooperation between Muravlenko, Lopukhin, and Khodorkovski developed rapidly after 1992, and when Lazard Frères ended their relationship with Lopukhin, Menatep was ready to assist Muravlenko and YuKOS. Unlike Promtekhbank, Menatep under Khodorkovski had strong links with the government and government structures, and its staff were also far more dynamic and business-minded.

Surgutneftegaz and Sidanko: Multiple Financial Affiliates

Other Russian oil companies, including Surgutneftegaz and Sidanko, did not attempt to forge tight links with a single financial investment group. Surgutneftegaz was similar to LUKoil with regard to its proactive strategy vis-à-vis financial institutions, but its financial operations were handled by several banks. Accounts were taken care of by Oneksimbank and a number of others, whereas share issues and the register of shares were under the direct and close attention of the company's head office.

However, in early 1995 Surgutneftegaz bought a 16.6 percent stake in Oneksimbank. This has given the oil company some of the benefits of having a proprietary bank, including credits on favorable terms. The bank has since invested $40 million in a joint project with the SNG refining subsidiary, Kirishinefteorgsintez, and is also involved with the company in a port terminal project in Luga near St. Petersburg. However, a major motivation for the oil company's move may have been to block the bank from buying it. The stake is not big enough to control the bank, but Surgutneftegaz was able to preclude unwanted moves. Nevertheless, Surgutneftegaz has maintained a clear distance from Oneksimbank. All issues connected to management and the restructuring of the oil company have remained under the strict control of the holding company. Surgutneftegaz has managed to consolidate its assets and has embarked upon a strategy to attract foreign financing through the issue of American depository receipts in cooperation with the Bank of New York.

The relationship that developed between Sidanko and its financial affiliates has been less independent and benign. Until mid-1995 Sidanko's leadership was preoccupied with internal affairs, trying unsuccessfully to consolidate the company and improve its structure. During 1994 and 1995 the holding company received scarcely any transfers from its subsidiaries, and did not control material and financial flows within the so-called vertically integrated company. It was thus forced to take up credits—mainly from Oneksimbank and Imperial—in order to maintain operations, and has become one of the largest clients and debtors of Oneksimbank.

THE EMERGENCE OF FIGS

Notwithstanding the dynamism and increased role and influence of the big Russian universal banks located in Moscow, their assets have remained very small indeed. This reflects the fact that the accumulation of capital in Russia is still in an early stage, and that there are too many banks in existence for the total capital available. Before the financial crisis of 1998, for example, the equity capital of Inkombank was only U.S.$327 million.

During 1993 and 1994 the center of gravity shifted from the proprietary banks to the big multi-profile banks. The oil companies preferred the latter not only for their healthy financial state but also for their growth potential, judged primarily on the basis of the qualifications of their staff and top management and their ability to establish and widen contacts with the government.

As the securities market developed and privatization progressed, the banks began to form investment departments. The main motivation of the banks in entering the oil sector was to secure very large clients with significant turnover, and clients oriented toward foreign economic operations. The development of the securities market greatly influenced the activity of commercial banks, many of which formed significant subsidiaries dealing with investment. Investment companies emerged from these departments and subsidiaries in some of the larger banks. These were in turn to become the nuclei of the so-called financial industrial groups (FIGs).[3] Typically, a division of labor was introduced between investment companies and commercial banks:

- *Interros.* The financial industrial group Interros was created around the MFK-Oneksimbank alliance by a presidential decree of 28 October 1994;[4]
- *Rosprom.* The management company Rosprom was formed in September 1995 within the framework of Menatep, to manage shares held in industrial enterprises;
- *Inkom-Kepital.* The investment company Inkom-Kepital was created under the auspices of Inkombank in September 1996, and a division of labor was agreed between the bank and the company. The main investment activity, the management of client assets, and corporate finance is taken care of by Inkom-Kepital, whereas Inkombank handles custody business and project finance.

The stimulus for creating investment divisions has been explained in an article in *Segodnia* (22 October 1996) by D. Shmarovich, General Director of Interros:

> When Interros was created, Oneksimbank was already a self-sufficient organism. It was interested in the financial-industrial group from the perspective of cooperation with the state. . . . Afterwards we realized that a joining of state and private capital would not happen. The state support was zero. So we decided to rely on our own strength. . . . Interros will select enterprises and companies which in our opinion are underpriced by the market. We will attract experts and form management groups, restructure the enterprise and improve its financial performance at the micro level. Only when this has been done will we form our own industrial portfolio. Some enterprises will be sold on our behalf or on behalf of the government whereas some will remain in the structure of the financial-industrial group.

An additional factor was the reduced profitability of operations on the financial market, connected with the decreased interest on refinancing from the Central Bank of Russia, which fell from over 200 percent in the fall of 1993 to 50 percent in December 1996. The introduction of a currency corridor in July 1995 and the strengthening of the system of state regulations and control of currency market operations also created a hole in bank profits. The currency corridor created a significant disparity between the nominal rates for hard currency and the real inflation rate, resulting in a fall in the purchasing power of foreign currency (see figure 2.1). Credit institutions with a large share of their working assets in hard currency were particularly hard hit—first and foremost the Moscow banks, including the universal banks.

Figure 2.1 Inflation and Exchange Rate, 1994–1998

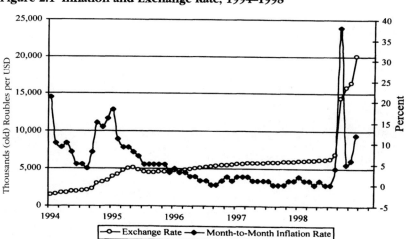

Source: PlanEcon Report, various issues

Thus toward mid-1995 the new banks' possibilities for growth as described above were largely exhausted. The profitability of simple cashier operations, especially in hard currency, was drastically reduced, and there was a marked tendency in 1994 and 1995 for banks of all sizes to turn from currency operations to operations with state securities, primarily state treasury bonds (GKOs). In 1996 the banking system in Russia was kept afloat largely by state securities—which were still relatively profitable at the time (see figure 2.2). However, there has been a gradual reduction in the profitability of these operations, which proved to be enduring for the GKO market.

A lower rate of inflation normally changes the structure of demand in favor of longer-term credits, requiring a corresponding increase in the share of long-term obligations provided by banks. Nevertheless, long-term credits in September 1996 amounted to only 19.6 trillion rubles out of the 314 trillion rubles managed by banks. Long-term credits amounted to no more than 0.04 percent of the balances of the ten leading banks at the time of peak inflation in 1993–94, and the situation has changed little since then. Almost half the assets of the credit institutions have circulated within the banking sphere itself, without entering other sectors of the economy.[5] A major problem is that the banks' best resources and best personnel have been oriented toward accounting and cashier services, purchase and sale of hard currency, and work with government securities as well as short-term loans.

This strategy has permitted the Russian banks to survive but not to develop, and the weaknesses were revealed in the currency collapse in 1998. Given the conditions prevailing in Russia, it is not enough for a bank to work well or to have a solid basis and a developed network of branch

Figure 2.2 Profitability of Three- and Six-Month State Treasury Bonds (GKO) 1995–1996

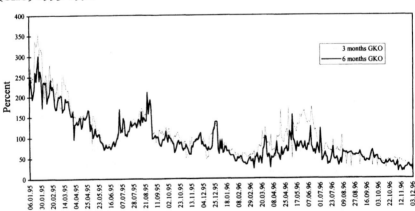

Source: Central Bank of Russia

offices to be successful: state support is a sine qua non. In our view, the development of relations between the banks and the oil sector in Russia amply supports this assertion. The state is interested not only in a stable financial system, but in the stability and development of production. Traditionally the most important productive sectors include the fuel and energy complex, with the oil industry as the main component.

As indicated in table 2.2, the share of assets derived from the state budget in the balance of some banks is very high. Five banks, including Oneksimbank and Menatep, accounted for 90 percent of the credits given to the state in 1995. In turn they received interest payments and other compensation corresponding to 27 percent of the credits they had issued.[6] Altogether these banks received 5.6 trillion rubles, or approximately $1.4 billion.

Table 2.2 State Monies in the Balances of Banks Working with the Oil Sector

Bank	Share of all deposits (from organizations financed by/via state budget, 1 July 1997)	Remaining rubles on accounts (of organizations financed by/via state budget, 1 September 1997)
Inkombank	0.242	82
Oneksimbank	12.163	427
Imperial	3.71	
MFK	0.409	
Stolichnyi Bank	0.928	
Sberezhenii/Agro Menatep	2.836	118
Nats. reservnyi bank	0.002	
Tokobank	0.154	
Alfa-Bank	0.74	
Neftekhimbank	0.493	
Gazprombank	1.156	
Promradtekhbank	12.429	
InterTekBank	0.119	
ZapSibKomBank	6.214	
Yugra	0.224	
Nefteprombank	0.087	

Note: Ruble figures have been converted to U.S. dollars at current exchange rates.
Source: Kommersant-reiting, no. 11, 1997, and *Profil*, no. 37, 1997.

The political and economic circumstances outlined above have determined the strategy of the major new banks with regard to increased participation in investments. Without taking steps in this direction it would have
been very difficult for them to keep state support or to reinforce their position as leading Russian banks.

LOANS-FOR-SHARES AUCTIONS:
PRIVATIZATION WITHOUT POLITICAL PAIN

When Russia's first vertically integrated oil companies were created out of the
horizontal ministries of the Soviet oil and gas complex, in accordance with the
1992 privatization program for the oil industry, as noted in chapter 1, the state
would hold controlling interests in the new oil companies. As a rule, 38 percent of ordinary shares, corresponding to 51 percent of voting shares, were to
be held as government property for three years. The first oil companies were
established in the spring of 1993; consequently, by the spring of 1996 the term
for government custody of a majority interest was starting to run out.

However, the expiration of the original three-year period was not in itself
a major motive for change, particularly as the political climate in the Duma
was not supportive of further privatization of the energy industries, and an
extension of government custody would have been easy to obtain. The
impetus for new measures came from a combination of two factors. First, the
financial position of the state was becoming increasingly difficult, with a
budget deficit corresponding to approximately 10 percent of GDP. This
placed the search for new income sources, or at least for temporary credit,
high on the government's agenda. However, since a straight sellout of state
assets was not politically feasible, liberals in the government were interested
in schemes that would soften the opposition to full privatization. Second, by
1996 professional bankers and banks had emerged whose initial areas of
activity, as depicted above, had become less profitable and who viewed participation in industry as a logical next step in their development.

It is thus no surprise that the new Russian banks came forward with a proposal to offer credit to the government on security in federal shares in privatized enterprises. The idea was first publicly voiced at a government session
on 30 March 1995, when the president of Oneksimbank, Vladimir Potanin,
made a speech on behalf of a consortium of commercial banks. Also present
at this session were the presidents of Menatep and the Stolichnyi Bank
Sberezhenii (SBS). In the scheme adopted by presidential decree on 31
August 1995, Russian investors would take over a part of the government
share in trust management for a specified period, in exchange for supplying
the government with credits.[7] The transfer would be organized through auctions, and foreigners were explicitly banned from participation. At the same
time, it was decided to organize investment tender competitions for state-

owned oil company shares exceeding the controlling interest that were to be placed under trust management. The winner would become owner of the shares, and would be required to commit himself to a specified amount of investment in the oil company, in addition to paying for the shares.

The first loans-for-shares auctions and the investment competitions were carried out almost concurrently at the end of 1995. At the time, allegations were made that both had been rigged, and some results were contested by the losers. However, shortly afterwards the results were approved by the authorities. The results are analyzed below.

An important feature of the loans-for-shares auctions was that without exception only new Russian banks participated, in other words, banks that had been built up de novo, not transformed Soviet banks. For these new banks, participation in the auctions provided a real opportunity to improve their reputation in government circles and shed their image as purely financial speculative institutions. The development of close relationships with the state remains an important business strategy in Russia. It would be naive to argue that the banks had a clear and elaborate strategy for their participation in the loans for share auctions and investment competitions. However, there was also an element of urgency as the banks did not want to miss out on the distribution of the best assets.

The banks had two main strategies for penetrating the oil sector, which could be described as "passive" and "active." The former concentrated on the development of a service function vis-à-vis the oil companies, namely to increase the volume and range of financial services that could be offered to the company. In contrast, an "active" strategy included intervention in the management of the oil companies and active participation in their restructuring. These two types of strategies are clearly illustrated in the development of relations between the main oil companies—LUKoil, YuKOS, Sidanko, Surgutneftegaz, Sibneft—and associated banks. For details of the changes in ownership, see Lane and Seifulmulukov, chapter 1.

In the case of LUKoil and Surgutneftegaz, the oil companies made use of the banks in the privatization process, but they were always in charge themselves, and in the resulting new ownership structure the oil companies' leadership remained very much in control. The banks were not allowed to intervene in the internal operations of these companies.

In the case of Sibneft, which was set up only in August 1995, the establishment of the company was connected to outside financial interests, with Logovaz-United Bank, controlled by Boris Berezovski, as a main force. During the loans-for-shares auction in the company, Stolichnyi Bank Sberezhenii (SBS) acquired the state shares for trust management, together with Neftiianaiia finansovaiia kompaniia (headed by Berezovski). The role of SBS during the auction was more that of an operator executing the wishes and plans of an important client—which indeed Sibneft was for the bank. In the end, a group consisting of Logovaz-United Bank and top management within Sibneft itself managed to concentrate 85 percent of the shares in the company in their hands.

In YuKOS and Sidanko, developments were different. Both these companies were plagued by a lack of internal cohesion, and Sidanko especially had a large debt problem when the loans for share auctions and investment tenders took place. The banks that won out in the auctions and tenders were, not coincidentally, banks that already had a relationship with these oil companies as main creditors and financial advisers. Soon after they had acquired temporary control over large blocs of government shares, Menatep and Oneksimbank started to play major roles in the development of YuKOS and Sidanko respectively. They did this through their respective financial-industrial groups, Rosprom and Interros.

As early as April 1996, at a session of the board of directors of YuKOS, representatives of Menatep were included in the steering organs of the company. The position of first vice president of YuKOS with responsibility for planning was filled by Mikhail Khodorkovski, the chairman of the management board of Rosprom as well as the board of directors of Menatep. Eight vice presidents came under him, twice as many as were allotted to the other two first vice presidents. Khodorkovski's area was defined to include oil refining, petrochemicals and chemicals, domestic market sales, exports, investment policy, finances, and securities. Other representatives of Menatep were also given leading positions in the company: By mid-1996 more than a hundred people from the Menatep group were working in YuKOS.

Through subsequent auctions and share issues, Menatep increased its control to the extent that by 1 December 1996 it held an overwhelming majority of shares either directly or through affiliated companies or in trust for the government (see table 2.3).

Table 2.3 Composition of Shareholders in YuKOS (1 December 1996)

Shareholder	Percentage
State share (held in trust by Menatep)	33.30
Yukos Invest	7.05
Companies controlled by Menatep	
Astarta	18.0
Makhaon	15.0
Tonus	5.5
Total	38.50
Russian Investors	12.79
Individuals	8.29

The original term for trust management of the shares received in the loans-for-shares auctions in 1995 expired on 1 September 1996. After that date, shares in trust management with the banks could either be bought back by the government, or would become the property of the trust managers. Since the government was in no position to repay the credits it had received from the banks, the second possibility began to be carried out. However, the government and the Security Council drafted a joint letter instructing that state shares held in trust management could be sold only on condition that the government be properly informed three months in advance, and that government representatives be invited to the auctions. Foreigners would be permitted to buy, but their stake would be limited to 15 percent of the total number of shares in each company. On the other hand, the government managed to extend the period during which it could hold shares in the oil companies until 31 December 1998.[8] But again the imperative was to sell, not to keep the shares.

After Menatep had secured key positions in YuKOS, on 20 November 1996 it announced that it would conduct a commercial competition for the 33 percent of shares it was managing on behalf of the government. (The government share was originally 25 percent, but it had been diminished by new issues.) Bidders were invited to commit themselves to investments in the company, under very much the same procedure as that of the previous year. The decision to sell the state share was not taken without the participation of the government, but it was on Menatep's initiative. According to the first deputy chairman of Menatep, K. Kogalovski, the main goal had now been achieved: for further cooperation with the company, the bank did not need to own the government shares.

Menatep's need for financial resources was the main reason behind the sale of the state share. The minimum sum mentioned in the conditions for the competition was $160 million plus an investment program of $200 million, approximately the same amount stipulated in the conditions for the loans-for-shares auction ($350 million) a year earlier. Thus if these sums were paid in, Menatep would have transferred all its financial obligations toward YuKOS to the new investor. The shares were sold to Monblan, an unknown company controlled by Menatep, which offered $160.1 million— just above the minimum price. Thus the bank decreased its exposure but not its control, and 94 percent of the shares in YuKOS were now directly or indirectly under the control of Menatep.

Even with the banks' exposure diminished, YuKOS continued to play a major role in Menatep's portfolio. A full 70 percent of the assets of the Menatep group were then linked with YuKOS. Total annual sales of the enterprises under Rosprom amounted to somewhat more than $6 billion, of which $5 billion stemmed from YuKOS. YuKOS is a very large company, and its investment requirements far exceed the capacities of Menatep. As of 1 January 1996, Menatep's equity stood at about 730 billion rubles, corresponding to 140–150 million dollars. Clearly, the group could not secure the development of the companies it then controlled from its own resources, which were sufficient only for survival. What the bank did was to use its own resources to restructure the industrial group and to invest in some highly efficient short-term projects.

The development of the alliance between Sidanko and Oneksimbank followed largely the same pattern as that of YuKOS/Menatep, discussed above. This included strengthening the bank's position in the top management of the company; establishing control over the flows of products as well as financial flows; transferring payments and accounts of the oil company to the bank as trust managers of the government share; acquisition by the bank of a significant portion of the shares as its own property through investment competitions; and further consolidation of the oil company. The final step in the process was integration of the oil company into a financial-industrial group.

The president of Oneksimbank, Vladimir Potanin, the chairman of the management board (president) of MFK, M. Alekseev, as well as his advisor Dmitri Maslov (who soon after became the oil company's vice president for economic and financial affairs) were included on the new board of directors of Sidanko. Also on the board of directors were two representatives of the Alfa Group consortium, and representatives from Oneksimbank and MFK were included in the management organs of the oil company's subsidiaries.

In September 1996 another investment competition was organized, for 34 percent of Sidanko's stock. This competition was used as an instrument to consolidate the company's assets. Conditions for participation included the investment of $100 million in the restructuring of credits to replenish the current assets of Angarsk Petrochemical Company, and $8.2 million to finance programs of Sidanko itself. An additional condition was that the successful bidder should transfer to Sidanko 13 percent of the shares in Chernogorneft. At the time, Oneksimbank was the only external owner in Chernogorneft with a package of shares this size.[9] Such conditions for an investment competition not only created an effective barrier to unwanted participants, but also to some extent weakened the separatist mood in Chernogorneft. The competition was won by a company called Interros-oil, belonging to the Oneksim-MFK group. Interros-oil had been specially set up within the Interros FIG to manage Sidanko. In November 1996, a shareholders' meeting was held in the financial-industrial group, and Sidanko was among the new shareholders announced. Participants in the FIG would immediately become shareholders in the joint-stock company, Interros-oil. Thus, indirectly Sidanko became part owner of itself, although Interros-oil clearly remained primarily the instrument of Oneksimbank. On 1 December 1996 the shares in Sidanko were distributed as shown in table 2.4.

When the state announced that its 51 percent holding in Sidanko, which was held in trust management by MFK, would be put up for sale at an

Table 2.4 Ownership Structure in Sidanko (1 December 1996)

Ownership	Percentage
State share (managed by MFK)	51
Shares sold at investment competition to Interros-oil	11
Shares sold at special auctions	11
Shares given by government to Menatap in exchange for shares in the bank	4

investment tender competition in January 1997, the stake was bought by Interros-oil for $129.8 million (with the minimum bid at $129 million) and an obligation to invest $100 million in the company within one year as well as securing the company $61 million in credits for financial stabilization and transferring 4.5 percent of the stock in the subsidiary Angarsk Petrochemical Company to Sidanko.[10] Thus the share of Interros-oil in Sidanko increased to 85 percent. This move must be seen as an attempt to deflect the negative consequences of a possible change in government policy on shares in trust management and on remaining state shares in the industry, after the extended term for trust management expired on 31 December 1996.

The Oneksimbank-MFK group has largely followed the same path as Menatep in obtaining permanent control of shares initially received in temporary trust management. But despite the many similarities between YuKOS and Sidanko, there are also differences. As noted above, YuKOS held 70 percent of the assets of the Menatep group. This proportion was much lower in the case of Oneksimbank-MFK. In addition to the shares in Sidanko, the group also received a controlling interest in the giant metals producer Norilsk nikel, which has an annual output worth some $3 billion, placing it in the same league as Sidanko. However, this meant that the banking group needed to restructure two extraordinarily capital-intensive and gigantic companies simultaneously. Whereas Sidanko had a surplus of about 2 trillion rubles in 1995, Norilsk nikel owed 6.3 trillion rubles as against the 4.3 trillion rubles it was owed. Like Menatep, the Oneksimbank-MFK group lacked the resources to cover the investment requirements of both Sidanko and Norilsk nikel. As of mid-1966, the group's equity capital was about 1,623 billion rubles, or approximately 700 million dollars.

In March 1997 it was reported that Interros-oil had transferred its original 34 percent stake in Sidanko to Cantupun, a company registered in Cyprus, in exchange for credits to Sidanko of approximately $80 million, thus shedding some of its financial obligations.[11] Cyprus is a well-known base for "foreign" Russian capital. Even if there are several foreign investors behind Cantupun, it is not improbable that MFK-Oneksimbank is among them. Nevertheless, with the remaining stake of 51 percent held directly by Interros-oil, the bank group did not risk losing control by placing shares under the temporary management of the Cyprus company. But gradually it became clear that there could be a conflict of interest between the oil company and its dominant owner. The bank and the FIG wanted to make use of Sidanko's financial resources in a broader strategy for the Oneksimbank-Interros group. This was a main reason why the two main oil producers within the company, Kondpetroleum and Chernogorneft, were practically lost for Sidanko after bankruptcy proceedings toward the end of 1998. The central office of Sidanko, dominated by representatives of Oneksimbank and Interros, forced the subsidiaries to pay very high commissions to the central office for the management of oil flows, at the same time as they were not allowed to sell to other buyers.[12] This helped fill the coffers of the holding company for a while, but it undermined the economy of the subsidiaries.

CONCLUSIONS: THE FINAL STAGES OF OWNERSHIP TRANSFER: LIMITATIONS AND POSSIBILITIES IN THE NEW SITUATION

Up to 1995, Russia's oil companies were nominally controlled by the state, since the state retained a majority of the voting shares in each company. However, there was at best only a limited direct state influence on the companies' current operations through the boards of directors. The passive role played by the state as owner meant that the top management of the companies had full control over company operations with no major interference from external owners. This is not to say that they were independent of the state in other respects. Because the institutional framework was unspecified and everchanging, every Russian oil company was engaged in complex negotiations with government authorities on vital issues such as access to credits, tax privileges, export quotas, and so on.

The first phase of privatization of the Russian oil companies during 1993–94 was a prime example of "insider privatization." The top leadership affirmed its control of the respective companies through the minority stakes the government put up for sale, as the state was passive and ineffective as majority owner. With the loans-for-shares auctions, new external owners were introduced.

The strategy of the banks after gaining control of oil companies has followed a common sequence:

- Transferring all accounts and payments to the bank;
- Changing the management of the oil company;
- Restructuring the oil company;
- Abolishing subsidiaries as joint-stock companies, creating a single shareholding in the company.

Similar developments took place in the companies where the oil companies themselves have been in the driver's seat. The latter are emerging from the process as tighter, better-managed organizations. But just as the banks overextended their financial resources, they were also stretching their decision-making and managerial capacity.

For the oil companies who had gone through the transformations described above and who wanted to expand, the purchase of other existing companies was a cheaper and easier solution than investment in new oil fields. When the fully state-owned oil company put forward a privatization plan in 1997, it was soon regarded not only as an object of interest for the banks—as was the case with the other verticals—it also attracted the interest of the other verticals themselves. In addition to Rosneft, the state also declared its intention to sell stakes in several smaller companies including ONAKO, Tiumen Oil Company, Eastern Oil Company, KomiTEK, East Siberian Oil and Gas Company, and the refining companies Sibur and NORSI-oil.

But at the same time as these options were opened, the financial situation of the dominant banks in the oil sector, as well as that of the oil companies, deteriorated. This deterioration was largely caused by two factors: the state started to transfer many of its accounts from the commercial banks to state banks, and the world market price for oil fell, leading to reductions in export income. The further growth and expansion of the big Russian oil companies was also complicated by the higher prices which were now demanded for the remaining objects of privatization.

While the auctions and investment competitions in 1995–96 had yielded little in terms of revenues for the state, strong voices were now arguing that the competition for Rosneft shares and the other remaining state assets should be freer and more open, thus encouraging higher bids. The cap on shares in Rosneft held by foreigners was lifted in July 1997. All this meant that a takeover of Rosneft would require significantly greater financial muscle than the purchase of substantially bigger oil companies had required only a year earlier. A new, more open tender process was already demonstrated in July 1997 when Alfa-Bank purchased 40 percent in Tiumen Oil Company for $820 million, far above the minimum bid.[13]

This was part of the background to the alliances and mergers in the Russian oil industry announced in the fall of 1997, although such alliances serve other purposes as well. In November 1997, Sidanko announced an alliance with BP, and almost simultaneously Gazprom signed a cooperation agreement with Shell. Both groups declared their intention to participate in the privatization of Rosneft. Shell had also already declared its interest in Rosneft. Very shortly afterwards, it was announced that the new alliance would cooperate with LUKoil in this matter.[14] The Gazprom-Shell consortium was expanded to include an Italian company, ENI, in February 1998.

In early December 1997, YuKOS acquired a controlling stake, 53.8 percent, in Eastern Oil Company for $800 million,[15] and one week later it was announced that Menatep was creating an alliance with Sibneft to bid for Rosneft.[16] The next logical step was the establishment of an alliance between Sibneft and Menatep's main oil asset, YuKOS. Thus the new company, Yuksi, was announced on 19 January 1998, after less than a month of negotiations.[17] In terms of crude production this would be the biggest oil company in Russia. In May 1998 the president of LUKoil, Vagit Alekperov, announced that his company was negotiating with Oneksimbank to take over Sidanko.

However, neither Yuksi (as the proposed new company was initially called) nor the amalgamation of LUKoil and Sidanko came to fruition. And no bids were delivered for Rosneft at the time designated for the auction, the end of May 1998. Three general factors were behind these developments: (1) insufficient capital in the oil companies and the connected banks to purchase shares at the expected price; (2) a general worsening of the economic situation in Russia in 1998, making the general economic outlook uncertain; and (3) a deteriorating economic situation in the oil companies caused by the fall in the world market price for oil and also in domestic prices.

But there were also more specific problems. A main reason for the collapse of the Yuksi plan was that the owners of YuKOS and Sibneft could not agree about how the new company's debt to the state should be handled. As of 1 May 1998, YuKOS had no such debts, whereas Sibneft had large, mature debts. At the same time, the ability of YuKOS-Rosprom-Menatep to attract foreign creditors was largely exhausted after the purchase of Eastern Oil Company, which required loans totaling $800 million from Goldman Sachs, Crédit Lyonnais, Merrill Lynch, and also from Russian banks—SBS-Agro and Most Bank.[18]

In addition to the financial limitations of Russian banks, these developments reflected still unresolved problems in the transformation of Russian oil companies into real business entities. The banks that involved themselves in the oil sector have carried out an important task in consolidating the various oil companies, getting control of material and financial flows at the level of the holding company. This was a prerequisite for increased efficiency, but not a sufficient condition. To help streamline activities further, the owners have chosen two strategies: to invite foreign partners and have foreign specialists take important positions, as was seen in Sidanko after BP purchased 10 percent, and to make the oil business a separate, independent activity within the financial-industrial conglomerates.

Thus in 1998 the management structures in the FIGs originally created by Oneksimbank and Menatep were changed. Now, Interros and Rosprom became holding companies where banking became one stream of activity, on a par with, for example, oil. Thus, the relationship between the FIG and the bank was inverted, with the bank becoming subordinate to the FIG. At the head of YuKOS was placed a new structure—Yukos-Moskva Ltd., headed by Mikhail Khodorkovski and including all the members of the management board of Rosprom. The Interros group created a new holding company with the task of determining the group's investment strategy, keeping financial control, and training leading personnel. The holding has three main divisions: finance (Oneksimbank), industry (Sidanko), and media. Oneksimbank received only 20 percent minus one share in the new holding company. During the final stages of the privatization process in the oil industry it is not quite accurate to say that the banks took control over major parts of the oil industry. Rather, the banks helped transfer ownership in the industry to new owners. In the case of YuKOS and Sidanko these new owners were holding companies representing the same owners as the banks that were instrumental in this transfer of ownership and control. So when in August 1998 a merger between Oneksimbank, Menatep, and Most Bank was announced, this did not mean that the industrial activities of the respective holding companies would be fused.

The planned merger of the banks was a result of the financial crisis. Whereas close contacts and links with the government had been a big asset in the development of many banks, now their tight links with state finances became a liability. Most of the banks active in the oil sector had put almost all their liquid assets into state bonds. Oneksimbank and Menatep had 82 and 70 percent respectively of their liquid assets in state securities. Even though between August 1998 and May 1999 only two banks lost their licenses, Menatep and Inkombank,[19] other oil-banks also found themselves in dire straits. Oneksimbank defaulted on its interest payments for Eurobonds, and Imperial Bank was declared bankrupt by the Moscow arbitration court in May 1999.[20] But because of the changes in the ownership arrangements between FIGs, banks, and the oil companies, the difficult position of the banks after August 1998 has not affected the oil companies as strongly as one would otherwise have expected. Of course, the banks' potential as lenders has become even more limited than before and their international credibility has been weakened, making them less attractive as channels for foreign credit.

The financial crisis in Russia has exposed the weakness of the banking system and generally reduced the influence of the banks on the oil sector. A comprehensive restructuring of the bank sector is expected, with mergers across the board. According to the president of the Central Bank, "two thirds of the banking system is living and will continue to live."[21] But the financial crisis has also revealed the role and significance of more tangible assets, such as development and production rights for hydrocarbons. Furthermore, the devaluation of the ruble has meant that oil exports have become a main arena for expansion by banks that find themselves in a relatively healthy position. A good example of this is Alfa-Bank, co-owner of Tiumen Oil Company, which is trying to acquire the assets of Sidanko. The internal consolidation process in the oil industry has continued despite the financial crisis. Tiumen Oil Company has gone from a holding structure to an integrated oil company with the top management in full control of the subsidiaries. According to its vice president, it has been strengthened by the crisis.[22]

The companies are responding to the capital squeeze by slashing investment programs, at the same time as the devaluation of the ruble brings increased ruble revenues from exports. A case in point is LUKoil, which reduced drilling by 47.4 percent in 1998, cut production costs by 12.7 percent, and increased exports by 30 percent.[23] Its president says clearly that there is overcapacity in the refining sector and refineries must be closed.[24] The fundamental investment problems have not been solved, however. A stronger competition for foreign investment among the FIGs and the oil companies should be expected. The managerial and financial streamlining of the oil companies is one prerequisite for increased foreign involvement. This development is mirrored in government policy: the operating conditions of foreign banks have been liberalized, and the limitation on foreign-owned shareholdings in the oil companies has been lifted. The most debt-ridden oil companies have to restructure their debt by offering shares to foreign creditors. Thus in Sidanko, by mid-1999 as much as 50 percent of the shares may be in the hands of foreigners (10 percent held by BP and 40 percent by the above-mentioned Cyprus-based Cantunpun, mainly representing foreign investors). The company's total debt amounted to U.S.$400 million; of this, U.S.$140 million[25] were owed to shareholders.[26] In other companies the foreign share has also increased substantially; as of May 1999, foreigners held 35.4 percent of the shares in LUKoil,[27] while in YuKOS their share had increased to 31.9.

Whereas the state as owner did not interfere in the internal developments of the oil companies, the large government stake had one important "external" function: it prevented the companies from taking over one another. With the end of state majority in the companies, the "truce" is over. The entire ownership structure has become liquid, even if there is good reason to believe, as argued above, that many of the banks will hold on to their new possessions, at least through indirect ownership that reduces their capital exposure. What we expect, and what is in fact already happening, is a reshuffling of the companies. Some units are likely to be transferred from one company to another, some companies will merge, and some may be bought up and dissolved altogether. Partly this is a response to a market process in which the industrial structure, initially formed by political decisions, is being realigned with market requirements. For example, traditional distribution areas for a particular refinery may be located far away from the plant. In a market economy it may not make sense to combine the distribution organization and the refinery in one company. And changes do not necessarily only entail more concentration. One should not rule out the possibility that some of the big conglomerates that are being formed will have to be broken up because of financial and managerial overload.

But in parallel with these market-driven developments there are changes in government policy that may affect the structure of the industry. The oil sector in Russia today may be characterized as a state-supported oligopoly. Starting in 1998, the government has repeatedly announced that it intends to establish a state oil company, Gosneft, composed of the unsellable Rosneft reinforced with Slavneft and ONAKO. At the same time it supports LUKoil's takeover of KomiTEK. Thus a market-oriented development is replaced by direct state intervention again. The government wants to reduce the number of companies.[28] This is happening at a time when the resource base is increasingly composed of small- and middle-sized fields, suited for development and operation by specialized production companies. There is no strong political opposition to this policy. The counter-force is precisely the financial needs and "objective" economic requirements that have been among the main factors behind the developments analyzed in this chapter.

NOTES

1. See *Kommersant-Daily*, 9 February 1995.

2. See *Izvestiia*, 22 May 1992.

3. Initially, FIGs were devised as a scheme to combine financial and industrial organizations, with the purpose of revitalizing Russian industry. FIGs were to be officially registered, and they enjoyed certain privileges according to legislation adopted in 1995. But there were also limitations on the freedom of maneuver of the participating financial institutions. Thus, so-called unregistered FIGs were formed, subject to neither special privileges nor limitations. In this paper we do not distinguish between these different types of FIGs. See Juliet Johnson, "Russia's Emerging Financial-Industrial Groups," *Post-Soviet Affairs*, vol. 13, no. 4 (1997), pp 333–365.

4. Presidential Decree no. 2023, 28 October 1994; *Segodnia*, 18 May 1995.

5. *Finansovye izvestiia*, 26 October 1996.

6. *Finansovye izvestiia*, 29 May 1997.

7. Presidential Decree no. 889, 31 August 1995. It was amended by Presidential Decree no. 986, 30 September 1995. *Sobranie zakonodatelstva RF za 1995 god* (Moscow, 1996), 3527, 3874.

8. Presidential Decree no. 1333, 9 September 1996, and Government Resolution no. 1415, 23 November 1996. "Ekonomicheskie i pravovye voprosy nedropolzovaniia v Rossii," *Geoinformmark* (Moscow, 1997), vol. 4, no. 18, p. 2, and no. 23/24, pp. 23–25.

9. *Ekspert*, no. 35, 16 September 1996.

10. *Delovoi mir*, 19 January 1997.

11. *Segodnia*, 14 March 1997.

12. *Rabochaya Tribuna*, 24 November 1998.

13. *Segodnia*, 21 July 1997.

14. *Segodnia,* 18 November 1997.

15. *Financial Times,* 9 December 1997.

16. *Segodnia,* 17 December 1997.

17. *Segodnia,* 20 January 1998.

18. *Kommersant-Daily,* 9 December 1997.

19. *Russia Today,* 7 June 1999; *Kommersant,* 19 May 1999.

20. *Kommersant,* 28 May 1999.

21. *Russia Today,* 7 June 1999.

22. A. Rumyantsev, "Silnye stanovyatsya silnee," *Neftegazovaya Vertikal,* no. 1, 1999, pp. 34–38.

23. *Neft Rossii,* no. 2, 1999, pp. 26–31.

24. *Ekspert,* nos. 1–2, 1999, pp. 46–47.

25. *Kommersant,* 18 May 1999.

26. *Kommersant,* 27 April 1999.

27. LUKoil press release, *Itogi,* 11 May 1999.

28. See Valery Kryukov, "Zachem i kakaya natsionalnaya kompaniya nuzhna Rossii?" *Neftegazovaya Vertikal,* nos. 2–3, 1999, pp. 40–42.

3

The Russian Oil Elite

Background and Outlook

by David Lane

In capitalist societies, the rise of oil companies is associated with the entrepreneurship of leading capitalists—Rothschild, Gulbenkian—and the quest of national governments to exert influence over oil assets, for both strategic and financial purposes. The position of Russia is unique. In the transition to capitalism Russia had no indigenous capitalist class able to purchase productive assets and provide economic entrepreneurial skills. The country's vast resources in oil and gas had been developed by the government. For political and economic purposes, the country has embarked on a transition to a capitalist economy. In chapter 1, we saw how the structure of ownership and control of the major companies has developed under privatization. Here I turn to consider the people who guide the companies. Two major questions are posed: who constitutes the new leadership (the economic elite) of the oil industry, and what are the values of the new elites?

The evolution of the oil elite must be considered in the context of the shift from state ownership and control that arose prior to and during the period of transformation. First, during the late Soviet period, under Gorbachev, private trade developed in services and commerce: medical consultations, private tuition, sale of agricultural produce, building, and repairs to housing. Second, during Gorbachev's term of office, "cooperatives" employing family labor were extended to a wide range of commodities and services. This development of trade gave rise to an incipient business class. Third, during the later Gorbachev period, government and Party property was utilized by people in these institutions for trade and the provision of services. These developments gave rise to a business class in two forms: those who organized production and exchange, and those in the state sector who illegally diverted the receipts from the sale of state produce. Fourth, during the period of the collapse of the Soviet Union and the formation of fifteen sovereign states, the USSR ministries were dissolved and their assets (production and units of commerce) were effectively controlled by their management. Fifth, in the process of mass privatization which took place from 1991, assets were sold or transferred to the public, and in this move managerial staff and financial institutions were privileged recipients. Finally, the state (in the institutional form of central, regional, or local governments) maintained ownership rights over certain assets, especially in key industries like oil, and placed its own representatives on the boards of companies which were formally privatized.

In this chapter, I am not primarily concerned with the formation of the new economic and capitalist class; the focus is on the economic elite, defined as people in positions controlling physical assets in the privatized (or semi-private) economy.

TYPES AND RECRUITMENT OF ELITES

The most popular interpretation of the origin of the new economic elite is that a "reproduction" of the previously dominant class has taken place. Explanations take two forms: The first is that the *nomenklatura* has converted political capital into private economic assets (private capital)—see principally points three, five, and six above. The second is that economic power derived from managerial control has been transformed into the ownership of productive assets—(points four and five above), that managerial and economic executives have turned managerial power into property rights. Both these approaches involve a shift of legitimating principles from administrative authority to ownership and market principles. An alternative scenario is the "circulation" hypothesis: this involves the collapse of the old system of recruitment and the rise of a different social stratum or class which, it is often optimistically assumed, will be the carrier of market orientation and democratic (or polyarchic) political values. (This process involves points one, two, and five above.)

Current interpretations of transition in Russia stress the "reproduction" of the *nomenklatura*,[1] with the implications that the elites lack commitment to a market system and that the pluralist institutions are merely a new shell for the previously dominant class. There are three problems with this approach: First, the *nomenklatura* was a very general category subsuming many different occupational groups and executive and administrative roles in diverse sectors of the polity and economy. Often persons with political capital (in the Komsomol and Party apparatus), are not distinguished from those with economic capital (in the economic administration and management) and those with general cultural capital (positions in higher education, research

capabilities, and command of symbols through the media).[2] A second problem lies in the nature of the new economic elite itself, and the fact that
researchers do not distinguish between the leaders of different sectors of the
economy—banking/financial services, manufacturing/construction, retail,
entertainment/show business, media, and energy industries. This is particularly important in a comprehensive and continental economy such as Russia. Third, existing research does not take account of the values and beliefs
of the elites. It is merely assumed that old wine in new bottles will taste like
old wine; in other words, there is no allowance for political "conversion" to
a new belief system.

In this chapter, I analyze the social origins of the oil elite, make some
comparisons with the financial services elite, and consider the values and
outlook of the oil leadership; finally, I make comparisons with the political
elite. I initially defined the oil elite as members of the boards of directors of
holding companies in post in 1995–96. To establish the background and origin of this elite, I searched biographical encyclopedias and databases for
details of their background and history. After excluding entries with very little information, I analyzed fifty-five biographies to give a composite picture
of the contemporary leaders of the oil industry. By way of comparison, I also
discuss the background of 118 leading people in banking and financial services. These were selected from published studies of the top hundred "most
influential" entrepreneurs and bankers[3] and from other leading entrepreneurs who were listed in handbooks of businesspeople published in
Moscow in 1996 and 1997.

Social and Political Origins

While it is sometimes contended that young people have been able to rise
rapidly under conditions of transition, a study of the oil elite severely mod-
ifies this view. On 1 January 1997, 49 percent of members of the sample
were aged over fifty and 89 percent over forty. (In banking the figures were
lower: 34 percent were over fifty and 73 percent over forty.) The first conclusion to be drawn is that the power and benefits of economic leadership
in contemporary Russia have accrued to middle-aged men. Very few in the
top business elite were female: only seven out of 118 in the sample of
bankers and financial services were women, and, out of the fifty-five members of the sample of the oil elite, none were women. Unlike other members
of the new banking/financial services elite, of whom 37 percent were born
in Moscow or Leningrad, all the oil leaders were born in the provinces of the
(former) USSR. In terms of higher education, 79 percent of the oil elite had
graduated in applied science and engineering (compared to only 34 percent
in banking and financial services), in economics the figure fell to only 11
percent (53 percent in banking and financial services). Just 3 percent of the

banking group had been to higher Party school, whereas none of the oil elite had done so.

Membership of the former Communist Party of the Soviet Union (CPSU) is one form of identification with the old regime. Data on Party membership from biographies, however, may be misleading for two reasons. First, former Party membership may be denied or minimized by respondents and second, membership may have been a formality with little, if any, political significance. Bearing these warnings in mind, approximately a third of the oil and banking elites in the sample had been Party members. When we consider those members who had had some position in the Party or Komsomol *apparat*, we find 37 percent in banking and 32 percent in oil. We need to distinguish between those who had a minimal position and those who had been prominent in the apparatus. So a further calculation was devised to determine the average political "saturation" of the two groups: positions in the Party apparatus were weighted by rank in the hierarchy (a weighting of ten was given for the post of secretary of the Central Committee of the CPSU, and other weightings were given, pro rata, down to one for a local Party secretary), and this figure was multiplied by the years in post (periods of Party membership were ignored). This gave an average Party/Komsomol index of eight per person for the bankers and four for the oil executives—showing a much greater salience of previous political capital for the bankers than for the oil elite. But the positions occupied in the Party were on the average middling ones (only one banker having been in the Communist Party Central Committee elite). It is worth emphasising, however, that particularly in the oil elite a large majority had had no participation at all in the Party *apparat*.

The other important elite sector of the Soviet political system was the government apparatus. Therefore all positions held in the Soviet government apparatus before 1 July 1990 were analyzed. A total of sixteen members of the oil elite (29 percent) had previously occupied positions in the economic administration (as members of Gosplan, the Central Bank), compared with sixty-six of the bankers (56 percent).

Occupational Histories

It is not a simple matter to determine the occupational background of members of the economic elite. Not only do people move, usually upward, between positions, but also in the period of perestroika there were important internal shifts as individuals sensed which way the ship of communism was going (or sinking). To solve this problem, the proportion of time that individuals spent in different positions in the seven years prior to the collapse of the USSR (the period August 1981 to December 1988) was calculated. It was from these positions that the elite moved in the postcommunist period.

A study of table 3.1 reveals the different career backgrounds of the oil and banking elites. For the oil elite, by far the most common activity was that of industrial executive (posts in production enterprises accounted for 54 percent of the career time of the elite in the period examined), followed by positions in the professions. Party and other government executive positions were relatively low in the proportion of time. For the banking/financial services elite, however, the largest group came from positions in the Soviet economic administration (such as Gosbank—24 percent of the time in post) and other government institutions (10 percent), while 14 percent were in professional positions). Since the banking sample was on average younger, many more had moved almost directly from higher education—this leads to the generally held impression that the new business elite is "young."

These figures suggest that we might distinguish between two career types among the new Russian economic elite. First, those with a career in the government, Party, and administrative elites of the Soviet system—people we might define as members of the "administrative" class. These people had had careers in the administrative organs of state and "reproduced" these forms of capital. Former elite members did not figure so highly among the new oil elites, and I suggest that this is a kind of "substitution" reproduction, where people move up the ladder, indicating that upward mobility progressed similarly in postcommunist Russia to what might have been expected under state socialism. In the new conditions, of course, the elites had individual rights to economic assets. However, the data also show that a considerable number of people came from outside the previous *apparat* and these people might be considered part of an elite circulation.

The conclusion we might draw here is that the transfer of executive capital was the most important asset of the oil elite, far more important than political capital. While it is true that many executives have had positions in the Party and state apparatuses, the former do not appear to have been particularly important. Among the banking elite, administrative capital and general cultural capital appear to have been more important assets. It is also evident in the study of the educational profile, which showed that the oil elite come predominantly from applied science and engineering, giving command of technical capital.

VALUES AND OUTLOOK OF THE NEW ELITES

The third problem of transformation/circulation defined above has to do with the values and beliefs of the new elites. Do they act in a market environment in the traditional *apparatchik* fashion or are they profit-seeking, accumulation-making entrepreneurs? What is their attitude to government control and to the market system? To answer these questions one would ideally interview

Table 3.1 Economic Elite, By Sector

Occupation/Status	Oil	Bank/Finance
Industrial executive (chief engineer, factory director)	54	11
Professional (doctor, lawyer, lecturer)	9	14
Student	7	14
Official (in Soviet economic organization, e.g., Gosbank)	4	21
Researcher	0	9
Entrepreneur	7	5
Government position holder	8	10
Party and Komsomol *apparat* member	6	8
Full/candidate CPSU CC member	0*	1
Other	5	7
Total	**100**	**100**

Positions held August 1981–December 1988. Figures refer to percentage of time all members of elite spent in the given occupational category.
*Expressed as zero due to rounding.

the members of the elites. In practice, this proved impossible as many of the major oil companies refused to allow their staff to be approached, and in other cases, top oil executives had insufficient time or interest to participate in the research. As noted in chapter 1, interviews were conducted[4] with sixty-five oil executives having the status of director, deputy director, president, or vice president; forty worked in Moscow,[5] five in Bashkiriia,[6] and five in Tatarstan.[7] Fifteen supplementary interviews including a limited range of questions were conducted with other oil executives in Moscow.[8] For comparison, thirty interviews were conducted with members of the administration and members of the Duma of the Russian Republic having an interest in the energy sector.[9] The interviews were conducted between June and October 1997.

The sample was similar in many ways to that of the oil elite in terms of biographies. (Personal characteristics of the two groups are given in an appendix to this chapter.) The oil and political executives were both male and middle-aged. The largest group had been educated in engineering, though a fair number of both the oil executives and the politicians had studied economics and management. A major difference with respect to the oil executives interviewed compared to the oil elite was that a much higher proportion of the executives had been born in Moscow, which indicates that they had worked in the commercial rather than the production and management aspects of the oil industry. Whilst all were "directors" or "presidents" or "vice presidents," there has probably been some inflation of language, and many of the respondents were in fact executives without a position on the board of directors (*soviet direktorov*) of the company. A large majority had not participated in the *apparat* of the Komsomol or CPSU. Identification with the new post-Soviet political parties was found to be weak—only a minority of the oil executives and about half of the politicians identified with a political party, and only half of the oil executives thought it important to be active in politics.[10]

In order to gauge their political and economic attitudes, questions were posed on the following: their evaluation of the effectiveness of the oil industry under the Soviet system and a comparison with the present one; their attitudes to the market, to money and inequality, to the role of the government, to influences on company strategic decision-making (discussed in chapter 1); their outlook on property and dividends; and their views on the effects of privatization.

Effectiveness of the Soviet and Current Systems in the Oil/Gas Sector

It is widely accepted that stable pluralistic and polyarchic politics are characterized by elites sharing fundamental beliefs: that the parameters of the economy (forms of ownership, management, mode of state intervention) are acceptable, and that change should occur within the existing framework of political interest articulation (parties and groups). For example, a study of Western European bureaucrats in "stable democracies" found that 60 percent of them thought the political system "fundamentally sound, with little need for change" and another 37 percent found it "fundamentally sound though some reforms were necessary."[11] I have shown that, unlike those in Western Europe, the political elites under Gorbachev and Yeltsin were divided: none of the Gorbachev elite and only 1 percent of the Yeltsin elite agreed with the first of the above responses, though 51 percent and 40 percent respectively agreed with the second. At the other end of the scale, none of the European bureaucratic elite believed their political systems to be "basically unsound and should be completely replaced," whereas the figure for the Gorbachev elite was 18 percent, and for the Yeltsin one 40 percent.[12]

Very little is known about the attitudes of the economic elites to the legitimacy and efficiency of the economic system. I therefore adapted the questions used in the political elite study to make them appropriate for executives of the oil industry. The respondents were asked about their perception of the efficiency of the Soviet oil industry before perestroika. In table 3.2, four alternatives were posed to the respondents, ranging from "fundamentally sound requiring no change," to "basically flawed precluding economic reform." The first column shows the responses of the oil elite (sixty-five

Table 3.2 Oil Elite's Perceptions of the Oil Industry and Type of Reform Required Before Gorbachev

Perception	Oil executives (N=65)	Politicians (N=30)	Gorbachev elite (N=116)
Effective and almost no need for change	7.7	13.3	1
Effective but needing some reform	43.1	50	40
Generally not effective, but reforms could be carried out under state system	18.5	26.7	19
Completely ineffective and reforms could not be carried out	23.1	10	40
No response	7.7	0	0

Columns in percentage, totaling 100.

Question: Consider the oil industry in the period before perestroika, before Gorbachev came to power: do you think the oil/gas industry at that time was . . .

respondents), the second column the responses of the thirty politicians. The third column refers to earlier research conducted on the Gorbachev political elite and to questions on the economic and political system.

The extent of disunity among the present oil interests, with its implications for reform, is shown by the fact that for the current oil executives the sum of the first two rows (on reform within the old Soviet system) comes to 50.8 percent of the respondents—indicating that basically, the Soviet system was sound, but needing reform. The views of the politicians are rather more positive toward the Soviet system than were the views of those interviewed in my earlier study of the Gorbachev elite. A significant minority, however, thought the system completely ineffective.

Further light is shed on the oil executives' perspectives for reform when we consider their attitudes to the changes which have taken place in the political system since 1992. (See table 3.3.)

Attitudes to the present political system are again divided, with a majority of the oil elite advocating considerable change, though it is noteworthy that half of the politicians here call for complete systemic change. This is obviously evidence of considerable doubt among the politicians and substantial concern by the oil executives as to the effectiveness of the present system.

I also asked more specifically about the present economic system, and the responses are shown in table 3.4.

Table 3.3 Effectiveness of the Political Reforms Since 1993.

Perception	Oil executives (N=65)	Politicians (N=30)
Effective and almost no need for change	4.5	0
Effective but needing some reform	27.7	10
Generally not effective, but reforms could be carried out under the present system	52.3	40
Completely ineffective and complete change is necessary	13.8	50
No response	1.5	0

Columns in percentage, totaling 100.
Chi-square=.003. Difference between the responses of the two sets is statistically significant.

Question: As a result of the political and economic reforms that have taken place since 1993, is the present political system . . .

Table 3.4 Effectiveness of the Current Economic System

Perception	Oil executives (N=60)	Politicians (N=30)
Effective and almost no need for change	1.5	0
Effective but needing some reform	32.3	10
Generally not effective, but reforms could be carried out under the present system	53.8	26.7
Completely ineffective and complete change is necessary	7.7	50
No response	4.6	3.3

Columns in percentage, totaling 100.
Chi-square=.00011. Difference between the responses of the two sets is statistically significant.

Question: The present economic system in the Russian Federation is . . .

There is a striking difference between the politicians and the oil executives. Of the former, again 50 percent call for a complete change. Of the oil executives, while only some 8 percent believe that a complete change is necessary, more than half believe that the system is not effective. It seems clear from the responses shown in these last two tables that a critical mass of executives has lost confidence in present policies and seeks more reforms but is prepared to work within the present structures to achieve change. Far greater disillusionment, however, is shown by the politicians.

The lack of confidence is also indicated by the very large numbers of respondents believing that corruption and lawlessness is widespread. Over three-quarters of the oil executives and politicians agreed that corruption is widespread (table 3.5), and 40.7 percent of the oil executives and 83.3 percent of the politicians thought that lawlessness is a characteristic of economic life (table 3.6). The inadequacies of the tax system led over 70 percent of the oil executives and over 50 percent of the politicians to agree that the prime task of the government should be "to establish order in the system of taxation." (table 3.7) The politicians had a significantly more negative attitude to the extent of corruption than the oil executives.

Table 3.5 Extent of Corruption

Perception	Oil executives (N=65)	Politicians (N=30)
Completely agree	76.6	83.3
Agree with reservations	20.3	16.7
Do not agree, with reservations	1.6	0
Completely disagree	1.5	0
No response	0	0

Columns in percentage, totaling 100.

Question: Today in Russian society there is a widespread prevalence of corruption.

Table 3.6 Extent of Criminalization of the Russian Economy

Perception	Oil executives (N=65)	Politicians (N=30)
Lawbreaking occurs from time to time (*edinichny*)	1.7	0
Lawbreaking occurs often, but, in general, the economy is healthy	57.6	16.7
Economic life, in general, has a criminal character	40.7	83.3
No response	0	0

Columns in percentage of those responding positively. Columns total 100.

Question: How do you evaluate the level of criminalization in economic life?

Table 3.7 Government and the Tax System

Response	Oil executives (N=65)	Politicians (N=30)
Completely agree	29	30
Agree but with reservations	43	23
Do not agree, but with reservations	15	33
Completely disagree	12	13
Scale	2.11	2.3

Columns in percentage, but do not total 100 because of rounding.

Question: The most important task of the government is to establish order in the taxation system.

Preferences for Type of Economy

The asymmetric attitudes to the present system may also be illustrated by views about the types of property which "should predominate in the near future": of the oil elite only two persons out of sixty-five chose state ownership, 61.5 percent were in favor of joint-stock company property, and 6 percent were for individual personal property. Comparisons with the politicians show a reversed ordering with 70 percent being in favor of government property and 23 percent favoring joint-stock property.

There was a considerable degree of agreement that the system would be a mixed one. The respondents were asked to choose between a liberal, a social-democratic, and a paternalist system. The overwhelming preference was for a social-democratic system, though just over a fifth of the politicians were in favor of a more paternalistic one. (See table 3.8.)

A number of questions were asked to gauge the ways in which the executives saw the development of their companies and the position of the company in the economy. Here I probed their attitude to profit maximization and the role of the government. (See tables 3.9–3.13.) Generally, the oil executives favored a market type system in which companies were market oriented with free pricing and little government control. However, there were significant exceptions, and a minority recognized the role of government intervention. There was strong disagreement between the politicians and the oil executives over whether regional political authorities presented one of the major problems facing the oil companies (table 3.10). The executives, unlike the politicians, were resolutely opposed to an increase in government control over the economy (see table 3.12): over three-quarters opposed further control by politicians over economic affairs, but more than 60 percent of politicians disagreed. The politicians, moreover, were more sceptical of market relations, and over 70 percent supported government

Chapter 3

Table 3.8 Models of Social Development

Social model	Oil executives (N=65)	Politicians (N=30)
Liberal (the state to a greater extent supports the rights of business than society)	0	0
Social-Democratic (the state aims to make equal the interests of business and society)	81.5	66.7
Paternalistic (the state administers a significant part of the economy and aims to support all strata of the population)	12.3	23.3
Other forms	6.2	10

Columns in percentage, totaling 100. No statistically significant difference between the two groups. No response=0.

Question: Which model of development of society do you think would be the most effective for Russia under present conditions?

Table 3.9 Market Effectiveness

Response	Oil executives (N=65)	Politicians (N=30)
Completely agree	41.5	26.7
Agree, with reservations	36.9	36.7
Do not agree, with reservations	10.8	10.0
Completely disagree	10.8	26.7

Columns in percentages, totaling 100. chi-square=.20. No statistically significant difference between the two groups.

Question: Do you agree that the oil companies should be governed exclusively by the owners and managers with the aim of maximum market effectiveness?

intervention over internal oil prices (see table 3.11). In terms of ideology, on oil policy there is some consensus among oil executives, but a considerable gap between their preferences and those of the politicians. It is premature to describe the development of a unitary elite of interests with respect to oil politics.

Table 3.10 Interference of Regional Political Authorities

Response	Oil executives (N=65)	Politicians (N=30)
Completely agree	24.6	6.7
Agree, with reservations	41.5	34.5
Do not agree, with reservations	26.2	37.9
Completely disagree	7.7	20.7

Columns in percentages, totaling 100. Chi-sq=.05. Significant at 5 percent level.

Question: Do you agree that regional authorities present one of the greatest problems facing the management of the Russian oil sector?

Table 3.11 Internal Oil Prices

Response	Oil executives (N=65)	Politicians (N=30)
Completely agree	15.4	36.7
Agree, with reservations	20.0	36.7
Do not agree, with reservations	29.2	13.3
Completely disagree	32.3	13.3

Columns in percentages, totaling 100. Chi-square=.01. Significant variation between the two sets of responses.

Question: The freeing of prices in the oil sector was a mistake, and the government should introduce control over prices of oil products in the internal market.

Table 3.12 Role of Politicans in the Economy

Response	Oil executives (N=65)	Politicians (N=30)
Completely agree	39.3	0
Agree, with reservations	42.6	36.7
Do not agree, with reservations	11.5	43.3
Completely disagree	6.60	20.0

Columns in percentages, totaling 100. Chi-square=.00002. Highly significant difference between responses of the two groups of respondents.

Question: At present, under existing conditions, it does not make sense to talk about an increase in control by politicians over economic matters.

Table 3.13 Internal Excise Duties

Response	Oil executives (N=65)	Politicians (N=30)
Completely agree	44.6	20.0
Agree, with reservations	26.2	33.3
Do not agree, with reservations	10.8	30.0
Completely disagree	7.7	3.3
Nonresponse/don't know	10.8	13.3

Columns in percentages, totaling 100.

Question: Internal excise duties now in place in Russia are unjustified.

Attitudes to Money and Inequality

Immense fortunes, particularly in the oil industry, have been made out of the move to the market and privatization in the post-USSR countries. I therefore asked about the legitimacy of making "big money" (defined as over $500,000).

The oil executives were divided in their views. More than 60 percent felt that making a large amount of money was justified if it was a reward for one's own labor; more than half agreed if it provided for capital investment and employment, and over 40 percent believed it justified support for charity and other interests (table 3.14). However, attitudes to money making are quite different among the politicians, almost all of whom felt that making "big money" in Russia was not justified at all. Moreover, over 60 percent of the oil executives supported government intervention to make the distribution of earnings and wealth more equal—in roughly similar proportions to the politicians (table 3.15).

Comparing both halves of table 3.14, the responses to all questions are highly statistically significant. Oil executives and politicians differ significantly in their views.

Attitudes to Property and Dividends

The propensity for investment, the continued and constant accumulation of capital, is one of the major features of modern capitalism. It is therefore important to study the attitudes of executives and politicians in postcommunist societies to find out how they regard the role of private companies in relation to the market and to government control. Their attitudes may also shed some light on whether entrepreneurs and management seek to maximize rents and income rather than take a longer-term view with investment

Table 3.14 Justifications for Making Money

Oil executive response	1	2	3	4	5
Reward for their own labor	25	37	18	20	--
Provision of employment	15	37	20	23	5
Formation of capital for investment in economy	20	34	21	21	3
Support of charity/other social interests	11	34	15	35	5

Politician response	1	2	3	4	5
Reward for their own labor	0	0	3	97	0
Provision of employment	0	0	0	100	0
Formation of capital for investment in economy	3	0	7	90	0
Support of charity/other social interests	0	0	0	100	0

Rows in percentages, totaling 100.

Key:
1=completely agree; 2=agree with reservations; 3=do not agree, with reservations; 4=disagree completely; 5=no response.

Question: In the transition to markets and privatization of wealth, many people have "made" a lot of money. Which of the following do you consider to be a justification for making such income?

Table 3.15 Government Role in Making Income and Wealth More Equal

Response	Oil executives (N=65)	Politicians (N=30)
Completely agree	32.3	23.3
Agree, with reservations	29.2	36.7
Do not agree, with reservations	20	26.7
Completely disagree	10.8	13.3
No response/don't know	7.7	0

Columns in percentages, totaling 100. No statistically significant difference between the frequency of answers.

Question: The creation of conditions for a greater equality of income and wealth is currently one of the main tasks of the government.

in mind. Table 3.16 illustrates the attitudes of the oil executives and, for comparison, the politicians with respect to investment and dividends and to the respective interests of companies, investors, and government.

First I asked about attitudes to paying dividends in the short run (see row A in table 3.16). Nearly 70 percent of the oil executives agreed with the proposition that paying dividends to investors in the short run should be a prime object of the company. Among the politicians, however, nearly the same proportion disagreed with such short-term policy. Second, I inquired about their attitudes to oil prices. Again there was an asymmetric attitude to

Table 3.16 Attitudes toward Dividends, Earnings, Investment, and Charity on the Part of Companies

		1	2	3	4	5	6	7
A. Short-term	O.E.	27.4	41.9	21.0	9.70	2.13	4.60	Y
dividends	P.	17.2	17.2	31.0	34.5	2.83	3.30	
B. Low oil prices	O.E.	7.9	33.3	34.9	23.8	2.75	3.10	Y
	P.	60.0	10.0	13.3	16.7	1.87	0	
C. Company's	O.E.	26.2	49.2	24.6	0	2.0	0	
interests first								
D. Asset control	O.E.	43.5	46.2	9.70	1.60	1.69	4.60	Y
	P.	26.7	13.3	26.7	33.3	2.67	0	
E. Promotion of	O.E.	29.7	42.2	17.2	10.9	2.09	1.5	Y
charity	P.	6.70	5.70	36.7	50.0	3.30	0	
F. Personal	O.E.	17.9	41.1	35.7	5.40	2.29	13.8	
income use								

Rows in percentages.
O.E.=oil executives; P=politicians

Key:
1=completely agree; 2=agree, with reservations; 3=disagree, with reservations; 4=completely disagree; 5=scale (average); 6=no response; 7=statistically significant difference between oil executives and politicians; Y=yes.

Questions:
A. To pay dividends to shareholers in the short term (1–3 years) should be the prime objective of your company.
B. Oil prices in Russia should be kept low in order to provide cheap energy for Russian industry.
C. The interest of your company in the furthering of its own investment is more important than satisfying the government's tax needs.
D. Company owners must have the rights over the control of the assets of the company, whatever the interests of the government.
E. Promoting charity is an outward sign of good company management.
F. It is beter to use your personal income for yourself or your family than to invest in the company (or some other company).

the price of oil: only 8 percent of the executives agreed unconditionally that oil prices should be kept low to provide cheap energy for Russian industry, compared to 60 percent of the politicians (row B). Third, the executives also believed that investing in the company and the rights of owners over assets were more important than satisfying the tax or other needs of government, whereas over half of the politicians did not concede the primacy of rights to owners of assets (rows C and D). Over 70 percent of the executives compared to 14 percent of the politicians took a positive view of charity (row E). However, more than half of the executives preferred to use their own income to meet personal needs, rather than to invest further in their own (or other) companies—only 5 percent disagreed completely with this proposition (row F). (This question did not apply to the politicians.)

We may conclude that the executives had a positive attitude to private property and to the rights of shareholders but an aversion to government control. They saw government intervention as an interest not compatible with the interests of the oil industry. The politicians, however, appeared to have a longer-term and wider view of the interests of the oil and other industries; they were critical of the market and sought controls of private rights over assets. These responses again showed a significant difference in values between the two sets of respondents.

Effects of Privatization

Finally, the respondents were asked about the effects of privatization on the functioning of the oil industry. (See table 3.17, first group of fifty respondents only.) As far as the quality of production was concerned, it appeared that privatization had made little difference, 82.6 percent indicating little change (though twenty-seven out of fifty people did not answer the question). There seemed to be either no change or change for the better with respect to relations with ministries (63.6 percent and 22.7 percent). The greatest positive difference was with respect to the introduction of new technology, where more than 70 percent said that things had improved. The overall evaluation of the oil executives is that the position is better or the same, relatively few believing that organization or procedures are worse. The high nonresponse rate is explained by the lack of privatization in some companies and lack of detailed knowledge by the respondents.

CONCLUSIONS

This study of the social background of the new economic elites suggests that, following the movement to a market economy in Russia, there are four forms of transformation of previous personal assets into economic ownership and control, in the following order of importance. First, there are people who

Table 3.17 Oil Executives' Responses to Company Changes

Responses	Number of responses	Percentage of positive responses
Improved		
a.	4	17.4
b.	17	70.8
c.	5	22.7
No change		
a.	19	82.6
b.	4	16.7
c.	14	63.6
Worse		
a.	0	—
b.	3	12.5
c.	3	13.6
No response		
a.	27	—
b.	26	—
c.	26	—
Total		
a.	50	100
b.	50	100
c.	50	100

Key:
Question: Compared to pre-privatization, how has the position in your company changed with respect to:
    a. the quality of production?
    b. the introduction of new technology?
    c. relations with the Fuel and Energy Ministry?

have turned their control and knowledge of "economic organization"—their positions of authority and expertise in the Soviet economy—into economic assets in the new capitalist economy: this has been particularly important in the creation of the oil elite. Second, there are those who have successfully converted "political capital"—their posts and networks in the Soviet political system—into economic assets: this appears to have been important among the new banking elite and to a lesser extent among the oil elite. Third, and to a lesser extent, many have converted their "intellectual capital"—higher education and the knowledge it gives, positions in state educational and research institutions, particularly in the scientific institutions—into economic assets. Finally, a relatively small number had started entrepreneurial activities in the late Gorbachev period and have built on the money earned in the private sector.

There has been, then, both a "reproduction" and a "circulation" of elites. It seems likely that the oil elite includes a larger proportion of people who have transferred economic organization and industrial executive capital into control of assets in the market economy, whereas the banking elite has come both from a Soviet administrative background and from posts outside the previous apparatuses of power. A more general conclusion is that the political economy of transformation should take into account different industrial sector profiles, and that large and diverse economies such as the Russian one will have different forms of "transition settlement" compared to the smaller, more specialized economies of Eastern Europe. In Russia, aspiring capitalists have found a place in the new economy, and this economy has also enabled the previous industrial executive class to perpetuate its control over the means of production.

The major conclusion to be drawn from the attitudinal study is the absence of a stable consensual structure of elites. As far as the views of oil executives are concerned, there is considerable division about the performance of the industry under state socialism: half of the sample of oil executives interviewed thought the previous system was effective. In general, the post-Soviet structure—both the economy in general and the oil sector—is considered to require considerable reform. There is an awareness of widespread criminality and corruption; the evolving system may be characterized as disorganized. The oil elite is more prepared for *internal* within-system change than the politicians with interests in the energy sector; for the majority of the former the joint-stock company is the preferred form of ownership in the context of a market-type society. Generally, since destatization, the oil executives have seen the greatest improvements in the introduction of new technology in the oil industry, though other aspects of organization had not been subject to significant change.

While a majority of both oil executives and politicians believe that the government has a duty to make income and wealth more equal, the politicians as a group do not accept the legitimacy of the large fortunes made in the transitional period. The majority of the oil executives, however, have moved to a more capitalist orientation—justifying very large earnings and the accumulation of wealth (even if this be of a speculative nature) through rewards for labor and for capital formation. They also condone the payment of dividends to shareholders as a "prime objective" of companies. Politicians take a longer-term view of investment and are more sympathetic to the support of other Russian industries through subsidized oil prices. In conclusion, one may generalize that the oil executives as a whole appear to accept the movement to a market company-owned oil industry, though the present system requires considerable changes. Politicians concerned with this sector, however, are more critical and skeptical about the market system; they support greater state involvement and control. The elite structure lacks cohesion and consensus.

NOTES

1. Khrystanovskaia, for example, in a study carried out in the mid-1990s, concluded that 61 percent of the Russian business elite came from the "Soviet nomenklatura." Of these, the largest share originated from the Komsomol (38 percent), 13 percent from Party executives, 3 percent from the Soviets, and 38 percent from the economic sector. Olga Khryshtanovskaia, "Finansovaia Oligarkhiia v Rossii," *Izvestiia*, 10 January 1996, p. 5.

2. A similar position is taken by a group of researchers in VTsIOM (the All-Russian Center for Public Opinion Research). In a work published in 1996, they reported that, of a sample of people forming the economic elite, one-third were in *nomenklatura* positions in 1988. The VTsIOM study also addresses the reproduction of the economic apparatus and concludes that 70 percent of the economic elite in place in 1993 held comparable places in the "economic nomenklatura" in 1988. B. V. Golovachev, L. B. Kosova, and L. A. Khakhulina, "Formirovanie Praviashchei Elity v Rossii," in *Ekonomicheskie i Sotsialnye Peremeny: Monitoring Obshchestvennogo Mneniia* (Moscow: VCIOM 1996), no. 1, pp. 33-35.

3. Chosen by a panel of Russian finance experts in 1996, these were listed in *Ekonomika i Zhizn'*, no. 33, August 1996, and *Interfaks-AIF*, no. 28, 8–14 July1996.

4. Most of the following were organized and conducted by VTsIOM, Moscow.

5. All were from the following companies: Moscow local companies (4), Tyumenneftegaz, Transnefteprodukt (2), Rostneft (5), Sidanko, YuKOS (2), Vostochnaya (2), Slavneft (2), Ritek (2), Uralneft, Nefteresursy (2), Tyumenimpeks, Intol, Rosa Mira, Nakhodka, Komiartiol, Bi-Gaz-Si, Rial, RRK, ZAO, Surgutneftegaz, Mostransnefteprodukt (2), Mezh. Ekon. Sotrudnichestvo, ONAKO, Vitolneft, and Sibur.

6. All five were directors of Bashneft.

7. Four were directors or deputy directors of Tatneft and one was a director of Tatnefteprodukt.

8. These were people contacted on a personal basis in firms inaccessible to the VTsIOM interviewers: they included seven directors or vice presidents of LUKoil, two from Transneft, two from Rosneft, two from Octan Plus, and two from Alfa EO joint-stock company. They were mainly in posts dealing with foreign or international contracts. A limited number of questions was put to these respondents.

9. The politicians' group included eight members of the government of the Russian Republic and twenty-two members of the Russian Duma selected from committees or areas with an interest in energy. For details see chapter 1, note 18.

10. We asked: "To promote the interests of a company such as yours, is activity in politics important or does it have no significance?" Just under half of those who answered the question (thirty-one out of sixty-five) thought it important, and the other half did not.

11. Joel D. Aberbach, Robert D. Putnam, and Bert A. Rockman, *Bureaucrats and Politicians in Western Democracies.* (Cambridge: Harvard University Press, 1981), p. 195.

12. See David Lane, "Transition under Eltsin: The Nomenklatura and Political Elite Circulation," *Political Studies,* vol. 45 (December 1997), p. 871.

APPENDIX

Table A.1 Type of Company

Type	Oil executives (N=65)
Holding	24
Subsidiary	3
Independent	28
Other (government)	9
No response	1

Table A.2 Position of Respondent

Position	Oil executives (N=65)
Director, president	19
Director, economics, finance	24
Vice president, deputy director	19
Other members of board of directors	2
No response	1

Table A.3 Politicians' Positions

Position	Politicians (N=30)
Members of administration, Presidential *apparat*	8
Members of legislature	22

Table A.4 Other Categories

Gender and Age	Oil executives (N=65)	Politicians (N=30)
Male	58	27
Female	7	3
Age (average in 1997)	50.3	46

Place of birth	Oil executives	Politicians
Village (<1,000 people)	4	10
Village (1,000–5,000)	5	0
Small town (5,000–10,000)	2	3
Midsize town (10,000–100,000)	14	2
Large city (>100,000)	13	8
Capital city	2	4
No response	2	3

Previous Officeholder in CPSU, Komsomol, or Other	Oil executives	Politicians
Komsomol, Secretary/Deputy Secretary	19	3
Other positions	2	1
CPSU Secretary/Deputy Secretary	8	7
Member of committee/other posts	16	8

Have Current Political Party Affiliation	Oil executives	Politicians
Yes	21	20
No	31	10
Other response	12	0
Party identity		
Communist Party of the Russian Federation	1	7
Liberal Democratic Party	0	2
Democratic Choice	6	0
Yabloko	8	3
Our Home is Russia	3	3
Others	2	4
No response	45	11

Education	Oil executives (N=50)	Politicians (N=30)
Mining engineer	2	1
Engineer	20	11
Lawyer	4	3
Economist/management	10	5
Liberal Arts	3	4
Other sciences	1	2
Place of education: Moscow	22	3

Corruption and Crime in the Russian Oil Industry

Heiko Pleines

When dealing with corruption and crime in Russia, one has to be aware that information on the topic, and especially statistical information, is not very reliable. This is due to a number of reasons. First, all those involved in these activities maintain a high level of secrecy. Second, changes in legislation distort the picture by changing the definition of what is criminal activity. Third, the different intensities of anti-corruption and anti-crime campaigns lead to biased statistics. Estimating the number of unreported cases is much more difficult in Russia than in Western countries, because post-Soviet experience with crime and corruption covers only a few years and because the situation in Russia is changing very rapidly. Fourth, public charges concerning corruption and criminal activities are part of the politics of confrontation. Accordingly, reports on corruption and criminal activities can often better be understood as an indication of power struggles between Russia's political and economic elites than as sound and reliable analysis.

CORRUPTION AND CRIME IN RUSSIA: AN ANALYTICAL FRAMEWORK

Corruption can generally be defined as the misuse of public power and/or public resources for personal gain. This definition, though, needs to be made more specific. In a narrow interpretation, corruption is directly linked to the payment of bribe money to a state official in return for a concrete favor. But critics argue that such a definition falls short of encompassing the full phenomenon. They prefer a wider definition that includes networks between state officials and entrepreneurs (or directors of Soviet enterprises). These networks are not necessarily based on direct transactions (bribe payments against favors) but on mutual trust, on the knowledge that granting a favor will offer the right to demand a favor in return.[1]

Especially in this wider sense, corruption is essential for understanding the Soviet economy from which much of present practice originates. The Soviet system promoted corruption and could probably only function through it. Because of political repression and the command economy, the Soviet system was very inflexible. It was unable to react to political dissatisfaction or economic needs of the population with adequate adjustment mechanisms. A logical consequence of this inflexibility was widespread corruption, which was employed to weaken the state's control and to allow for more flexibility.

Managers had to break the law in order to obtain supplies they needed to meet the plan for the enterprise. Normally they were only punished for underfulfillment of the plan, not for offenses against the law. Therefore "it seems a fair generalization that all Soviet managers are, ipso facto, criminals according to Soviet law."[2] Moreover, in order to avoid punishment and to get preferential treatment from relevant authorities, managers were tempted into giving false reports about their performance.

But it was the desire for personal advantage that led many executives in the Soviet economy into criminal activity. In an economy where nearly everything was scarce, nearly every manager could make big profits through embezzlement. In such a system, all managers needed unofficial connections with other managers and with influential party officials in order to make deals and to feel secure in their performance.[3]

After the collapse of the Soviet Union, the situation in Russia fundamentally changed. In the wake of economic reforms, corruption spread to the privatization process and to the partially liberalized foreign trade regime. Moreover, the transition to a money economy changed the nature of corruption. Under socialism, power and influence were the most important criteria, which also ensured personal wealth. In postsocialist Russia, personal wealth has become a central value and a career in state structures is no longer necessary to achieve it.[4]

Nevertheless, as noted in chapter 3, it is widely asserted that large parts of the Russian economy are still dominated by Soviet-style corruption networks between state officials and managers. As a Russian commentator has put it:

> Today we have an economy which is to a certain degree regulated by the rivalry between corporate-bureaucratic structures (clans), by their fight for power and their regulative activities. One of the main consequences of the new mechanisms for the allocation of resources is the division of the national economy into a sector where these structures are dominant and a sector where they are not really influential.
>
> The first sector is characterized by a large number of companies, which are monopolies, . . . [have] liquid monetary resources and bureaucratic-corporate power. The fuel energy industry, the finance and trade complex and some industrial branches belong to this sector of the national economy.[5]

If one accepts the introduction of democracy and a market economy as objectives of the transition process, corruption considerably hampers the further development of post-Soviet Russia in a number of ways, including the following:

An anti-democratic effect. Widespread corruption makes democratic decision-making impossible, since politicians are regularly "bought." The rule of law is weakened.

An image-effect. The extensive media coverage of cases of corruption discredits the political leadership and its policy of reforms.

A negative overall economic effect. Whereas a single company can reduce its transaction costs through corruption, widespread corruption leads to an increase in transaction costs at the national level. A single company can, for example, profit from offering a bribe to a judge. But the resulting legal uncertainty considerably hampers overall economic development. Bribe payments to avoid taxation will increase the company's profits, but the resulting state budget deficit might fuel inflation and make an efficient economic policy impossible. Moreover, corruption networks between managers and state officials can prevent competition in some markets. Companies turn to the state for support instead of adopting market-oriented behavior. In the case of widespread corruption, rent-seeking gets out of the control of political decision-makers, since corrupt state officials multiply the possibilities for rent-seeking.[6]

A distributive effect. Because of corruption, some businessmen had the possibility of making immense profits in the privatization process and in foreign trade activities. At the same time, some state officials could increase their real income considerably through corruption.[7]

Criminalization. After the end of state repression, corruption also led to the spread of organized crime.

Whereas a crime can be conducted by any individual without preconditions, the criminalization of a society or a part of society is impossible without widespread corruption. Only corruption offers protection from criminal prosecution and thus allows for the persistence of criminal behavior on a large scale. It is, for example, possible for an individual oil company to smuggle oil out of the country without being detected. But the total amount of oil smuggled out of the country can be estimated by comparing the relevant export statistics with the import statistics of those countries buying the oil. The same is true of illegal capital transfers abroad. A specific oil company might be able to cover up its capital flight, but the total amount of capital flight from the oil sector can be estimated by comparing actual total exports with their monetary equivalent in world prices.

That means an individual Russian oil company can evade the law enforcement agencies. But the criminalization of the whole oil industry cannot remain unnoticed. Nevertheless, Russian efforts to fight this criminalization have been slow and at best halfhearted. This may be explained by the high level of corruption among state officials and the tight connections between the oil industry and state. As a result of this situation, state officials receive money for offering all kinds of "preferential treatment." Police forces, customs authorities, and other investigative bodies are paid to cover up criminal activities. In addition, banks are used to avoid taxation and launder illegal profits.

THE OIL INDUSTRY'S CORRUPTION NETWORKS

The original post-Soviet oil elite consisted of the top managers of the leading oil-producing companies and of financial institutions. "Most of these people have maintained personal working and business contacts with each other for many years. That is why in recent years the oil elite has been able to rally in defence of its common economic interests."[8]

As noted in chapters 1 and 2, since 1995, Russian banks and financial groups have secured stakes in Russian oil companies through more or less hidden insider deals allowing the purchase of assets at prices far below their estimated value.[9] This is also a serious form of corruption.

In order to defend its interests on the federal level, the oil elite has formed a lobby among government officials and parliamentary deputies. But the leading figures in the oil industry do not pay too much attention to official lobbying activities. "They seem to believe that 'keeping in touch' with the organs of executive power is sufficient for the defence of their interests."[10]

Many state officials are most interested in obtaining personal profits from the business operations of the oil industry. Accordingly, "the interests of government agencies and officials are best served not by laws which outline their powers and responsibilities in a very precise way, but by a system in which they enjoy as much freedom as possible to enter into 'negotiations' with individual clients, to request certain kickbacks and bribes in return for particular favours. . . . It was not in the interests of government officials for a law to be passed which would clarify the industry's regulatory structure, and thus reduce their opportunities to promote their personal gain."[11]

It is sometimes claimed that some state officials at the federal as well as at the regional level have formed corruption networks with the oil elite that have allowed both groups to redirect some of the industry's profits into their own pockets. Since governing the oil industry promised a high additional income from bribes, many state institutions tried to become involved in decisions concerning the industry. In 1996, altogether fifteen different federal state bodies as well as the governments of Russia's regions were responsible for reforms in the oil sector.[12] The number of state bodies responsible for the administration and taxation of the oil industry is even higher.

A good example of the resulting "intertwined network of mutual favours" is the system of oil coordinators. The interministerial commission chooses oil companies and exporters to be coordinators of oil ports and foreign markets. Reportedly the commission bases its decision upon the oil companies' expressed interests. "The coordinators assist in deciding who will export oil to which destination and how much; they too must approve the quarterly schedule. The coordinators also regulate the tanker schedules and loading at pipeline sea port terminals. . . . Evidently, the oil companies benefit financially from their coordinating role, and it gives them the means to disadvantage their competitors or punish companies with whose actions they disagree."[13] Most of Russia's domestic oil market is divided between the large companies on a regional basis. There are only a few regions where oil producers engage in real competition. The same applies to the markets for oil products.[14]

On the regional level the Republic of Komi, in Russia's Far North, provides a good example of comprehensive corruption networks in the oil industry. Investigative journalists revealed in spring 1999 that the republic's political leadership and the management of the regional oil company Komineft had embezzled more than U.S.$10 million from oil exports with the help of a single scheme. In similar cases, money had been moved to Western companies and bank accounts.[15]

In summary, oil executives continue to engage in rent-seeking activities instead of developing market-oriented behavior. "It is becoming increasingly clear that the current oil market in Russia is developing an oligopolistic structure with a state-backed cartelisation of external flanks."[16] We might generalize that the managers of the oil industry have used their close connections with state officials to promote the following:

- to keep control over the oil industry and to ensure favorable market conditions;
- to increase profits through illegal activities, especially smuggling;
- to launder illegal profits and invest them for their personal benefit, avoiding taxation if possible.

The aim of managers to keep their company under their control and to create favorable market conditions does not necessarily require corruption or criminal activities. Most of the oil industry's actions meant to promote favorable legislation and regulation of oil production and sales can be interpreted as lawful lobbying.[17] But these activities, with the resulting close cooperation between oil companies and state bodies, promote the development of corruption networks.

SMUGGLING

The fear that liberalizing oil prices would fuel inflation caused the Russian government in January 1992 to exclude oil (and some other products) from the general freeing of prices. The low oil prices on the domestic market acted as subsidies to industry and private households. In order to guarantee supplies to the domestic market at the lower prices set by the state, oil exports were restricted and subject to licensing. Only "skilled exporters" were allowed to export "strategic goods" like oil. The total quotas for Russian exports of these goods were determined by the Ministry of Economy.

Since it was much more profitable for a Russian oil company to export oil than to sell it in Russia, where prices are lower and customers are often unable to pay, the foreign trade regime led to widespread fraud. And the foreign trade regime was designed in a way that allowed individual state officials to cover up smuggling activities. About a dozen competing bureaucracies had power over customs, and the regulations were frequently amended. As a result, Russian customs regulations were incomplete and sometimes even contradictory. Whether and under what conditions oil could leave the country depended to a large degree on the state official concerned.[18]

Moreover, quotas for oil exports were often granted to regional authorities, which had no experience with oil exports. This offered oil exporters the chance to receive commission for organizing the sale of the oil on behalf of the authorities. Sometimes the oil exporting company simply disappeared after it had received the oil.[19] But often oil exporters collaborated with the regional authorities and both made illegal profits.

For example, when in 1993 the administration of Tomsk Oblast obtained the right to export about 1 percent of the oil extracted in the area, it decided to buy grain from abroad. The only purpose of this procedure was to make an exchange possible. The administration then transferred the deal to the local monopolists, Tomskneft, an exporter of oil, and Tomskkhleboprodukt, an importer of grain. The monopolists used their intermediary firms in Moscow to get a contract with a foreign firm. The oil was delivered at once, but the grain supply was delayed by the Russian intermediaries in order to make speculations on commodity exchanges possible. When grain prices were at a low level, the grain was delivered to Tomsk Oblast. Brokerage was paid to intermediaries, monopolists, and functionaries. United in one corruption network, all parties involved profited from the deal at the expense of the oblast's finances.[20]

In order to smuggle oil out of the country, Russian oil companies mainly used two methods. First, they could send the oil to a dummy company they had set up in the Russian enclave of Kaliningrad. To reach Kaliningrad the oil had to be transported through Lithuania, where the cargo was readdressed and then exported to Western countries. In Russia the oil was booked as a loss. Second, the Russian company could sell the oil directly to a Western partner and then claim that the oil had been rejected. Officially the oil was then returned to Russia. But in reality the returned cargo contained some other goods or considerably less oil than stated in the customs declaration.[21]

Russian institutions abroad also offered the possibility of exporting oil or oil products without paying custom duties. A good example of this is the Western Group of the Soviet (and later Russian) army, which was stationed in

Germany until 1994. According to a report presented to Russian President Boris Yeltsin in November 1992, the Western group received considerable amounts of fuel supplies from Russia. But these fuel deliveries were not used for the Russian forces; instead they were forwarded to two private companies, which then sold the fuel at dumping prices. The profits from these illegal sales were estimated at U.S.$13 million.[22]

Another way to smuggle oil out of Russia was to export it through an organization that had been exempted from paying customs duties by a presidential decree. The idea of such decrees was to offer non-profit organizations an alternative source of finance after the state was no longer able to provide funding. The income from duty-free foreign trade activities had to be used for the declared purpose of the non-profit organization. But commercial companies and criminal gangs gained control over a number of Russian non-profit organizations and forced them to act as middlemen in deals to import consumer goods and export raw materials.[23] In 1995–96 about a dozen leading figures in non-profit organizations were killed, probably as the result of struggles over the control of their organizations.

The criminalization of foreign trade combined with pressure from the International Monetary Fund influenced the Russian government to gradually liberalize foreign trade in oil. The system of state-set export quotas was abolished in March 1995.[24] The decision to cancel the crude oil export tax was finally made in November 1996. The liberalization of oil exports brought large-scale oil smuggling to an end in 1997. Most of the shady oil-exporting companies have left the market. In 1997 the number of Russian companies engaged in oil exports came to a mere 150, and seven leading oil companies were responsible for about half of Russia's exports to countries outside the former Soviet Union.[25] Once oil exports were no longer subject to special restrictions, a different problem emerged. Instead of hiding oil exports, traders now started to report more oil exports than they had actually made, in order to get higher refunds of value-added tax.[26]

Finally, the end of the era of oil smuggling did not bring an end to the criminalization of the oil industry. Criminal gangs had already accumulated considerable financial means, and when the operation of oil export companies became less profitable, these gangs tried to take over oil-producing companies in order to ensure future profits. "With the change in the quota and license system for exports a rise can be observed in the number of criminal firms, entering 'legal' businesses and trying to control profitable enterprises of the industry."[27]

MONEY LAUNDERING AND CAPITAL FLIGHT

Capital flight means the transfer of legally gained money abroad in order to avoid taxes and to find better investment possibilities. In Western countries this behavior is considered to be a normal part of international transactions between financial markets. Money laundering, on the other hand, describes financial schemes designed to cover the criminal origin of income and is subject to criminal prosecution. Until the introduction of a new criminal code in January 1997 Russian legislation made no distinction between money laundering and capital flight. They both meant the unlawful transfer of capital abroad and its investment in a way that was meant to disguise its origin.[28] In both cases, offenders were accused of tax evasion and of violating foreign currency exchange regulations.

The Russian oil industry had two reasons to engage in illegal capital transfers abroad. First, the need to launder illegal profits from oil smuggling, and second, the wish to invest legal profits abroad in order to find better investment opportunities and avoid taxation in Russia. It has been estimated that capital flight from the Russian oil industry amounted to a total of U.S.$7.4 billion in the period from 1992 to 1995.[29]

There are two main ways to illegally transfer capital abroad. The first way exploits the fact that banks are able to transfer hard currencies across borders without being controlled. The second way is based on import-export contracts. Since the Russian banking system was underdeveloped until 1995, and since Russian oil companies did not have close connections with Russian banks until that time, they mostly used false import-export contracts with foreign firms in order to transfer money abroad illegally. Under such a scheme the Russian company exports oil to a Western firm. The Western firm directs the payment (or parts of the payment), not toward the Russian account of the delivering company, but toward its hard currency account in the West.[30]

The following diagram illustrates this method:

Figure 4.1

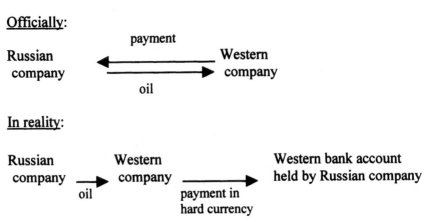

Bigger companies often use their own offshore subsidiaries for illegal transfers of capital abroad. Under such a scheme, the Russian company delivers oil or oil products to its offshore subsidiary at prices far below world market levels. The subsidiary then sells the oil or the oil products at world market prices and pays the profit into a hard currency account.[31] Thus the Russian company does not make any profits and, therefore, does not pay taxes. The offshore subsidiary makes a huge profit, which is deposited in Western bank accounts and is actually at the Russian company's disposal. Such a scheme reduces the risk of detection even further, since all transactions are carried out in accordance with legal contracts.

Russia implemented a number of different controls to prevent such deals, and the controls have been revised and tightened several times. But it proved to be impossible for the customs authorities to check all foreign trade transactions. Besides, if irregularities are detected, the Russian company cannot be prosecuted when it claims that it was deceived by the foreign firm. Accordingly, there are no indications that Russian authorities can effectively hamper illegal capital transfers abroad without reversing the liberalization of foreign trade.[32]

Russia's new criminal code, which came into effect in January 1997, marked an important reform step in the fight against capital flight and money laundering. The foreign exchange regime was liberalized, and for the first time in Russian history money laundering was introduced as a criminal offence. Thus it became possible to fight money laundering activities more efficiently.[33]

Figure 4.2

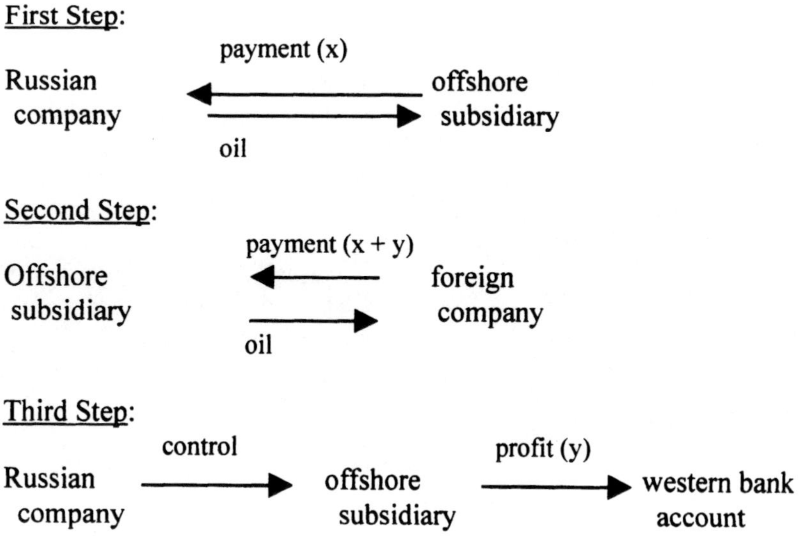

<u>First Step</u>:

<u>Second Step</u>:

<u>Third Step</u>:

Capital flight, on the other hand, is becoming more legalized, and the Russian leadership seems to hope that it will lose relevance with the improvement of investment opportunities in Russia. However, the Primakov government introduced some new restrictions in late 1998 after the August crisis had led to a new upsurge in capital flight from Russia.

ORGANIZED CRIME AND THE OIL INDUSTRY

The profits of the oil industry and the dominance of corruption networks in its operation attracted not only banks but organized crime as well. Since criminal gangs made considerable profits from the illegal activities of the oil industry, their influence continued to grow as long as the criminalization of the oil industry went on. Accordingly, the influence of organized crime in the Russian oil industry probably reached its peak in 1995–96.

In February 1996, Russia's minister of the interior, Anatoly Kulikov, stated that the oil industry was included in the spheres of interests of organized crime and that three leading oil companies, YuKOS, Rosneft, and LUKoil, already had strong connections with criminal groups.[34] According to a report by the Russian newspaper, *Izvestiia*, a number of leading managers in the oil industry of the Tiumen Region had ties with a criminal group that controlled a leading bank, an insurance company and an oil exporting company.[35]

The influence of organized crime led to an escalation of violence within the industry. A good example of this is the case of Megionneftegaz. Megionneftegaz is the single oil producer of the vertically integrated oil company, Slavneft. Anatoly Kuzmin, who had become head of Megionneftegaz in 1993, was engaged in a conflict with two banks, which were connected with the company. These two banks, Iugorsky Bank and the International Bank for the Development of the Fuel Energy Complex (MBRTEK), were operating four trading companies in Europe and the United States, which were responsible for most of the acquisitions of equipment needed by Megionneftegaz. The annual turnover of these trading companies amounted to several million dollars. When Kuzmin tried to become head of the newly founded Slavneft oil company, he was shot by a contract killer. Subsequently, a candidate of the two banks was chosen as head of Slavneft. One year later, the head of Iugorsky Bank, too, fell victim to contract killers.[36]

The criminalization of the oil sector is not limited to producers and exporters. Russia's domestic market for oil products has become subject to a mafia-like fight for influence. Illegal sales of gasoline made up nearly a quarter of all detected tax frauds in 1998.[37]

A striking example is the gasoline market of Moscow. When the capital's government decided to merge the two leading companies in the market, MPKA and TsTK, a power struggle evolved between the managers of these companies, and in August 1997 the director of MPKA was killed. There are persistent rumours that the rival company, TsTK, headed by the former energy minister, Iury Shafranik, has close connections to high-ranking state officials and to Moscow's most notorious criminal gang.[38] A main trader in oil products in the Moscow region, the Iunios company, lost its two founders in contract killings in 1996 and 1998.[39]

The criminalization of the Chechen oil industry is a special case. During the war between the separatist republic and the Russian army, Chechens started to sink their own makeshift oil wells and to siphon oil out of the Baku-Novorossiisk pipeline that runs through the Chechen capital of Grozny. The oil was processed into gasoline in underground refineries. After the war ended, the new Chechen leadership tried to regain control over the oil sector in order to finance reconstruction of the devastated republic. In August 1997, Chechen President Aslan Maskhadov issued a decree, which, in the words of the head of the Chechen oil company, Iunko, "will help to eradicate completely the illegal oil business and this is of great importance for ensuring the safety of the Baku-Novorossiisk pipeline."[40] Following a campaign in which more than fifteen hundred police and national guardsmen took part, Chechen security forces had shut down about a thousand illegal oil refining operations by late September.[41] The Baku-Grozny-Novorossiisk pipeline, following repairs, was re-commissioned in October 1997, and Chechnya started to receive transit fees for the transport of oil from Azerbaijan's offshore fields.

While the Chechen oil industry experienced some measure of stabilization in 1998, the situation deteriorated greatly in the neighboring republic of Dagestan, where serious unrest broke out in summer 1998. The head of the republic's oil company, Dagneft, Gadzhi Makhachev, has been described by Liz Fuller as "a criminal individual who has accumulated enormous fortunes by dubious means," and whose support base is a private army masquerading as a movement of Dagestan's ethnic Avars.[42]

CONCLUSION

The corruption network that connects the Russian oil industry with state officials had already emerged in Soviet times. The reorganization of the foreign trade regime after the end of the Soviet Union offered this network a new source of illegal income. Between 1992 and 1995, oil smuggling caused immense losses for the Russian budget. At the same time, oil smuggling and the laundering of profits brought corrupt managers of oil companies into contact with organized crime. With that development, the criminalization of the Russian oil industry was completed.

But whereas the Russian press routinely assumes that the existence of an organized criminal in the management of an oil company means that organized crime controls that company, it may well be that oil companies are powerful enough to use criminal groups only for their own interests, such as for smuggling and money laundering. This interpretation is backed up by the fact that criminal gangs active in the oil industry are in most cases employed at banks or shady export companies but not at the big oil companies themselves.

Criminal gangs were trying to change that situation in 1995–96. At that time they had already accumulated considerable capital, and the privatization process offered the chance to buy a stake in leading oil companies. But banks had the better contacts with the relevant state officials and acquired nearly all the stakes offered. These banks are part of corruption networks, and it is likely that most of them engage in illegal activities. But they also operate legally and they can make profits by working according to the laws. Moreover, the liberalization of foreign trade has made criminal activities in the oil industry much less profitable.

The banks, which now play a leading role in the Russian oil industry, are, therefore, likely to concentrate on legal ways to make profits from their engagement in the oil industry. The result of this development is a conflict between old Soviet-style managers and modern capitalist-style managers in nearly all the big oil companies. It is also in part a conflict between members of criminal gangs and new managers. The new managers consider it much more important (and more profitable) to modernize the oil industry, to stop the decline in production, and to make profits through legal operations. In order to achieve that goal, the industry is in urgent need of foreign investment. Thus the financial situation of the oil industry may encourage the transparent accounting and fair dealing that foreign investors normally require.

Accordingly, the drastic decline in profits from illegal activities, together with the growing influence of banks, may lead to a decriminalization of the Russian oil industry. Under the new conditions it will no longer be profitable for oil companies to cooperate with organized crime, and the connections between oil industry and criminal gangs are likely to loosen. However, the corruption network of the oil industry will remain in place, because good connections with the state will continue to be vital for the Russian oil business.

NOTES

1. For a brief overview of different definitions of corruption, see Natasha Kogan, "Thinking about Corruption," *Transitions,* vol. 5, no. 3 (March 1998): 40–45; Michael Johnston, "The Search for Definitions: The Vitality of Politics and the Issue of Corruption," *International Social Science Journal,* no. 149 (September 1996): 321–35.

2. David Granick, *The Red Executive: A Study of the Organization Man in Soviet Industry*, (New York: Doubleday, 1969): 43.

3. On corruption in the Soviet economy, see, for example, William A. Clark, *Crime and Punishment in Soviet Officialdom* (New York: Sharpe, 1993): 71–99; Nicholas Lampert, *Whistleblowing in the Soviet Union* (London: Macmillan, 1985): 13–60; Alec Nove, *The Soviet Economic System* (London: Allen & Unwin, 1968): 13–60; Konstantin Simis, *USSR: Secrets of a Corrupt Society* (London: Dent & Sons, 1982).

4. Leslie Holmes, "Corruption and the Crisis of the Post-Communist State," *Crime, Law and Social Change*, vol. 27, nos. 3–4 (December 1997): 275–97.

5. Svetlana P. Glinkina, "Prichiny usileniia i spetsifika tenevoi ekonomiki na etape perekhoda Rossii k rynku," in *Izuchenie organizovannoi prestupnosti*, ed. American-Russian Center for the Study of Organized Crime (Moscow: Olimp, 1997): 249–268 (here: 251–252).

6. For a more elaborated version of this point, see Anders Aslund, "Reform vs. Rent-Seeking in Russia's Economic Transformation," *Transition (OMRI)*, vol. 3, no. 2 (January 1996): 12–16.

7. See, for example, R. Frydman, K. Murphy, and A. Rapaczynski, "Capitalism with a Comrade's Face," *Transition (OMRI)*, vol. 3, no. 2 (January 1996): 5–11.

8. Yakov Pappe, "Fuel and Energy Complex Elites in the Political Economy of Contemporary Russia," in *Post-Soviet Puzzles, vol. III*, ed. K. Segbers and S. de Spiegeleire (Baden-Baden: Nomos, 1995): 459–77 (here: 468).

9. See, for example, Isabel Gorst, "Oil Industry Privatization, Russian Style," *Petroleum Economist* (February 1996): 3–4.

10. Pappe, "Fuel and Energy Complex Elites": 459.

11. James Watson, "Foreign Investment in Russia: The Case of the Oil Industry," *Europe-Asia Studies*, vol. 48, no. 3 (1996): 429–455 (here: 447).

12. C. P. McPherson, "Political Reforms in the Russian Oil Sector," *Finance and Development (World Bank)*, vol. 33, no. 2 (June 1996): table 1.

13. U.S. Embassy, Moscow, "A Primer on Pipeline Access and Its Politics in Russia," *Pipeline News*, no. 66, 5–11 July 1997. Although Russian President Boris Yeltsin announced the liquidation of the system in his 1998 "state of the nation" message, pipeline access remained subject to negotiations between state officials and companies.

14. V. Iu. Alekperov, "Vertikalnaia integratsiia i konkurentsiia na rynke nefti i nefteproduktov," *Neft i biznes* no. 2, 1997: 2–5.

15. East-West Institute, Russian Regional Report, New York, 25 March 1999.

16. Eugene M. Khartukov, "Bankers Becoming New Masters of Oil Companies," *Petroleum Economist* (February 1997): 6–8 (here: 8).

17. See, for example, Vladimir Rasuvaev, "Zachem neftianikam 'khodit' vo vlast'?" *Neft Rossii*, no. 4, 1997: 26–28.

18. D. N. Bakhrakh, "Tamozhennoe pravo kak institut administrativnogo prava," *Gosudarstvo i pravo*, no. 3 (March 1995): 13–21; B. N. Gabrichidze and N. A. Suslov, "Tamozhennye organy rossiiskoi federatsii," *Gosudarstvo i pravo*, no. 3 (March 1995): 22–29.

19. Vadim Belykh, "Chernaia krov," *Izvestiia*, 4 January 1997.

20. Heiko Pleines, "Organized Crime and Corruption in Russia since 1987," *Russia and the Successor States Briefing Service*, vol. 3, no. 5 (October 1995): 3–20 (here: 9).

21. Belykh, "Chernaia krov."

22. Altogether, the report estimated the losses caused by the Western Group's illegal activities at U.S.$60 million. The head of the supervisory administration, Iury Boldyrev, was dismissed by Yeltsin in March 1993. His post was abolished and the report was shelved. The commander of the Western Group, General Matvei Burlakov, became deputy defense minister after his return from Germany. The report was published in *Moskovski komsomolets,* 28 October 1994. Burlakov was suspended from his position in November 1994 and dismissed three months later.

23. Mikhail Berger, "1.374.172.715.572 rub.," *Izvestiia,* 21 February 1995; Stanislav Govorukhin, *Velikaia kriminalnaia revolutsiia* (Moscow: Andreevskii flag, 1993): 23–26; Interfax, "Tri neftyanykh SP pretenduyut na poluchenie eksportnykh lgot," *Segodnia,* 17 March 1995.

24. Since the export capacities of Russian pipelines and ports are limited, there are still export quotas in place (see above).

25. Eugene M. Khartukov, "Incomplete Privatization Mixes Ownership of Russia's Oil Industry," *Oil and Gas Journal,* 18 August 1997: 36–40 (here: 39–40).

26. Interfax, 16 January 1997.

27. Russian Ministry of the Interior, "O sostaianii i merakh usileniia borby s ekonomicheskoi prestupnostiu i korruptsiei v RF (1996)," quoted in *Nezavisimaia gazeta,* 17 January 1997.

28. As long as the money was not laundered in Russia itself.

29. Vladimir Tikhomirov, "Capital Flight from Post-Soviet Russia," *Europe-Asia Studies,* vol. 49, no. 4 (1997): 591–615 (here: table 3).

30. A. Kozyrin, "Pravovoe regulirovanie poriadka peremeshcheniia valiuty i valiutnykh tsennostei cheres rossiiskuiu granitsu," *Dengi i kredit,* no. 8 (1994): 33–38.

31. *Segodnia,* 27 September 1995.

32. Tikhomirov, "Capital Flight": 595–598.

33. *OMRI Daily Digest,* 10 December 1996; *Segodnia,* 15 January 1997.

34. Analytical Centre Izvesty, "Lukoil. Politika i biznes," *Izvestiia,* 15 May 1997.

35. Sergei Leskov, "Ostorozhno: vo vlast idet Atroshenko," *Izvestiia,* 10 January 1997.

36. Belykh, "Chernaia krov."

37. "Levye dollary iz podpol'nykh khranilishch," in *Rossiiskaya gazeta,* 6 November 1998: 2.

38. A. Nogina, T. Lysova, and N. Kalinichenko, "Koroli benzokolonok," *Ekspert,* 8 September 1997: 32–34. Andrei Ovciannikov, "Delo pakhnet benzinom i dengami," *Literaturnaia gazeta,* 24 September 1997.

39. Sergei Topol', "Neftyanaia firma teryaet rukovodstvo," *Kommersant-Daily,* 3 November 1998: 5.

40. Interfax, 9 August 1997.

41. Itar-Tass, 20 September 1997.

42. *RFE/RL Caucasus Report,* 2 June 1998.

Part 1 Appendix

Company Profiles: LUKoil, YuKOS, Surgutneftgaz, Sidanko

David Lane and Iskander Seifulmulukov

LUKOIL[1]

LUKoil was not only the first Russian vertically integrated company to be established, but it also remains unquestionably the leader of the country's oil industry. It is in first place in amount of oil production, is very much ahead of other companies in the size of market capitalization and liquidity of its equities, enjoys a superior level of management and a stronger financial position than others, and has proceeded on its way to the consolidation of its subdivisions. It is also active outside the former USSR with markets in the countries of the Commonwealth of Independent States and elsewhere.

LUKoil was established in the form of a state *konsern* as early as 1991. The company is made up of three large oil-extracting enterprises from Western Siberia—Langepasneftegaz, Uraineftegaz, and Kogalymneftegaz (the first letters of these names were used in the "LUKoil" abbreviation), one from the Urals Region—Permneft, two from the Volga Region—Nizhnevolzhskneft and Astrakhanneft, and one from the Kaliningrad Region on the Baltic. The downstream operations are carried out by refineries in Perm and Volgograd and by eight regional oil products distribution enterprises.[2]

According to an estimate by Miller and Lents, the proven reserves of oil of the three Western Siberian extraction enterprises included in LUKoil, on 1 January 1996, constituted 7.9 billion barrels (about 1.1 billion tons) of oil and 11,519.4 billion cubic feet of natural gas.[3] LUKoil claims proven oil reserves in Tiumen Region and the European part of Russia of 14.9 billion barrels (roughly 2 billion tons), not much less than those of YuKOS, which in this respect occupies first place among Russian companies. For comparison, Royal Dutch Shell, which is a leader among the non-state oil companies of the world, has 9 billion barrels of oil resources and Exxon (second after Shell) 6.5 billion barrels.[4] LUKoil is first in Russia in the amount of oil extraction and fourth in the world.[5] The scale of these holdings indicates the economic importance of LUKoil and its strategic and political importance. It is clearly the jewel in Russia's oil crown.

LUKoil's six-year program foresees considerable investment in petrol stations in different regions of Russia and abroad.[6] It plans, in the United States alone, two thousand service stations by the year 2003. In 1997, it already partly owned Nexus Fields, which gives five thousand U.S. supermarkets sites[7] that it intends to develop to sell petrol. In this way, LUKoil may become like the classical Western oil giants (before the nationalization of Middle Eastern and other oil fields) owning (or having under direct control) extraction, production, refining, marketing, and sales.

LUKoil was also the first Russian oil holding to begin consolidation of its internal structure. This implies transition to a single vertically integrated stock company involving an exchange of shares of the subsidiaries for those of the holding company. This facilitates control by the company's management of the marketing activities of its subdivision and centralization of intra-firm financial flows. It has developed its own trade network, particularly in the retail sale of oil products. One reason for this is that, consequent on the move to the market and the insolvency of large-scale industrial (and domestic) users, there has been widespread default in payment. Private car owners are the only completely reliable category of solvent Russian fuel users. The aim of the company for the years 1997 to 2002 is to sell no less than 50 percent of its production through its own retail distribution network.[8]

As to the internal organization of the company, present intentions are to establish structures on a functional basis: a single center for analysis of financial aspects, and a single drilling subdivision. The other forms of administration will have geographical subdivisions bringing together units on a regional basis. The main oil extraction facilities of the company are in the Tiumen Region, which is an area of activity of its subsidiary enterprises Langepasneftegaz, Uraineftegaz, and Kogalymneftegaz. By the end of 1996 these units were organized in a single filial unit, the operational company, "LUKoil-Western Siberia."

The addition of the new extracting enterprises has allowed LUKoil to create territorial-industrial complexes (TPKs) covering the complete cycle (extraction-processing-trade). The first of them is situated in the Volga Region and is represented by the production companies, Nizhnevolzhskneft and Astrakhan'neft, the Volgograd refinery, and the trading enterprises, Volgogradnefteprodukt and Astrakhannefteprodukt. Using Astrakhan'neft,

LUKoil intends to study the possibility of development of the oil/gas resources of the Russian part of the Caspian shelf.

There are multi-profile subdivisions of LUKoil in many other regions of Russia—LUKoil-Moscow, LUKoil–St. Petersburg, LUKoil-Tatarstan, and others. LUKoil's interests in the Commonwealth of Independent States countries are represented by the joint-venture (in Russian an SP) especially established for the purpose (LUKoil-Kazakhstan, LUKoil-Baku, LUKoil-Ukraine, LUKoil-Bel, LUKoil-Uzbekneftegaz). Finally, international projects of the company are entrusted to the registered Viennese firm, LUKoil-International.

Despite the relative prosperity of LUKoil, the company is facing the same problems as the whole of the Russian oil industry. These include a declining domestic demand for oil and petroleum products, significant non-payments, a heavy burden of taxes, expensive bank credits, and a reduction in export earnings due to the continual fall in world prices. Finally, while LUKoil's financial position is slightly better than that of most other Russian oil companies, it is considerably worse than that of large Western oil corporations. To make one comparison, Mobil Oil extracts roughly the same amount of oil but makes seven to eight times more profit.[9] In the first half of the nineties, LUKoil experienced a considerable decrease in investments and only in 1995–96 did investment stabilize and gradually begin to increase. The company's debts by the end of 1995 exceeded 2.6 trillion rubles (more than 0.5 billion dollars).[10]

The company's interests cover the whole of Russia, the areas of the former USSR, and other countries.[11] It is active in the former republics of the USSR, it is actively exploring in Azerbaijan and Kazakhstan, and it has retail outlets in the Baltic countries, Kazakhstan, Kirghizia, Belarus, Moldova, and Ukraine.[12] The company is also carrying out exploration work in Algeria, Tunisia, and Egypt and has an agreement (in principle) to participate in the development of the large oil field of West Kurna in Iraq.

Expansion into other regions is necessary for LUKoil, both to establish new markets and to enlarge its resources. Although 55 percent of LUKoil's economically viable resources and 70 percent of its overall resources are situated in the territory of Western Siberia, development of the probable resources in this region demands considerable investments. Hence LUKoil plans to pay special attention to the development of oil fields in the European part of Russia and abroad, where costs are lower and development is more profitable. Its president, Vagit Alekperov, in his report to the shareholders' meeting in June 1997, pointed out that oil reserves are increasingly difficult to extract and another spokesman, Alexander Vasilenko, anticipated that the company would produce up to at least a quarter of its oil outside Russia by the year 2000.[13] According to the company's own prognoses, by the year 2005 LUKoil's production will reach the level of 67 million tons, and of these 20 million will be extracted outside Russia.[14]

In a number of its projects in Russia and abroad, LUKoil is supported by
strategic collaboration with Western oil companies: the American Atlantic
Richfield Company (ARCO), Pennzoil, and Italy's Agip. ARCO owns 7.99
percent of LUKoil's stock, and along with LUKoil is taking part in one of the
North African projects. In September 1996, the two companies established
the LUKARCO SP (joint venture) for carrying out projects in the exploration
and development of gas and oil fields in Russia and the countries of the
Commonwealth of Independent States. It is estimated that the overall
amount of investments will be 5 billion dollars within the course of the next
fifteen years.[15] Pennzoil and LUKoil have established a joint venture to
develop the Karabakh oil field in Azerbaijan, as well as to manufacture and
trade lubricants in Russia. LUKoil and Agip cooperate in the North African
projects. LUKoil is more successful than other oil companies in attracting
foreign credits.[16]

While LUKoil at present is not in the same global league as the leading
Western international oil companies, it clearly aspires to a similar role. The
significance here is that in the process of economic transition in the post-
communist states, one indigenous company has the potential to become a
world actor in its own right. Not only to ensure a flow of capital as a source
of finance for exploration and extraction, but also in order to spread its
operations downstream, it is in its interests to have foreign collaborators and
joint ownership. Given its leading role in the Russian economy, particularly
as a (potential) earner of foreign currency, it has a truly global impact on the
Russian government. Its interests are not compatible with the indigenous
metal manufacturing and agricultural industries, which are local in scope
and incapable of achieving a world profile. Such industries seek a low price,
high-output fuel industry with domestic subsidies.

YUKOS

The YuKOS oil company was established in April 1993. At the beginning of
1997, it was made up of 20 subsidiaries, the largest of which are the Yuganskneftegaz (Tiumen Region) and Samaraneftegaz oil production associations. YuKOS has three oil refineries in the Samara Region: Kuibyshev,
Syzran, and Novokuibyshev NPZ. YuKOS is the top Russian oil company in
terms of total recoverable and proven oil reserves.[17] Its greatest strength lies
in the quantity of its total recoverable oil resources, which are the largest in
Russia, totaling 2.1 billion tons (Yuganskneftegaz's share is 85 percent, and
Samaraneftegaz's 15 percent).

Yuganskneftegaz is the largest oil production corporation in Russia, having some 350 oil and gas fields—including thirty large ones. However, more
than half of the exploited fields are at the stage of declining extraction

returns (emptied to 60–70 percent). That fact, as well as the economic difficulties of recent years, explains why the total extraction of oil and gas condensate is on the decline: in 1986 it was 71 million tons, in 1990 58.9 million tons, and in 1995 27 million tons.[18] Oil extraction by Samaraneftegaz company in the nineties has also greatly decreased, from 15.1 million tons in 1990 to 8.6 million in 1994, though extraction increased to 9.1 million tons in 1995.[19]

In 1995, combined YuKOS oil output (including Yugansksneftegaz's share in joint ventures) totalled 36 million tons, second in rank to LUKoil—though production declined in 1996. The company exported about 8.5 million tons of crude oil and 3.4 million tons of petroleum products. The company's oil production decreased to 35 million tons in 1996.[20] It expects not only to halt the decrease in amounts of extraction, but to increase it up to 40 million. tons by the year 2000.[21] There are a number of oil fields where extraction is growing, and in 1995 the company received licenses to exploit the resources of eleven areas next to Yuganskneftegaz's territories in the South of Tiumen Region and Khanty-Mansi National Autonomous District. In 1994, the company also received a thirty-year license for prospecting and development of the oil/gas region in Peru (at present this project is suspended due to lack of finance).

The most promising of YuKOS's oil fields are located in the far north where, however, there is no economic infrastructure and, before an increase in extraction can take place, a great deal of exploration and development needs to be carried out. One of the most important tasks of the company is to find the necessary investment resources. This problem can be partially solved by the attraction of foreign partners to provide financial resources and modern technology. In particular, YuKOS is associated with the American corporation, Amoco, in the extraction of oil from the large Priobskoe oil field, where the resources are estimated as being 600–700 million tons of oil. YuKOS and Amoco also intend to cooperate in the modernization of NPZ, geological prospecting, and transportation and retailing of oil products. YuKOS and its subdivisions cooperate with other foreign firms in a number of smaller projects, in particular in the reconstruction of non-working oil wells through Yuganskfrakmaster, a joint venture established in 1989 by Yuganskneftegaz and Canadian Frackmaster.

The oil processing complex of YuKOS is one of the most advanced and potentially valuable in Russia. The sum of its crude distillation capacities in direct oil processing is 33 million tons per annum, though in 1995 only 16.2 million tons were processed. In 1994 the amount of petrol manufactured by YuKOS was 12 percent of the total manufactured in the country, and of diesel fuel the share was 14 percent.[22] The company has plans to update all three refineries in order to increase the yield of light and middle distillates from 62 percent in 1996 to 78 percent at the beginning of the next decade.[23]

YuKOS provides oil products in nine regions of Central Russia and the Middle Volga, as well as Khanty-Mansi Autonomous Okrug, north of Western Siberia. The retail network of the company includes 940 filling stations, or 11 percent of the number in Russia. In 1995, its trade subsidiaries sold 6 million tons of oil products on the home market, and in the future the company intends to increase the amount of sales to 20–22 million tons. It also intends to extend its operations to areas outside its present boundaries. In 1997 plans were made to build eighteen new retail outlets and to rebuild twenty-five of the existing ones.[24]

Following LUKoil's example, YuKOS has also begun expansion into new regional markets: in 1995 and 1996 it opened several filling stations in Omsk, Novosibirsk, and Krasnodar Regions, areas of other companies' activity. In the future the company intends to start selling oil products in Ukraine and Belarus. In Turkey, a joint venture, YUSAT Petrol, has been established, which processes the oil of Western Siberia and retails oil products on the local market.

The most serious problems for YuKOS are caused by the poor financial performance of the holding company and the majority of its subsidiaries. These firms are subject to a high level of consumer payment arrears; they owe large debts to the state and salaries to their own workforce. In 1995–96 Yuganskneftegaz, an extraction subdivision of YuKOS, became one of the largest debtors to the federal and local authorities. Though the government has rescheduled payments in order to ease this burden, by the end of 1996, Yuganskneftegaz still owed 295 million dollars to the federal government budget alone.

In the regions of YuKOS's operations, the main customers are from the agricultural sector, which is notorious for non-payment. Moreover, for some years the local governments of these regions have forced YuKOS's trade subdivisions to sell fuel to such users on credit, with no real prospect of eventual repayment. As a result of non-payments, the oil products' distribution enterprises themselves have become insolvent, and YuKOS's refineries have sought to sell oil products to outside clients. The company's difficult financial situation can be attributed to a large degree to its poor management and lack of real control over its subsidiaries. Due to these factors, YuKOS lost ground from its position in 1993–94 when it was regarded as Russia's second most important oil company. By 1995 YuKOS lagged far behind LUKoil and Surgutneftegaz in financial strength and corporate character.

The future of the company is strongly linked to its partnership with the leading bank, Menatep, headed by Mikhail Khodorkovski and which acquired a controlling stake in YuKOS in late 1995. Although this bank does not have sufficient resources to make YuKOS solvent and technologically advanced, it is capable of considerably improving YuKOS's financial management, of increasing the attractiveness of the company to outside investors, and of acting as an intermediary in attracting necessary finance. However, the shares held by Menatep in 1998 were to Western banks as collateral to losses.

Since its acquisition by Menatep, efforts have been made to improve YuKOS's management, to consolidate its subsidiaries, and to rationalize their operations and money flows. YuKOS has tightened control over its subdivisions by introducing "external management" (in particular, this means that managers of all affiliate companies are nominated by the holding, rather than being elected by shareholders' meetings). A joint team from YuKOS and Menatep has been seeking to lower costs. Early in 1996, following LUKoil's example, the company's management intended to take a controlling interest in its subsidiaries.

In January 1998, it was announced that there would be a merger with Sibneft, making the new company, Yuksi, the largest in Russia. However, due to the financial uncertainties, both nationally and internationally, by the summer of 1998, the merger was cancelled.

SURGUTNEFTEGAZ

Surgutneftegaz was founded in April 1993. It is made up of Surgut (Tiumen Region) oil production association (AO Surgutneftegaz), the Kirishinefteorgsintez refinery (in Kirishi, Leningrad Region), and retail enterprises in St. Petersburg and other regions of northwestern Russia.

The company's recoverable oil reserves are estimated at 1.5 billion tons. AO Surgutneftegaz has licenses to develop more than fifty oil fields, though in 1997 extraction was carried out only in twenty of them. The average depletion rate of all the oil fields, according to 1995 data, did not exceed 38 percent, indicating considerable potential for future oil production.[25] However, conditions of extraction on the developed fields are worsening: in the last ten years, average productivity per well has decreased by a factor of more than four, and there is a growing cost of extraction as marginal costs rise. In this situation, the amount of oil and gas condensate extracted by AO Surgutneftegaz decreased from 51 million tons in 1990 to 34.3 million tons in 1994. In 1995, the rate of extraction decrease considerably slowed down, and by 1996 it remained at the level of 33.3 million barrels of oil, while gas production increased from 8.4 billion cubic meters to 9.6 billion.[26]

The Kirishi refinery, with a capacity of 19 million tons per annum, is among the five biggest in Russia and is the only refinery owned by the company. The amount of oil processed by Kirishi has grown considerably in the last two years and in 1996 exceeded 15.3 million tons.[27] But the oil processing facilities of the company are noticeably inadequate for the amount of extraction. Also, the distance between oil fields and refineries is greater than in any other Russian company—hence transport costs are higher, making the prices at the Kirishi refinery among the highest in Russia. One compensating factor, however, is that since the refinery is situated near the western border of the country, it can export a large part of its production to Germany, Finland, Denmark, the Baltic countries, and Ukraine at competitive prices. A complex modernization of the enterprise is underway at an overall estimated cost of 750 million dollars; when completed this will increase the yield of light and medium distillates from 55 percent to 75 percent.[28]

In 1996, the company started a program of reconstruction and building of a filling station network. In 1996–1997 it was planned to build twenty-six new outlets and to refurbish five old ones. Future plans include the expansion of markets for oil and oil products in Russia and the development of foreign markets.[29] This will confirm Surgutneftegaz as a major oil exporter, second to LUKoil. In 1995 the company exported 11.8 million tons of crude oil.[30] Support has also been given by the Russian government to Surgutneftegaz in the development of an oil port at Batareinaya (Leningrad Region).

Of all the Russian companies, Surgutneftegaz has the strongest financial position. It is one of the few Russian oil companies to pay dividends and it also pays tax punctually. By the end of 1996, Surgutneftegaz was not in debt to the federal government; and the company also owed no arrears of pay to its workforce. It finances itself through revenue and has no bank credit. Much attention is paid to the control of costs, and in the extraction sphere average wage costs are 1.5 to two times lower than in most other Russian oil companies.[31] Non-payments by its clients amount to considerably less than those of the majority of other vertically integrated oil companies.

Originally, the policy of Surgutneftegaz was to be self-sufficient and independent of outsiders. Before 1996, it had no foreign projects, and had neither established joint ventures nor sought credits from Russian or foreign banks. The management of Surgutneftegaz had often emphasized its role as a "people's company," and had sought to spread its own shares and those of its subsidiaries among the largest possible number of small investors. The company's charter initially prevented the selling of more than 5 percent of its shares to foreign investors. It had no plans to sell shares on Western stock markets. A relatively hostile attitude toward outside investors was emphasized by a lack of transparency with respect to the company's operating and financial performance. Symbolically perhaps, the company has its headquarters in Surgut rather than in Moscow.

However, in 1996, Surgutneftegaz began to shift away from this rather parochial tradition by announcing that it welcomed foreign investments. It has also rescinded the regulations limiting foreign investors to a maximum of 5 percent and has moved toward more transparency by disclosing more information about its operations. An ADR (American Depository Receipts) program was launched in order to improve the marketability of the company's shares. Surgutneftegaz is expected to establish a joint venture with Neste, and is developing a program of cooperation with Slovenia and Yugoslavia. It is also possible that Surgutneftegaz will participate in a refinery project in Leuna (Germany) together with the French company, Elf Aquitaine.

Reorganization of the inner structure of NK Surgutneftegaz is done along different lines from those of LUKoil or YuKOS. This is due to the fact that the management of Surgutneftegaz's holding company and the extraction subdivision, AO Surgutneftegaz, are very closely interrelated. The holding company's president (Vladimir Leonidovich Bogdanov) is general director of the subsidiary. Unlike LUKoil and YuKOS, there is no large management structure associated with the holding company; most functions remain with the subsidiaries.

Having been able to exercise full control over its main production subsidiary, the holding company's management has for several years neglected the integration of the company's refining and marketing subdivisions located in the Russian north-west. The movement toward more consolidation began only in 1995. As a result, Surgutneftegaz has had problems with regional authorities in St. Petersburg and the Leningrad Region, as well as with minor shareholders of the company's downstream subsidiaries. In 1996, for example, shareholders of three distribution subsidiaries from St. Petersburg did not approve the stock exchange with the holding company or with AO Surgutneftegaz on the grounds that the ratios of exchange were unfair. Nonetheless, these difficulties are not expected to hinder development into a vertically integrated company.

Surgutneftegaz is now clearly emerging as LUKoil's main rival in Russia in terms of corporate operational and financial performance as well as foreign investment potential.

SIDANKO

The Siberia and Far East Oil Company (Sidanko) was established in May 1994. In 1997 it was made up of seven oil extracting companies: Chernogorneft, Varyeganneftegaz, Varyeganneft, Kondpetroleum (Tiumen Region), Novosibirskneftegaz (Novosibirsk Region), Udmurtneft (Republic of Udmurtia), and Saratovneftegaz (Saratov Region); three oil-processing enterprises: Angarsk Petroleum Company (in the town of Angarsk, Irkutsk Region), Khabarovsk and Saratov refineries; and twelve petroleum products marketing enterprises. Initially, the company also included a large Western Siberian extracting enterprise, Purneftegaz, which in 1995 joined the Rosneft company.[32] Despite the loss of Purneftegaz, Sidanko still remains one of the largest Russian oil companies, being the fourth or fifth largest in terms of the amount of oil extracted. In 1995, the overall amount produced by its subsidiaries was 22.9 million tons of oil, and together with joint ventures the total was 27 million tons. Its exports exceeded 5.4 million tons.[33]

During the period 1996–2000, the company plans to start exploitation of fourteen new oil fields, among which the largest is Verkhnii Tar in the Novosibirsk Region and Verkhnii Chon in the north of Irkutsk Region. The latter is the largest in Eastern Siberia (probable recoverable resources are estimated at 500 million tons). The 7 million tons of oil per annum from this field will be supplied to the Khabarovsk and Angarsk refineries. Among the more promising of Sidanko's projects is the exploration and development in 1997 of the Kovyktinsk field of gas condensate in Irkutsk Region, where the amount of gas extraction by the year 2005 is expected to reach 32 billion cubic meters. It is planned to export this gas to Mongolia, China, and Southern Korea, for which it is planned to build a large oil pipeline. Also Sidanko intends to explore and develop oil and gas fields in Mongolia, for which purpose the joint venture Monrusneft has been established.[34]

In overall capacity, (about 40 million tons per annum) Sidanko is second only to the oil-processing complex of Bashkiria. Of the three refineries that are part of Sidanko, the biggest and the most up-to-date is the Angarsk Petrochemical Company (its capacity is 24.6 million tons). This enterprise is the main supplier of fuel to the regions of Eastern Siberia and the Far East. The Saratov refinery, Cracking, is of average capacity (10 million tons per year) with rather old technology, and the Khabarovsk refinery is a small enterprise requiring major reconstruction.

In 1995, Sidanko's refineries processed nearly 20 million tons of crude oil. The company is carrying out a large modernization program with respect to its refining facilities, the plan being to increase by the year 2000 the volume of oil processed to 31 million tons, and to raise the yield of light and middle distillates by 75 percent.

Sidanko owns 159 oil storage units with a capacity of 3.4 million cubic meters, and 766 retail outlets capable of dealing with up to 40 million tons per annum. In 1995, 13.5 million tons of oil products were sold on the home market.[35] The sphere of trade activity of the company is Eastern Siberia and the Far East (Sidanko fulfills more than 80 percent of demand for oil products in these regions). The Saratov refinery serves the regions of the Volga, and in the past it also supplied its products to the republics of Central Asia.

The total investment in the reconstruction of the Angarsk refinery will be in the order of 1.9 billion dollars, including 1.1 billion for updating oil chemistry production and 800 million for oil processing. Eximbank of the United States will provide a credit of 400 million dollars to finance the first stage of reconstruction. A Spanish company, Dragados, has developed a project for the first stage of reconstruction of the Saratov refinery, at an estimated cost of 357 million dollars. It is estimated that 85 percent of this sum will be provided by American and Spanish banks, and Sidanko will act as a guarantor. It is planned to complete the reconstruction by the year 2002. Other foreign interests include the Japanese companies Marubeni and Chioda, which have carried out a feasibility study concerning the reconstruction of the Khabarovsk refinery. Completion of the project will considerably improve the structure and quality of production.[36]

Compared to other Russian oil companies, Sidanko is notable for the very weak technological, organizational, commercial, and financial integration of its subsidiaries. The extracting, processing, and trade subdivisions of the company are scattered on the vast territory from the Volga Region to the Far East. The company does not have a large extractive capacity, which could become a nucleus of consolidation (unlike YuKOS or Surgutneftegaz). Hence Sidanko is not a "proper" vertically integrated company because it has not developed a company strategy in terms of allocating resources, setting the objectives, and monitoring the performance of its subsidiaries. All the exploration and production units of Sidanko are relatively independent from the holding company, especially in the disposal of their oil and their contacts with foreign partners. For example, Chernogorneft participates in three joint ventures with foreign firms.

Unlike LUKoil, in which the subsidiaries have been brought under direct central control, Sidanko's management has conceded that the subsidiaries will continue to have powers. The program of corporate management, approved by the company's board of directors in September 1995, envisages a "mild" form of integration. The activities of the holding company and its subsidiaries will be coordinated through a consolidated business plan, based on the business plans of all affiliated production, refining, and distribution enterprises. Sidanko also intends to sign operating contracts with its subsidiaries to define the levels of extraction and processing by subsidiaries, as well as the volume of centralized deliveries of oil and oil products within the framework of the company. Subsidiaries are allowed to keep up to 30 percent of profit for investment projects.[37]

Sidanko thus offers its production units something which they cannot achieve themselves: supply, retailing, strategic planning, and political lobbying. It will also financially support the reconstruction of its refinery and provide raw materials and markets. Sidanko also intends to guarantee markets and their own export arrangements to the oil-extracting units, and the company intends to develop large-scale cooperation with foreign firms in investment, engineering, and consultancy.

According to Sidanko's vice president, Yuri Burlinov, the company's corporate development takes into account the historical peculiarities of the subsidiaries' structures. In his view, in order to run the company effectively and to attract foreign investors, over-centralization, depriving subsidiaries of their legal status, is not necessary. It is quite sufficient, he claims, to exert control through the ownership of stock of the subsidiaries by representatives of the holding company, to block undesirable policies.[38] This, however, may not always be easy to achieve.

Sidanko's lack of internal consolidation is exacerbated by long-standing conflicts with regional authorities, who seek control over some of the company's subsidiaries. Such was the case with the government of Udmurtia. The problem was that an agreement, signed in October 1995, had been made about the sphere of influence of the Udmurtia Republic and the Russian Federation, in which the former was given twenty oil fields located on its territory. However, almost all these fields have been developed by AO Udmurtneft, which is a part of Sidanko. Concerned that Sidanko would independently dispose of the oil and would receive most of the profit from its trade, the government of the republic, having only a 0.1 percent share in Udmurtneft, tried to obtain an additional 20 percent from the state stock package. But this attempt failed—probably because the Udmurtia Republic's political lobby is not powerful enough to change the rules of privatization in the oil industry.

In the summer of 1996, an attack on Sidanko's positions was undertaken by the local government and allied commercial structures of the Saratov Region. In this area are located three subsidiaries of the holding company: Saratovneftegaz (extraction), Cracking (Saratov refinery), and Saratovnefteprodukt (retailing). A group of shareholders of Saratov refinery, and the local oil traders, with the support of the director of the enterprise, attempted to pass a resolution to transfer the preference (non-voting) shares (25 percent of the overall stock) into ordinary (voting) ones. Consequently, the stock package of Cracking owned by Sidanko (51 percent of voting stock, 38 percent of overall stock) would have ceased to be a controlling one. Since the main fraction of preferred shares belonged to the refinery workers, control of the enterprise could very easily have passed from the holding company to the local shareholders. The plans of the local interests went as far as the establishment of a regional holding, which would include an extracting, a processing, and a trade enterprise. This was publicly announced by the regional administration. Again, however, Sidanko succeeded in stopping these proposals from coming to fruition.

Sidanko managed to resolve to its advantage the conflict in Saratov by threatening to cease completely the supply of oil to Cracking and of oil products to retailers. It also proposed a compromise deal by which the regional authority was guaranteed fuel and Cracking secured a loan from Oneksimbank, which is a major shareholder in Sidanko (as discussed in chapter 1). Local oil retailers were also offered long-term contracts for oil products. In order to preempt such conflicts in the future, the management of Sidanko intends to sign a series of agreements with the administrations of Saratov Region and Udmurtia and also with the governments of the Far East, where the majority of its distributive subsidiaries are situated.[39]

In summary, Sidanko is moving away from being a loosely organized vertical company. Its recent history shows that the subsidiaries have limited sovereignty—they are dependent on the holding company for finance, export, and distribution. The future expansion of the company will depend on finance from banks and foreign capital.

NOTES

1. LUKoil was the original name; since 1997 the capitalization of the first three letters has been dropped and it is now Lukoil. However, in this text, for consistency, I have adopted the original style.

2. The reorganization of LUKoil into a vertically integrated oil company was legalized by the President's Decree no. 1403 of 17 November 1992. A corresponding resolution of the government confirming the structure of NK LUKoil was issued in April 1993. Accordingly, the company, apart from the three above-mentioned oil extracting enterprises, was to include the Perm' and Volgograd NPZ, seven regional enterprises producing oil products, and a number of additional enterprises. In 1995 LUKoil accepted another group of oil extracting enterprises, Permneft, Nizhnevolzhskneft, Astrakhan'neft, and Kaliningradmorneftegas. The company owns more than fifty subsidiary multi-profile firms and joint ventures operating in thirty regions of Russia and sixteen countries.

3. *Neft i kapital*, no. 4, 1996, p. 31.

4. *Finansovye Izvestiia*, no. 33, 28 March 1996; *Segodnia*, 16 July 1996.

5. *Business MN*, 19 April 1995.

6. *Kommersant-Daily*, 9 December 1995.

7. *Houston Chronicle*, 6 September 1997.

8. *Ekspert*, no. 34, 9 September 1996, p. 20.

9. *Neft i kapital*, no. 1, 1996, p. 43.

10. *Neft i kapital*, nos. 7/8, 1996, p. 25.

11. Since 1994 the company has been selling oil products to some regions within the sphere of action of YuKOS's trade subdivisions (Samara, Ul'anovsk, and other places). In Rostov Region, LUKoil has bought two oil storage facilities and eight filling stations. In Kaliningrad Region, where the whole trade net belongs to Surgutneftegaz, LUKoil in 1995 opened several retail filling stations. With Marii-El Republic, which is in the zone of NORSI-oil, LUKoil has signed an agreement to provide oil products and establish an alternative trade net. A similar agreement has been signed with Tatarstan, which has its own Tatneft oil company. LUKoil's filling stations have also appeared in Moscow and Moscow Region.

12. In Azerbaijan, LUKoil is part of three international consortiums that are exploiting oil fields in Azeri, Gineshli, Chirag (where it has a 10 percent share), Karabakh (32.5 percent), and Shakh-Deniz (10 percent). In Kazakhstan, LUKoil is participating in the development of the large Kumkol' oilfield. The company is carrying out negotiations about acquiring a 5 percent share in the Tengizshevroil joint venture, in the development of the Tengiz oil field in the north of Kazakhstan. In addition, a preliminary agreement has been made that LUKoil will have a 20 percent

share in an international consortium to develop oilfields in the Kazakh part of the Caspian Sea shelf, where resources are estimated as being several billion tons. LUKoil is also pursuing research work in the Karachaganak oil field in Kazakhstan. In Kazakhstan, LUKoil also plans to take part in updating the Chimkentsk and Atyraussk refineries, in the development of Kenbai oil field, and in the restoration of boreholes in the Uzen' oil field. *Delovoi Mir*, 19–25 July 1996; *Ekspert*, no, 27, 15 July 1996; *Kommersant-Weekly*, no. 31, 29 August 1995.

13. Cited in *Pipeline News* no. 63, 7–13 June 1997. Three reasons were put forward for the reluctance to raise production in Russia: pipeline capacity, small export terminals, and low domestic demand.

14. *Neft i kapital*, nos. 7/8, 1996, p. 25.

15. *Segodnia*, 20 September 1996.

16. For the reconstruction of its oil-processing facilities, for example, it is hoping to attract credits from Great Britain ($35 million) and Canada ($20 million). *Segodnia*, 26 August 1996.

17. *Business MN*, no. 34, 20 September 1995; *Segodnia*, 18 July 1995.

18. *Business MN*, no. 44, 31 October 1993; *Kommersant*, no.43, 25–31 October 1993, p. 20; *Neft i kapital*, no.2, 1996, p. 77.

19. *Segodnia*, 14 September 1995; *Neft i kapital*, no. 6, 1996, p. 88.

20. *Neft i kapital*, no. 6, 1996, p. 88: *Kommersant-Daily*, 21 December 1996.

21. *Business MN*, no. 34, 20 September 1995.

22. *Moskovskie Novosti*, no. 8, 25 February–3 March 1996.

23. *Moscow Tribune*, 17 February 1996.

24. *Moskovskie Novosti*, no. 8, 25 February–3 March 1996; *Moscow Tribune*, 17 February 1996.

25. *Finansovoe Delo*, no. 2, 21 February 1995; *Kommersant-Daily*, 23 February 1995.

26. *Neft i kapital*, nos. 7/8, 1996, p. 66; *Business MN*, 24 May 1995; *Segodnia*, 24 January 1997.

27. *Segodnia*, 24 January 1997.

28. *Business MN*, 24 May 1995; *Neft i kapital*, nos. 7/8, 1996, p. 66.

29. *Neft i kapital*, nos. 7/8, 1996, p. 66.

30. *Business MN*, 5 July 1996, p. 4.

31. *Ekspert*, no. 22, 10 June 1996, p. 8.

32. In summer 1996, Sidanko made a claim to a court of arbitration for the return of AO Purneftegaz, but it was rejected.

33. *Neft i kapital*, no. 5, 1996, p. 42; no. 6, 1996, p. 89.

34. *Kommersant-Daily*, 18 October 1995; *Business MN*, no. 2, 17 January 1996.

35. *Kommersant-Daily*, 6 February 1996; *Neft i kapital*, no. 6, 1996, p. 89.

36. *Neft i kapital*, no. 6, 1996, p. 89.

37. *Kommersant-Daily*, 6 February 1996.

38. *Kommersant-Daily*, 22 July 1995, 21 February 1996.

39. *Segodnia*, 20 July 1996.

Part 2

Oil and the Regions

5

Tiumen, Decentralization, and Center-Periphery Tension

Bruce Kellison

Though Russia remains the world's third most productive oil state in the late 1990s, the political struggle over its huge oil resource between Moscow and the producing regions is fierce. However true it might have been to portray Moscow as a ravenous "core" devouring the natural resources of the "periphery" during the Soviet period, the development of Russia's oil sector in the post-Soviet era has been marked by a significant decentralization of political and economic control over these resources. Indeed, the very development of the resources by the Soviet authorities in the 1960s and 1970s necessitated the devolution of decision-making authority to the producing regions themselves. This in turn set the stage for production association managers to seize control of oil assets under conditions of quasi-privatization in the late Gorbachev and post-Soviet periods. But the devolution of power and authority in the Russian "oil patch" goes beyond a one-way or zero-sum model in which the periphery gains control and Moscow loses it. As we shall see below, there are a number of powerful and distinct levels of government competing for a share of the revenues generated by Tiumen's oil wealth. Local governmental bodies in Western Siberia increasingly demand the authority to direct investment and to tax oil and gas companies, often but not always at Moscow's expense.

This chapter highlights the roles played by political bodies at the federal, oblast, and okrug levels in the functioning of Western Siberia's oil sector. The political role played by oil enterprises is also examined. Local control of resource development and use is a source of political conflict at the national level, but also, perhaps surprisingly, at the local level. The collapse of the vast ministerial structure, the destruction of the Communist Party of the Soviet Union (CPSU), and the swift withdrawal of the Soviet Union's constituent republics has presented Western Siberian leaders with both opportunities and challenges. Local leaders are excited about the opportunity to exploit an enormous oil resource with less interference from Moscow than ever before. The problem for local legislatures, however, is deciding *which* local level will have the most authority to direct production. Conflict on a variety of issues, from taxes to foreign policy, among oblast and okrug leaderships—including the oil companies themselves—is in many ways more important for the future of Siberia than the center-periphery struggle often referred to by analysts of Russian affairs. Moscow still retains many means of control over the Siberian oil resource, but as in so many areas of the economy, Moscow's will far exceeds its abilities.[1]

The term "Moscow" is used throughout to refer to the Ministry of Fuel and Energy and the Yeltsin government. The chapter focuses on local politics in Tiumen Oblast—the "periphery"—in Western Siberia and on the ways in which local governments are using newfound authority to take control of natural resources. I use the terms "center" and "periphery" because I believe that a center-periphery framework most adequately describes the unbalanced, exploitative relationship that used to exist between Moscow and the provinces and the general axis around which issues relating to the regions are believed to revolve in Russia today.

The provinces are much more politically autonomous now than they have been at any time since 1917. This is not to say that devolution of political power to the provinces has been intentional. On the contrary, much of the political decentralization has been unintentional and unwanted and began prior to either Gorbachev's or Yeltsin's leaderships. I hope to illustrate this decentralization with this study of the recent politics of the Western Siberian oil region, and to suggest that movement away from the command administrative economic system toward some type of market system has its own political implications for the relations between Moscow and the provinces. The provinces have taken much more control over the resources in their geographical jurisdiction since economic reform began. I conclude, however, that political decentralization is by no means unidirectional; that is, the devolution of political authority is not proceeding solely away from the center (Moscow) toward the periphery (Western Siberia in this instance). The provinces themselves are grappling with an altered political and economic landscape that is blurring and eroding old lines of regional authority.

In this chapter I discuss the recent experience of four different levels in the Russian polity: Moscow and the national government, Tiumen Oblast, Khanty-Mansi Autonomous Okrug, and Yamal-Nenets Autonomous Okrug, then I consider the political interests of oil companies and joint ventures in Tiumen Oblast.

DECENTRALIZATION AND MOSCOW'S CONTROL
OF THE OIL INDUSTRY IN THE 1980s AND 1990s

Investment funds in the oil sector have always flowed out of Moscow to the producing regions of Siberia. Thane Gustafson has examined the periods of crisis in oil investment.[2] What is important here is that industrial investment in the oil sector began to decline in the late 1980s and, as a result, oil output peaked in 1988 and began declining after that. The ministries simply ran out of money to invest in the industry.

With the decline in investment has come a loss of control over oil production. Decisions are now made locally on how and where to produce, and with whom to barter for materials. This gives much greater leverage to the oil companies in their negotiations with the ministry over the amount of oil to be allocated to Moscow instead of sold to suppliers, smuggled out of the country, or legally exported for hard currency.

There is a limit, however, to the autonomy of the oil companies in their relationship with Moscow. One of the most powerful tools still left for the center to use is control over the pipeline system. The Ministry of Fuel and Energy regulates the export schedule for all companies wishing to sell their oil abroad through the pipeline system. Transneft was the ministry that controlled the pipeline system during the Soviet period, and it was transformed from a ministry into a joint-stock company in 1993 with 100 percent state ownership. (Privatization is planned, though in 1998 the government owned 75 percent, and Transnefts' employees the remaining 25 percent of the assets.)[3] Transneft as a business operation has been very profitable, reporting a net profit of $213 million in 1997.[4] The current Deputy Fuel and Energy minister, Victor Ott, is chairman of Transneft's governing board, as was his predecessor, Sergei Kirienko. Since spring 1998, the Russian government's formal representative on Transneft's governing board has been Sergei Generalov, who replaced Kirienko when the latter became prime minister. The separate Federal Energy Commission creates and maintains the system of pipeline tariffs, but the Ministry of Fuel and Energy jealously guards its role as oil export broker.[5]

Yet the image of oil companies as supplicants to an independent federal ministry staffed by professional bureaucrats is facile. The job of arriving at export quotas and prices falls to the oil "coordinators," who are responsible for setting quarterly prices and quotas for particular export markets. The coordinators, however, are not ministry officials but the oil companies themselves, each of which is given a particular export market as a quasi-monopoly to operate on its own. The result is higher export prices and lower competition, an arrangement of great benefit to the oil companies. The physical location of the pipelines is an attractive target for localities wanting a share of the tax revenues the pipelines generate, or outright ownership of the pipelines. The conflict in Chechnya, for example, is widely believed to have had its roots in the struggle between the Russian government and the Chechens over control of the oil pipelines running through Chechen territory.

Another powerful financial tool available to the state in its regulation of the oil industry in the post-Soviet period has been the program of exporting oil to fulfill "state needs." Until President Yeltsin scaled it back by decree in 1997, the program had pitted the coordinators against export traders who were able to handle "state needs" exports. Under the program, exporters would buy oil at low prices from domestic producers, sell it at world market prices with guaranteed pipeline access, and then split the proceeds with the state. According to a U.S. Embassy report, exports through the state needs programs were 27.5 million metric tons in 1996, or between 15 and 25 percent of total exports, amounting to gross revenues of between $1.25 and $3.6 billion in 1996. And since these exports were guaranteed pipeline access, they reduced the space available to other exports from oil companies.[6] Part of the rationale for reducing the states needs program, to an estimated 8 percent of exports, was political. Former Fuel and Energy Minister, Boris Nemtsov, acknowledged that the program had enriched an entire segment of oil traders at the expense both of the state and of domestic producers hoping to export their own oil. "You probably know that a lot of oil was supplied for state needs, and to our great regret, the effectiveness of the programs was very low," he said in an interview.[7] By allowing domestic producers to export more oil, the Fuel and Energy Ministry can garnish a percentage of the revenue from exports and reduce oil producers' collective $521 million debt to the state. This, in turn, enables the Russian government to pay wage arrears in other industries.

Controlling access to export pipelines is a public policy tool the center can use to leverage what remaining authority it does have over the sector. In its effort to comply with IMF guidelines to limit its budget deficit and increase tax revenues, the center can limit the ability of oil companies to sell their output on the international market by restricting their pipeline access and force them to pay the back taxes they owe the federal government. On 30 June 1998, former deputy prime minister Viktor Khristenko announced that the government would reduce pipeline access for Bashneft, Sidanko, Tiumenneft (TNK), Tatneft, and ONAKO until their back taxes were paid. An exception would be made, however, for companies like LUKoil and YuKOS that export oil as collateral for foreign loans.[8]

One of the biggest restrictions on Moscow's ability to direct development in the oil sector is budgetary: in light of low and declining rates of tax collection, the federal government is under tremendous pressure to use the oil sector to finance the federal budget. Furthermore, the federal budget is so reliant on the value of its shares in the oil companies and the taxes generated by oil production that Moscow is constrained in what it can order the companies to do. Yeltsin's recent decision to revoke the ownership restrictions on oil companies and allow foreign companies to purchase controlling interests in oil companies is a result of this fiscal pressure. With tax collection falling, Moscow has been generating revenue by selling its shares in oil companies in the "loans-for-shares" program as detailed in chapter 1. The fall in the world market price of oil saw oil export revenues drop 25 percent in the first quarter of 1998 from the same period in 1997. Russian oil companies actually exported 9 percent more oil during the first quarter of 1998 but earned only U.S.$2.9 billion.[9] In the year 1997, Russia exported a total of 126.856 million metric tons of crude oil worth U.S.$14.972 billion. In addition, Russia exported U.S.$7.205 billion in petroleum products in 1997, earning a total of over U.S.$22 billion for Russian companies.[10] With the rise in world oil prices in 1999, earnings and profits will increase.

Of most relevance to the content of this chapter is that the federal authorities retain the ability to tax oil exports. Oil excise taxes are established by Moscow, but frequently, the center makes special deals with politically powerful oil company executives, especially those with joint ventures. Former prime minister Sergei Kirienko had said in April 1998 that excise taxes would be lowered from fifty-five rubles per metric ton to forty-five rubles per metric ton. But in June the Ministry of Fuel and Energy reversed its position in the face of a financial crisis brought on by the center's inability to generate revenues.[11]

The center's methods of enforcing compliance with its tax provisions, however, are more and more reduced to bluff and bluster. The center has few real sanctions it can place on the companies besides the restrictions on access to the pipelines examined above. Former first deputy prime minister, Boris Nemtsov, in the summer of 1998 gave the heads of oil concerns LUKoil, ONAKO, Sibneft, and Sidanko two weeks to clear their debts to the federal government, without specifying what penalties they would face if they did not comply. Since the taxes they pay on exports are responsible for a huge share of the federal budget, the center is dependent on their success for its operation. The federal government no longer dictates how much oil it will expropriate from the companies to fill state orders. The companies have now all been privatized except for Rosneft, which was scheduled to be auctioned in late 1998, though this was then delayed due to the financial crisis. If the companies do not pay their taxes, however, the federal budget deficit worsens.[12]

I have outlined first the strengths and weaknesses of Russia's executive branch because the Russian presidency holds vastly more power than does the Duma. One of the Duma's resources, however, in its struggle for influence in the oil sector is its legislative power, which it has used to shape (and amend) the contentious production-sharing agreement (PSA), which was passed in December 1995. The most important body here is the Duma's Committee for Natural Resources, which has the authority to oversee the oil extraction industry. The PSA stipulates that contracts involving foreign investment in certain named natural resource deposits in the Russian Federation must include clauses that provide for a portion of the resources extracted during the life of the contract be "shared" with the Federation. The PSA is an attempt by lawmakers, who fear that Russia's natural resources are being "stolen" by foreign investors, to ensure that Russia's richest natural resources remain under Russian control. The Duma has been trying to decide which resources to put on the list and at what rate to tax them. Before 1999, many joint ventures and other international projects were held up.

Other interests involved (often in opposition to the Duma's committees) are the Yeltsin government, regional governments, and the Russian and foreign companies themselves. The Yeltsin government decreed that there is no legal limit on foreign ownership of the oil sector, and that foreign companies can buy up to 100 percent of the assets of a particular company. However, companies themselves may decide to limit foreign ownership, and the Duma (with respect to privatization) attempts to impose restrictions.[13] The Duma continues to delay, if not block, the opening of lucrative oil fields to foreign companies and investors, but it recently approved amendments to the December 1995 PSA law. The amendments then stated that foreign investors can acquire no more than 20 percent of Russia's natural resources through PSAs and no more than 10 percent of "strategic natural resources," the list of which has not yet been finally determined. The revised law would require that production-sharing agreements be approved by regional legislatures as well as federal agencies.[14]

TIUMEN OBLAST: FROM KING TO PAUPER

In a sign that the newly elected regional governors take their authority very seriously, Kemerovo Oblast governor Aman Tuleev demanded recently that his oblast be allowed to allocate all federal investment in the coal industry, and that state orders should dictate the pace of coal production, not the market. Tuleev's radical rhetoric, although emanating from a region that produces coal and not oil, is typical of the way in which resource-rich oblasts are using whatever means possible to control resources in their territory.[15]

Tiumen Oblast, in Western Siberia, is twice the size of Texas and produces 91.5 percent of Russia's natural gas and 65.8 percent of its oil. Tiumen's industrial output comprises 7.2 percent of the national GDP. The city of Tiumen, located in the southwestern corner of the oblast, is the oblast capital and home to many of the Soviet planning bodies that directed all of the investment in the region's oil industry. According to one estimate, as of 1997 the oblast was one of only ten regions that had been able to maintain their industrial production at more than 60 percent of their 1990 level.[16] Today, however, its role as the center of the oil industry and political capital of the region is being challenged on a number of fronts, as the decentralization of the political system proceeds in the wake of economic restructuring and reform.

Much is made of the relative contributions to, or share of the revenues from, the federal budget from a particular region. Leaders from oblasts that claim to contribute more to the federal budget in taxes than they receive in subsidies or services, or that contribute more than ethnic-based republics do, like to portray themselves as victims of an unfair federal system.[17] The growth of "independence" movements in the regions has been well documented by analysts as evidence of the unresolved tension in Russia's federal system between the rights granted to the republics and those granted to the oblasts.[18]

A more complex situation emerges, however, if one looks at how taxes are actually collected by the center from the regions. Regions, as such, do not pay taxes themselves. Taxpayers and businesses in the regions pay a range of taxes, including income, excise, and value-added taxes. In a recent research note, Steven Solnick has argued that the real tax collection issue for Russia is not tax withholding by regions or the individual tax treaties signed between Moscow and individual regions, but the change in the amount of federal taxes collected in the regions that actually goes to Moscow before being distributed by the government. The regions have been lobbying effectively for increased authority to retain *in regional banks* the federal taxes collected locally but previously bound for Moscow. These revenues are then distributed by regional Ministry of Finance officials, whose appointments presumably are approved by the regional governor, to cover federal budget obligations in the region. This is significant, Solnick argues, not only because of the ascendance of regional banks at the expense of Moscow-based banks, but because officials in the regions "will be deciding which federal bills get paid in a particular region, rather than bureaucrats in different federal ministries. This represents an enormous devolution of power." Changing the *mechanism* by which federal taxes are distributed to the regions, however, does not affect the *amount* of money a particular region pays to or receives from the federal government. Furthermore, Solnick argues, the difference between "donor" and "recipient" regions is now less significant, because of the general collapse of the Russian budget and the trend toward more funds flowing to the regions and not to huge government programs like defense, science, and space development. "Given the massive regional economic inequality so apparent across the federation, we should not be surprised, or dismayed, that a very few regions constitute the bulk of federal revenues."[19]

The former centrally planned oil industry was extraordinarily complex, with at least nine ministries overseeing oil exploration, production, refining, and distribution. All of them had offices in Tiumen, and all have now disappeared. The companies privately decide the strategic issues, and investment decisions, in particular, are taken privately. This means that, politically, the oblast is much more autonomous now than it used to be under Soviet administration. Even before the formal collapse of the USSR, Tiumen Oblast's Supreme Soviet had reserved for itself the right to pass laws that could not be abrogated by Moscow, including the right to set prices of oil, gas, and wood products. The "transition to the market" is mentioned often in the Oblast Supreme Soviet's declarations, as a way of demonstrating its commitment to reform.[20] Perhaps paradoxically, its political connections to Moscow have always been impeccable, with reappointed Prime Minister Chernomyrdin having served as chairman of Gazprom, and former Fuel and Energy Minister and current chairman of Tiumenneft, Yuri Shafranik, having served as oblast first party secretary prior to the collapse of the Union. Leonid Roketskii, appointed governor by Yeltsin in the early 1990s, was elected oblast governor by a landslide over his challenger, Sergei Atroshenko, head of Tiumenskii Kredit, a local bank, by 59 to 33 percent in the fall 1996 elections. But the integrity of the oblast itself is in doubt. The threat to oblast-level control over resources and authority to tax lies not in Moscow but with Tiumen's autonomous okrugs, Khanty-Mansi and Yamal-Nenets, which contain the bulk of the oil and gas there.

THE AUTONOMOUS OKRUGS: IN THE DRIVER'S SEAT

Khanty-Mansi Autonomous Okrug, located just north of the city of Tiumen, contains most of the oil-producing areas of the oblast. Its capital is the city of Khanty-Mansi, situated at the confluence of the Irtish and Ob rivers. Yamal-Nenets, located north of Khanty-Mansi and extending to the Kara Sea, contains over 90 percent of Russia's vast natural gas reserves. Its capital is the city of Salekhard.

The 1993 Russian Constitution clearly states, in Article 66, that the okrugs are a part of the oblasts in which they reside and are subject to oblast law. On the other hand, Article 5 grants these okrugs special authority out of deference to the ethnic minorities living there.[21] It gives okrugs the same political status as oblasts, even including the right to secede with the permission of the Russian Duma.

It is safe to say that Tiumen Oblast has had the most difficulty of any oblast in the country in reaching a political settlement with the autonomous okrugs existing within its borders, and it is not difficult to see why: the real source of tension between the oblast and the okrugs is the struggle over the energy resources themselves and the rents and revenue streams that are derived from them. In recent years the okrugs have used their constitutional powers to create parallel structures in banking, budgeting, and taxation that compete directly with those of the oblast. The entire budgeting process, which used to flow in a linear fashion from Moscow through Tiumen and on to the okrugs, now goes directly from Moscow to both Tiumen and the okrugs simultaneously. Many of the conflicts between the oblast and the okrugs, then, are a result of the blurred constitutional lines of authority between levels of government. Russian federalism is and will remain in perpetual crisis as long as constitutional authority is ambiguous.

Power-sharing treaties between Moscow and the regions have attempted to paper over the shortcomings of the federal arrangement. There are now thirty-eight such treaties in force among Russia's eighty-nine regions. In November 1997, President Yeltsin and Deputy Prime Minister Boris Nemtsov signed the first treaty with a region (Krasnoyarsk Krai) and two of its constituent parts (Taimyr Autonomous Okrug and Evenk Autonomous Okrug) at the same time, supposedly outlining areas of authority for each level of government, which, as in Tiumen Oblast, had been contested. On a certain level, however, Moscow hopes that by using these treaties instead of revamping the Russian Constitution to clarify contradictory lines of authority, the wealthier, more productive regions like Tiumen will be unable to wield political power commensurate with their economic power. Just as it does in the Caucasus, Moscow plays off regional actors one against another and then steps in to broker a compromise that does not really solve the core problems, but serves only to prolong the conflict. Such a policy is destabilizing to the regions affected, but it preserves Moscow's position as the arbiter of last resort.

In Tiumen, a power-sharing agreement between the okrugs and the oblast leaderships seems unlikely. After deliberating the issues surrounding the conflict among the contending parties, the Russian Constitutional Court in July 1997 was unable (more likely unwilling) to resolve the disputed status of the okrugs. Yamal-Nenets' incumbent governor, Yurii Neelov, won reelection in October 1997 after ignoring Yeltsin's decree to hold the okrug elections on the same day as the oblast elections.[22] Neelov won his election by a wide margin and promptly vowed to continue to push for his okrug to secede from Tiumen Oblast.[23] Aleksandr Filipenko, governor of Khanty-Mansi, easily won his reelection campaign by garnering 72 percent of the vote. Both candidates ran and won espousing secession from Tiumen Oblast. And in a sign that the okrugs are growing ever more independent of the oblast leadership, Yamal-Nenets announced in early 1997 its intention to float $250 million in Eurobonds and to open a $150 million line of credit with Western banks.[24]

Bond sales and credit lines are not the only sources of funds for the okrugs. In a recent interview, Khanty-Mansi governor Filipenko said that the tax on resources is the only tax that oil enterprises have to pay to the okrug. (Oil companies pay significant excise, transport, and other fees and taxes to Moscow.) Because of a special arrangement with Moscow, Filipenko said that 60 percent of the tax revenue from this source is allocated to the okrug, 20 percent goes to Moscow, and 20 percent goes to the oblast government.[25] As an example of how important the economic activity of the oil companies is to the okrug budgets, Filipenko went on to say that taxes collected on resources produced by just one company, Surgutneftegaz, amount to 27 percent of the okrug's budget.

Oil towns in the okrugs, like Nizhnevartovsk, were developed in the 1960s to house temporary workers flown in to work the giant Samotlor oil field and other petroleum reserves in the Ob River basin. Workers rotated out after three- to nine-month shifts in the harsh tundra climate. Over time, city government became more complex as the local economy became more diverse and institutionalized. Nevertheless, Nizhnevartovsk's main employer, Nizhnevartovskneftegaz, was chiefly responsible for the provision of food, health services, and education. With the collapse of the command economy, the responsibilities of city governments all over Russia have mushroomed. While enterprises are no longer required to build and maintain a social infrastructure for their workers, and firms have been "downsizing" activities not related to their core businesses, city governments have been saddled with the construction of social safety nets and other basic services that used to be provided by employers. They have found, however, that the money to pay for them is not available.

The only tax on oil production available to the oblast, okrug, and city governments in Tiumen is a resource tax, the bulk of which goes to the okrug government, not the city. The city of Nizhnevartovsk is almost completely dependent on the okrug government to provide it with revenue. The tax system is complex enough without the added worry for city planners of competing with raion- and oblast-level administrators who are arranging their own tax deals with firms and enterprises. Officials in the financial department of the city administration complain that the existing tax laws are not clear enough to prevent joint ventures, for instance, from establishing separate tax payment arrangements with the raion Duma and shutting out the city Duma.[26]

OIL PRODUCERS: MANAGING THE WEALTH

The 1990s have seen the consolidation of the Western Siberian oil sector, as the Soviet system of production associations gave way to more vertically integrated holding companies. Even though oil production in Russia has plummeted to less than half what it was at its height in 1987, the rig count is once again on the rise, and some of Russia's largest oil producers, like Tiu-menneft (TNK), are based in Tiumen Oblast. What is the political role of the oil producers in Tiumen Oblast? How has "privatization" contributed to a decentralization of political power in the oblast? Why is Moscow less able today to control the oil sector than it used to be? To answer these questions I turn to consider the experiences of three oil producers in the oblast (Tiu-menneft and its subsidiary Nizhnevartovskneftegaz, Sidanko's subsidiary Chernogorneft, and the joint venture Chernogorskoe).

In the early 1990s, managers at Nizhnevartovskneftegaz claimed they wanted to take the first steps toward privatization by converting their firms into joint-stock companies. But until late 1993 and early 1994, they were quite comfortable existing in a quasi-privatized environment, in which they had enormous control over oil production and the sale of oil products but did not have to answer to powerful shareholders. It was a time of dramatic cutbacks in investment in upstream development, bartering oil for parts and supplies, and tremendous political flux in Moscow. While there was great uncertainty in the industry, managers were gaining more and more control of their companies and especially of revenues from oil sales abroad. I have already highlighted the huge financial benefit "state orders" held for traders with good connections in the Fuel and Energy Ministry.

Beginning in 1993, however, the industry began to consolidate in verti-cally integrated holding companies. Nizhnevartovskneftegaz was absorbed by Tiumenneft (TNK) in 1996. Even Chernogorneft, which began life as Neftyanoe Gosudarstvenoe Dobivayushchoe Upravlenie, a subsidiary of Nizhnevartovskneftegaz and the first oil company to "secede" from its par-ent company, became co-founder of Sidanko in 1994 and by 1996 was largely controlled by the Oneksim financial-industrial group.[27] Chernogorneft has been among the most aggressive companies in seeking financial help from the West. With guarantees from the U.S. Export-Import Bank, Chernogorneft quickly exhausted a 1996 $43.7-million credit from Société Générale in France to buy U.S. equipment to rehabilitate two thousand wells.[28] What is more, Moscow has sold off so much of its stake in oil companies to raise funds to cover for its budget deficits that the planned sale of the state-owned shares of Tiumenneftegaz will be among the very last holdings left to sell.

These vertically integrated holding companies are so steady on their feet, relatively speaking, that TNK can afford to encourage Moscow to put TNK's largest producer, Nizhnevartovskneftegaz, into receivership to pay off state-owed debts. From TNK's perspective, the sale of 40 percent of its own state-owned shares, combined with the sale of its Nizhnevartovskneftegaz unit, will attract the foreign investment needed to maintain and increase output from the giant but aging fields around Samotlor. Viktor Paly, general direc-tor of Nizhnevartovskneftegaz, promised that preference would be given to Russian investors who contribute the estimated $8 billion needed to increase yields from Samotlor, which is believed to contain an additional 1.17 billion metric tons of oil.[29] In fact, one of the reasons a production-sharing agreement was delayed in the Russian Duma is the nationalist fear that foreign investors will buy up shares in a famous but aging Russian resource like Samotlor. In a strange twist to the story, TNK allied with Khanty-Mansi tax police in October and November 1997 seized 700,000 metric tons of oil from Nizhnevartovskneftegaz to repay tax debts to the okrug and oblast. Nizhnevartovskneftegaz currently produces approximately 1.3 million metric tons of oil per month.[30]

From Moscow's point of view, the taxes owed to the federal government by the oil sector are staggering. The Russian State Tax Service says that all of Russia's fuel and energy companies, 466 firms in all, owed 28.31 trillion rubles (about $4.7 billion) to the federal government as of 1 April 1997. Nizhnevartovskneftegaz owed 1.334 trillion rubles and was not even the largest debtor. Chernogorneft had paid 39.618 billion rubles of its debt by 1 April 1997. The Tax Service report, however, indicated that the total debt of these companies had decreased by 10 percent from the start of the year 1997.[31] However, the tax situation is complex, and not just for oil companies. In 1998, there were signs that the entire Russian economy was moving increasingly to a barter economy and away from one based on cash payments. In-kind exchange between companies is common and therefore difficult to tax.

Some mention of the joint ventures operating in the region should be made in this discussion of political decentralization. Even though their overall production was just a small share of Russia's oil production (6 percent in 1996), joint ventures attract foreign investment to the okrugs, something the okrug governments in Tiumen certainly would like to see increase. Because of the potential for much more foreign participation in the oil sector, okrugs are eager to establish their own contacts with foreign companies and help arrange deals with Russian producers in their areas. Even okrug-level contacts with foreign governments are growing fast enough for the Russian Duma recently to have passed a law ordering any region to register contacts or agreements with the federal government for approval. Such activity, though, is occurring at the okrug level and not at that of the oblast. Indeed, conversations with managers of the Chernogorskoe joint venture between the Anderman-Smith oil company of Denver and Chernogorneft in 1993 revealed that one of the keys to success for a joint venture was to keep negotiations as local as possible and to avoid unnecessarily early involvement by Moscow. Foreign managers found that it was far better to rely on their Russian partners to negotiate with Moscow. Another key was to start slowly and limit expectations, something many foreign businesses have discovered working in Russia.

CONCLUSION

Decentralization of political authority in the Russian Federation has produced a proliferation of power bases in the oil sector. There are now more
actors in Moscow and in the regions that can affect the sector politically and
economically, and I have attempted to summarize the roles of the most
influential players. Competing interests within the bureaucracy in Moscow,
which had been partially but not totally obscured prior to the Soviet collapse, are now in full view. The devolution of power has not meant that
Moscow has lost all its influence. Rather, it has meant that traditional actors,
like the Ministry of Fuel and Energy (Mintop), have waned in influence, and
others, like the Privatization Committee, have gained. Turf battles between
the Federal Energy Commission, which regulates pipeline tariffs, and
Mintop, which is responsible for the system of export brokers, is one example of how power within Moscow has been spread among many actors in a
much more decentralized political environment than before. Both are playing a major role in the struggle to force the oil companies to pay taxes.
Reducing access to export pipelines—and therefore to hard currency earnings, as was discussed in the cases of Bashneft, Sidanko, and Tatneft—is one
way the center can limit the exports of companies it no longer directly controls. But the budget constraints the center faces are making the outright sale
of its state-owned shares more, not less, likely in the future. Rosneft, for
instance, remained for sale in 1998, although it was not attracting many
potential buyers.

For the oil-producing region of Tiumen, decentralization has brought with
it a loss of influence at the oblast level. The administrative and bureaucratic
centers in Tiumen, so powerful during the 1970s and 1980s, have almost all
disappeared. Authority over production sharing agreements, environmental
regulations, and tax issues has fallen to the okrug governors, who are
closely associated with the oil companies themselves. This has exacerbated
the long-simmering tension between the two okrugs (Yamal-Nenets and
Khanty-Mansi) and Tiumen Oblast, which is based on the vague wording of
the Russian Constitution that makes the okrugs both independent of and
subordinated to the oblast in the federal hierarchy. However, the okrugs
have been far more aggressive than the oblast government in attempting to
secure a more prominent position in the industry. Physically closer to the
source of the oil, the okrug governments in Khanty-Mansi and Yamal-Nenets
have exploited their ambiguous constitutional position and sought the legal
status of oblasts. Tiumen, which under the Soviet ministerial system was the
base for oil operations in Western Siberia, was slow to reposition itself after
the Soviet collapse and has struggled to remain "relevant" in the ensuing
years. The government of the oblast is finding that it is difficult ruling a

region twice the size of Texas when property and constitutional rights are so vague.

From Moscow's point of view, the constitutional questions that fuel the struggle between the okrugs and the oblast government enhance its power in the industry. Just as Moscow has played to all sides of the Caucasus conflicts in Georgia, Chechnya, and Armenia, Moscow chooses not to resolve the conflict in Tiumen as a way of continuing to act as a broker to the parties. Moscow knows the Constitutional Court does not have the institutional authority, let alone the power, to settle the conflict. A power-sharing agreement signed by Moscow, the okrugs, and the oblast government is the only conceivable solution short of changing the Constitution to clarify the lines of authority between the okrugs and the oblasts. But such an agreement is unlikely to happen because of the stakes involved. The okrugs are quite comfortable asserting their constitutional authority and courting international financiers and oil companies. Moscow controls access to the pipeline system. Omitted is the oblast government, which continues to petition Moscow for help in resolving the crisis.

The race for control of the region's vast oil wealth has energized a number of powerful political entities. Some, like the okrug governments, are creating new political space for themselves, whereas others, like the oblast government, are struggling to retain their former influence. Moscow is pressured by national fiscal restrictions to make choices in the oil sector that it would rather not make, like selling off state-owned shares in oil companies. Political decentralization has opened up competition for control of economic assets. It is not unidirectional but complex. The tensions between center and periphery in Russia are likely to continue, especially in the crucial public policy arena of Siberian oil. Decentralization of the Russian polity and economy has definitely encouraged Russia's regions to chart their own futures, which in turn has produced political turf battles among localities in Western Siberia over control of the enormous oil wealth there.

NOTES

1. The literature on center-periphery relations in Russia is extensive and growing. Geographers have long studied the destructive and exploitative impact of the metropolis as it has integrated the hinterlands into its political and economic sphere without significant regard for indigenous societies. See Leslie Dienes, *Soviet Asia: Economic Development and National Choices* (Boulder, Colo.: Westview Press, 1987) for a comprehensive treatment of this view. See See Donna Bahry, *Outside Moscow: Power, Politics, and Budgetary Policy in the Soviet Republics* (New York: Columbia University Press, 1987), and Thane Gustafson, *Crisis Amid Plenty: The Politics of Soviet Energy under Brezhnev and Gorbachev* (Princeton: Princeton Univer-

sity Press, 1989) for examples of regional political elites that may have been effective in lobbying the center for a share of investment in the periphery but were far less able to alter the direction of policy itself to correct uneven economic development patterns. For more recent treatments of the subject, see Edward Walker, "The Dog That Didn't Bark: Tatarstan and Asymmetrical Federalism in Russia," *Harriman Review*, vol. 3 (1996); Alastair McAuley, "The Determinants of Russian Federal-Regional Fiscal Relations: Equity or Political Influence?" *Europe-Asia Studies*, vol. 49 (1997); and Darrell Slider, "Russia's Market—Distorting Federalism," *Post-Soviet Geography and Economics*, vol. 38 (1997).

2. Gustafson, *Crisis Amid Plenty*, especially chapter 2.

3. *Energy and Politics*, no. 21, part 1, 11 June 1998.

4. *Energy and Politics*, no. 23, part 1, 8 July 1998.

5. The Federal Energy Commission charges a set amount for every thousand kilometers that oil travels in a pipeline. It recently cut by 50 percent the tariff it charges producers, from $3 to $1.50, in response to the dramatic reduction in crude oil prices on world markets. The result not only is less revenue generated for the center's federal budget but also less revenue available for the maintenance and construction of the pipeline system itself. See *Energy and Politics*, no. 12, part 1, 7 April 1998.

6. "A Primer on Pipeline Access and Its Politics in Russia," a report from the U.S. Embassy, Moscow, cited in *Pipeline News*, no. 66, part 1, 14 July 1997.

7. Reuters interview, cited in *Pipeline News*, no. 66, part 1, 14 July 1997.

8. *RFE/RL Newsline*, vol. 2, no. 125, part 1, 1 July 1998.

9. *Energy and Politics*, no. 19, part 1, 28 May 1998.

10. *Energy and Politics*, no. 18, part 2, 20 May 1998.

11. *Energy and Politics*, no. 21, part 2, 11 June 1998.

12. *Energy and Politics*, no. 20, part 1, 4 June 1998.

13. *Pipeline News*, no. 78, part 3, 10 November 1997. Amendments to the 1996 federal law on production sharing have centered on drawing up a list of oil fields in which foreign companies may operate. The proposal is to limit to twenty-five the number of large deposits available to foreign-based firms. See also Jane Upperton, "Duma Sets Back Hearing on PSA," *Platt's Oilgram News*, vol. 75, no. 31, 13 February 1997, p.1.

14. *RFE/RL Newsline*, vol. 2, no. 135, part 1, 16 July 1998.

15. *Segodnia*, 5 November 1997.

16. Natan Shklyar, "Leading Geographer Evaluates 'The Race of the Regions,'" *Institute for East/West Studies Russian Regional Report*, 5 June 1997, citing an article in *Rossiiskie vesti*, 20 May 1997, by Presidential Council member and geographer, Leonid Smiriagin.

17. Many oblasts and krais have complained that republics have unfair constitutional advantages over them. Khabarovsk Krai governor Viktor Ishaev in 1995 wanted to create a Far Eastern Republic because, he said, his krai sends 50 percent of its tax receipts to Moscow, whereas other ethnically based republics send less than 25 percent. *Omri Daily Digest*, no. 231, part 1, 29 November 1995.

18. See, for example, Gail W. Lapidus and Edward W. Walker, "Nationalism, Regionalism, and Federalism: Center-Periphery Relations in Post-Communist Russia," in Gail W. Lapidus, ed., *The New Russia: Troubled Transformation* (Boulder, Colo.: Westview Press, 1995), and Elizabeth Teague, "Center-Periphery Relations in the

Russian Federation," in Roman Szporluk, ed., *National Identity and Ethnicity in Russia and the New States of Eurasia* (Armonk, N.Y.: M. E. Sharpe, 1994).

19. Steven Solnick, "Russian Federalism," in *Johnson's E-Mail Russia List*, 28 April 1997.

20. See, for instance, "Polozhenie o status Tiumenskoy Oblasti" ("The Position Paper on the Status of Tiumen Oblast"), *Tiumenskie izvestiia*, 5 January 1991, p. 5, from the second session of the Oblast Soviet.

21. Various versions of the Soviet Constitution gave okrugs the same rights.

22. The leaderships of both okrugs initially refused to allow the okrugs to participate in oblast-wide gubernatorial elections. They then capitulated, but the turnout in both okrugs for the election was below the threshold mandated by Russian law and the returns were invalidated. Since the populations of both okrugs as a percentage of the oblast population, however, are so small, the outcome of the oblast election was not affected. See *IEWS Russian Regional Report*, 17 July 1997.

23. *Omri Daily Digest*, no. 199, part 1, 14 October 1996.

24. *Kommersant-Daily*, 10 October 1997.

25. *IEWS Russian Regional Report*, vol. 2, no. 36, 23 October 1997.

26. Interviews conducted by author with Nizhnevartovsk city officials, including V. S. Grabovskii, then First Deputy Head of Administration, July 1993.

27. S. Volkov had skillfully used the Law on Enterprises to privatize Chernogorneft in 1987. At the time it was a remarkable coup, and it heralded a new era in the Russian oil industry by marrying entrepreneurial assertiveness with good connections in Moscow to avoid the "war of laws" that began soon after Gorbachev lost control of his reforms in the late 1980s.

28. *Pipeline News*, no. 44, 18 January 1997.

29. *Pipeline News*, no. 66, 14 July 1997.

30. *Pipeline News*, no. 78, part 3, 10 November 1997.

31. *Pipeline News*, no. 58, part 2, 13 May 1997.

6

Federalization, Fragmentation, and the West Siberian Oil and Gas Province

Peter Glatter

The process of federalization in Russia has led to the fragmenting of Tiumen Oblast—"The West Siberian Oil and Gas Province"—while cementing the relationship between the fragments on the one side and the big oil and gas concerns on the other. Tiumen is a special case of a general phenomenon at the elite level in post-Soviet Russia: a marked continuity combined with a high level of conflict. This chapter reviews the Tiumen variant of the continuity and conflict, which are inseparable from the issue of access to revenue from the vast oil and gas reserves of the region.

"Regions" here has usually been taken to mean the oblasts and krais which make up by far the greater part of the territorial-administrative system in terms of population, area, and economic importance. These correspond most closely to the general notion of a region as a simple administrative division. The rest—autonomous okrugs, republics, and the one autonomous oblast—are supposed to be ethnically linked but the titular nationality is often in the minority. Seven Siberian regions contain autonomous okrugs, Tiumen Oblast being unique in having two: gas-rich Yamal-Nenets (YaNAO) and oil-rich Khanty-Mansi (KhMAO). Russians in these okrugs predominate both in the general population and in the elites, the indigenous population is a small minority.[1]

ELITE CONTINUITY IN TIUMEN

This section compares the profiles of four key regional figures: the governors of the okrugs and the oblast, and Iurii Shafranik, the former oblast governor and Minister of Fuel and Energy.[2]

The head of the oblast administration (or governor) is the fifty-six-year-old Leonid Iulianovich Roketskii, a native of the Ukraine, who in 1966 worked in one of the first student construction brigades in Surgut, one of the main towns in the KhMAO. He returned to Surgut after graduating in 1970 to work in the Soviet Ministry for Construction of Oil and Gas Enterprises (*Minneftegazstroi*), rising, by the early 1980s, to the position of chief engineer in Surgutgazstroi. Roketskii left the industry in the early 1980s to work his way up the Soviet ladder, becoming chairman of the Surgut executive committee and of the Tiumen town executive committee in June 1988. In March 1990, he was elected to the Surgut Soviet. On 22 April 1990, he was elected to the Tiumen Oblast Soviet, becoming chairman of its executive committee, and he joined the Tiumen Communist Party oblast committee (*obkom*). Roketskii remained a member of the Communist Party until the abortive coup of August 1991, which he opposed. He was appointed first deputy governor in November 1991, shortly before the final collapse of the USSR, and governor on 20 February 1993. Roketskii's wife, whom he describes as "a powerful woman," had a senior managerial position in Surgut and now heads the Tiumen branch of Neftekhimbank.

The current head of the KhMAO administration is the fifty-seven-year-old Aleksandr Vasilievich Filipenko, who pursued a career as a bridge-building engineer in Surgut in the mid-1970s before heading the construction department of the KhMAO Communist Party committee from 1977 to 1982. A brief promotion to first deputy chairman of the KhMAO Soviet executive committee was followed in 1983 by five years as secretary of a Communist Party district committee (*raikom*). Filipenko's upward progress resumed in 1988, when he became secretary of the KhMAO Communist Party committee. In 1989, he became chairman of the KhMAO Soviet executive committee, a post which he continued to hold after having been elected as a deputy to the Tiumen Oblast Soviet for the town of Khanty-Mansiisk (the okrug capital) in March 1990. He remained a member of the Communist Party until the abortive coup of August 1991, which he opposed. He was appointed to his present position shortly before the final collapse of the USSR at the end of 1991 and declared that he would attempt to create a favorable climate for the useful activities of businessmen.

Iurii Vasilievich Neelov is the forty-six-year-old head of the YaNAO administration. He qualified as an engineer at the Tiumen Industrial Institute in 1974 before going from mechanic to director in a motor transportation unit within a couple of years, by which time he was also a member of the Soviet executive committee in Salekhard (the main town of the YaNAO) and chairman of the Surgut Soviet. His rise seems to have lost momentum in 1976, when Neelov shifted his focus into unspecified Komsomol and Party activity for some eleven years. Between 1987 and 1990, however, he chaired the Surgut Soviet, the Surgut Soviet executive committee, and the USSR

Supreme Soviet committee on transportation, communication, and information science. Neelov then became deputy head of the Tiumen Oblast administration until February 1994, when he was appointed governor of the YaNAO. As YaNAO head of administration, Neelov is a member by right of the board of directors of the gas monopoly, Gazprom. He has been known to blame central government for lack of investment in the okrug, resulting in idle oil and gas wells and unfinished industrial construction programs.

Another important regional figure to have spent a period in office in Moscow is Iurii Konstantinovich Shafranik, who was Russian Minister of Fuel and Energy for three and a half years. Like Roketskii, Shafranik has a Ukrainian background and like Neelov he is forty-six years old and graduated from the Tiumen Industrial Institute as an engineer in 1974 (he later acquired an external qualification in oil and gas technology). He appears to have started working for Nizhnevartovskneftegaz, an oil company based in the KhMAO, as early as 1972, and rose through a variety of posts in the enterprise until 1983. From 1983 to 1985, Shafranik was secretary of the Langepas district committee of the Communist Party in the KhMAO but for the following two years he was second secretary of the Party's Langepas town committee, a probable demotion. In 1987, however, he became one of the youngest general directors in the Soviet oil and gas industry as head of Langepasneftegaz, a position which he held for the next three years. Langepasneftegaz now accounts for over a quarter of the oil reserves of LUKoil, into which it has been incorporated. In 1990, Shafranik was elected chairman of the Tiumen Oblast Soviet by an overwhelming majority, despite being one of the least known of the six candidates. Although he joined the Communist Party *obkom*, he refused to enter its top leadership. Shafranik became oblast governor in October 1991, in the first wave of appointments to the new Russian regional administrations, and devoted strenuous efforts to keeping the oblast fuel and energy complex—and the oblast itself—together. He accompanied President Yeltsin to Britain in 1992 and agreed to a memorandum on cooperation between Tiumen Oblast and the European Bank for Reconstruction and Development. Yeltsin appointed him as Minister of Fuel and Energy on January 12, 1993, thus enabling Roketskii and others to move one step up the political ladder. In December 1993, Shafranik won the election in a KhMAO constituency for a seat in the Federation Council (the upper house of the Russian Parliament) with 49.5 percent of the vote, beating Filipenko (with 37.1 percent) into second place (the Council ceased to be an elected chamber in 1995). Shafranik lost his ministerial position in the clear-out which followed the 1996 presidential election and has since returned to the oil industry, though there have also been reports that he has been involved in electoral maneuvers against Roketskii (see below).

This evidence suggests that many members of the political elite in the oblast share a common ground. Our four leading regional figures have career profiles that are typical of Russian regional elite leaders (the *obkom* first secretaries) in the immediate post-Brezhnev period: they are all successful local insiders, for example, and their Soviet and Communist Party careers were inextricably intertwined.[3] The main differences between this post-Soviet group and other elites are that this post-Soviet leadership group is younger and has not been educated in Moscow. Second, these career profiles exhibit two important characteristics for which the Tiumen elite was noted in the late Soviet period. One is the high level of integration between oil and gas and the regional politico-administrative system. The other is the likelihood of promotion from the region to a region-related ministry in Moscow. Third, the steady progress of this leadership group up the promotion ladder in the 1980s is a remarkable common feature, given the purges which rocked the Tiumen regional elite until late in the decade. Shafranik, for example, made a fortuitous move from Nizhnevartovskneftegaz to Langepas just before the initial wave of purges. The second wave followed the arrival in power of Gorbachev, who visited Tiumen in the autumn of 1985 and accused top officials of lying about oil output. The first casualty was the oil minister himself, who was followed by most of the top management of the industry in Tiumen and several hundred on the level below. The four leading regional figures profiled here not only survived this prolonged crisis (albeit at some temporary cost to their prospects), they all came out of it in better positions than before.

Elite continuity in Tiumen is typical of the general picture in post-Soviet Russia. According to Olga Kryshtanovskaia and Stephen White, for example, there has, at most, been a certain level of renewal from within the ranks of the Soviet elite, this being reflected in a more youthful composition. Kryshtanovskaia and White "largely shared the conclusions of those who have argued that *plus ça change* in the composition of post-communist elites."[4] A critique by James Hughes, based on research into seven regional elites (including Tiumen), argues that these were much less variegated than Kryshtanovskaia and White have supposed. For Hughes, the sub-national political elite, "broadly uniform . . . in terms not only of occupational structure and status but also as regards age, gender and lack of overt party affiliation," is composed of an increasingly interlocked or integrated group of political-administrative and economic leaders. The old Soviet *nomenklatura* has not only recomposed itself but has also succeeded in dramatically eclipsing other social groups in the elected regional assemblies—professionals, women, young people, non-manual employees, and workers. Taking into account the scale of "administrative entrepreneurship" and of "rent-seeking" *nomenklatura* privatization, Hughes discounted the idea that leaders in privatized business, who constituted almost a quarter of the regional deputies elected in his seven regions in 1994, were likely to open up the closed elite. He concluded: "This is not the differentiated elite that one might have expected to emerge after a sustained period of democratisation." He went on to speculate that the importance of networks and coalitions between private and public elites in Russia was likely to increase.[5]

THE FRAGMENTATION OF TIUMEN OBLAST

The YaNAO, which lies in the far north and has a population of about half a million, produces 90 percent of Russia's gas and 12 percent of its oil.[6] The KhMAO, immediately to the south with a population of about 1.3 million, contains over two-thirds of the country's oil fields and produces 70 percent of its oil.[7] It also has a strategic role in the transportation of gas from the YaNAO.[8] The okrugs, which occupy 89 percent of the oblast's territory, have an overwhelmingly dominant economic position in the region as a whole, accounting in 1993 for more than 90 percent of gross output and over 95 percent of profits.[9] "Tiumen proper" (the extreme south of the oblast), on the other hand, produces a significant proportion of the region's food supply. Some six hundred thousand of its population of about 1.3 million live in the town of Tiumen, which remains a center of health, educational, and other facilities (one local academic remarked that a survey of students at Tiumen State University would be a reliable guide to the profile of the entire regional elite).

Tiumen Oblast is the richest region in Russia, outproducing Moscow by one-and-a-half times and accounting for one-third of all Siberian imports.[10] Yet the main political struggle has not been between Tiumen and Moscow but between the okrug and oblast leaderships. In Soviet times, the okrug authorities were subordinate to the authorities of the region in which they were located. The 1993 Constitution made them equal "subjects of the federation," which not only released the okrugs from their subordination to the oblast but gave them a great degree of independence from it. Their budgets, for example, are now separate. The okrugs are also legally entitled to charge for the right to use their natural resources and to receive regular payments for such use. In 1993, bonus and royalty charges brought in 15.4 percent of budget revenue in the YaNAO as a whole. In 1995, payment for use amounted to more than 70 percent of budget revenue in the Pur district of the YaNAO.[11] The okrug authorities were entitled to keep 60–70 percent of such payments, passing 20 percent to the oblast and 10–20 percent to the federal budget (not to speak of the other forms of revenue which the okrugs received from oil and gas companies, and of which the oblast authorities were demanding a similar share). If they were to secede from Tiumen completely, they might be able to claim the oblast authorities' 20 percent share.[12] Interestingly, the KhMAO has been receiving more money from Gazprom for transmitting gas than the YaNAO has for producing it.[13] In 1995, payments for the use of natural resources constituted 18 percent of the budgetary

income of the KhMAO and 20 percent of that of the YaNAO.[14] In losing political control of the okrugs, the oblast authorities have also lost the chance of
direct access to a major source of revenue at a time of extreme pressure on
public budgets. At the same time, the okrugs still form part of the oblast,
much the greater part, in fact. If they did not, Tiumen proper would fall to
fiftieth place among the eighty-nine regions, while the KhMAO would remain
in first place, with the YaNAO falling to fifteenth.[15] The relations between
oblasts (or krais) and their okrugs is one of the issues left unresolved by the
Constitution. In this case, the result has essentially been friction between different types of regions rather than between regions and the center.

The oblast leadership has accused the okrugs of separatism and has
alleged that their failure to unite with it in the defence of joint interests has
resulted in an overall loss of oil and gas revenue to the region as a whole.
Leaders of the okrugs have accused the Tiumen authorities of continuing to
treat them as raw material appendages, of holding on to their monopoly of
educational, medical, and cultural facilities, and of manipulating joint economic programs for their own benefit.[16] The oblast authorities submitted a
draft law to an apparently sympathetic Duma, which would place energy
supply, pipelines, and law and order within their exclusive jurisdiction, and
the use of natural resources in joint jurisdiction.[17] However, the issue has
remained unresolved. A year and a half later, the legislative assemblies of all
three federation entities concerned asked for a ruling from the Constitutional Court. The latter did little more than restate the constitutional provisions according to which the okrugs formed part of the oblast but were also
equal to it.[18] A coordinating council set up under the provisions of a treaty
between the three federation entities in the region had earlier run into difficulties when it came to practical decisions.[19] The okrugs effectively withdrew from the election for oblast governor in late 1996, each of them elect-
ing their incumbent administrative head.

Though governor of the oblast in name, Roketskii was returned only by
the electorate of Tiumen proper. Tiumensky Kredit, the bank headed by
Roketskii's challenger, Sergei Atroshenko, is alleged to be at the center of a
criminal and political web reaching deep into the oil industry and involving,
among other prominent regional figures, Iurii Shafranik, with whom
Atroshenko has been associated for some years.[20] Roketskii described this as
part of an attempt by unnamed forces to divide the oblast into three parts in
order to gain control of Tiumen's oil—"only the oil, they do not need any-
thing else."[21] The extent of the split between Roketskii and Shafranik may be
evidenced by Atroshenko's announcement at an early stage that his real aim
was to win the governorship at the next election, hence the name of his
electoral organization: "Tiumen-2000."

It seems a matter of common sense to identify continuity as a stabilizing
factor in a time of change. Yet elite continuity in Tiumen—as in post-Soviet

Russia in general—has gone hand-in-hand with a historically high level of conflict in the upper reaches of society. If post-Soviet Russia is essentially ruled by the same group or groups as in Soviet times, why has so much of its brief existence been dominated by conflict among the elites? One answer is the apparently permanent and worsening economic crisis. In the absence of effective measures for economic stabilization and recovery, power-holders are reduced to bickering amongst themselves about their share of the take from a shrinking pot.

Another possible answer is that the collapse of the Soviet Union went hand in hand with the disintegration of the old Communist Party (CPSU), which had structured elite relations into a hierarchy for sixty years. This led to shifts in the balance of power between different elite groups. One of these was the shift to the "Financial-Industrial Groups" (FIGs) and banks that are closely connected to central and regional government. Two of the FIGs particularly relevant to our purposes are LUKoil and Gazprom, the gas monopoly, the creation of which has been described as a model of large-scale *nomenklatura* privatization.[22] Other changes include a shift in the balance of power from central to regional elites. Such elite power shifts, plus the loss of the CPSU, destabilized relationships between the very groups of people most intimately involved in the business of the new state. They are a little like an officer corps which has survived some military disaster almost intact but at the cost of a breakdown in the chain of command, in other words, in the very thing that made it an effective officer corps. Their cohesiveness has deteriorated, and the lack of clarity about who is subordinate to whom and to what degree has stimulated competing claims and conflicts. The pressure of economic crisis is not conducive to the considered resolution of such disputes.

It is the particular combination of continuity and change at the elite level which is important. Had the *nomenklatura* been able to go on ruling with its traditional mechanisms, it might have been able to cope in the short term, perhaps even in the medium term, with the ups and downs of different elite groups without too much in the way of internal disruption. Had the *nomenklatura* been overthrown, then this kind of problem simply would not have arisen. Ironically, the elite conflict which typifies post-Soviet Russia is largely the result of a relatively peaceful, relatively gradual process of reform which was initiated and led largely from within the political establishment.[23]

OIL, GAS, AND THE FRAGMENTATION OF TIUMEN

In 1995, a commission of the YaNAO administration found that Gazprom had deprived the okrug of well over $400 million through non-payment of debts and tax revenues lost as a result of the system of transfer pricing, which greatly undervalued gas at the point of production. Despite this, Gazprom has continued to extract concessions from the YaNAO, not the other way round, and similar concessions have been made by the KhMAO.[24] The big oil and gas companies operating in the region are essentially extra-territorial, with refineries, head offices, and marketing operations located elsewhere. They also have close relationships with the federal government. Little benefit has been derived by the public authorities in the region from the restructuring and partial privatization of the oil and gas industries, as the region has been largely excluded from acquiring a shareholding in the major oil companies.

In the case of LUKoil, for instance, over 92 percent of available shares were sold in Moscow and only 0.4 percent in the region. On the other hand, the giant new joint-stock companies have been only too keen to burden the regional authorities with unwanted inherited responsibilities such as housing.[25] Where shares have been distributed, it almost seems that this has been done with an eye to exacerbating inter-regional tension. Thus, the KhMAO administration protested against the distribution of 15 percent of the state's package of shares in Sibneft to the YaNAO, Tiumen, and Omsk administrations, when 30 percent of the company's oil extraction took place in the KhMAO.[26]

But criticism by the regional leadership either of the federal government or of the oil and gas companies has generally been remarkable for its absence. Sergei Sobianin, the chairman of the KhMAO Duma, has claimed that his okrug contributes more than 50 percent of its net tax receipts to the Federation.[27] If this is so, then it must be particularly galling, since the okrugs had been hoping to benefit in terms of tax from the removal of the oblast from budget arrangements. According to one set of figures (for 1992), Tiumen Oblast as a whole stands out among the Russian regions as making by far the largest per capita contribution to the federal budget.[28] Although this underlines the region's economic importance, it is not a cause for rejoicing either in the oblast or the okrugs. Sobianin, for example, has accused the republics of Tatarstan and Bashkortostan (whose contribution rates to the federal budget are much lower) of "creaming off our oil," thanks to their refining capacity.[29] This is a local variant of the argument common in the regions that the "ethnic" republics are getting preferential treatment from the federal government at the expense of the regions. It is noticeable that Sobianin did not target the neighboring "Russian" region of Omsk, although its refining capacity is one of the biggest in Russia.[30]

Legalities aside, the real balance of forces is one in which giants like Gazprom can deprive the producer regions of tax revenue or obtain a development license by presidential decree for fields in the YaNAO without reference to the okrug authorities, in defiance of the law on underground resources.[31] Some oil companies have been set up with the participation of regional authorities but these have a weak financial base, mainly because of the weak financial positions of the authorities themselves.[32] But the giant, vertically integrated oil and gas companies control not only the production process inside the region but also transportation, distribution, and foreign sales. The okrugs have asserted their independence from Tiumen but not from the companies that dominate their main towns and exercise considerable influence on central government.

The friction between Tiumen and the okrugs—and the comparative lack of friction between them and the oil and gas companies—indicates that the relationship between center and region must be understood in its economic as well as in its political form. This is not the only such indication. In 1997, for example, the government was planning to restructure such "natural monopolies" as Gazprom, Unified Electrical System (the major energy supplier), and the railways. But the leaders of the regions and republics in the Urals declared their opposition.[33] They claimed that breaking up the energy system in particular would encroach on the interests of the regions and damage the energy industry. They also made known their fear that it would open the way to incursion by foreign multinationals and that this would threaten the security of the industry and of the country. The opinions of these provincial advocates of the natural monopolies were apparently shared by most of the other regional leaders.

How much the majority of Russians benefit from energy revenues is another question:

> About 45 percent of Russia's exports are oil and gas. . . . There is nothing wrong per se for a country to enter the international division of labor as a source of raw materials, notwithstanding the complaints from nationalists about the "Kuwaitisation" of the Russian economy. The question is whether this export performance is an indicator of future economic potential, or a relic of the Soviet past. The revenues being generated by foreign trade are not being ploughed back into investment in these sectors. They are not even finding their way back to cover current costs. Oil and gas firms are also among the worst offenders when it comes to arrears with their federal taxes, and in paying their workers.[34]

The fact that such elected regional authorities tend to line up with large, centralized corporations that operate against the interests of the majority of voters indicates how narrow is the scope of such provincial power and how much it is in thrall to an unelected economic power based on control of the means of production. The nature of regional economic differentiation in Russia is the key to this dependency.

Regional differentiation in Russia since the collapse of the Soviet Union has taken place against the background of a catastrophic decline in the economy as a whole and in manufacturing industry in particular. The regions that in some sense stand out against the trend—by declining more slowly, for example—are those that make a net contribution to the federal budget—the "donor" regions. There are probably no more than eight of them at the moment out of a total of eighty-nine: Moscow (which, like St. Petersburg, has regional status as a "city of federal significance"), Nizhnii Novgorod Oblast, the YaNAO, the KhMAO, Irkutsk Oblast, Sverdlovsk Oblast, Krasnoiarsk Krai, and the Republic of Sakha, formerly Yakutia.[35] The last six regions listed here are exporters either of raw materials such as oil and gas, which account for about 45 percent of Russia's exports, or of semi-processed goods, chiefly metals, which account for another 15 percent.[36] These six regions then, account for about 60 percent of Russia's exports, with the other eighty-three regions accounting for just 40 percent.

The critical importance of the donor regions to Russia's economic survival appears to provide a number of them with the basis for significant political assertiveness. Three of them in particular—Moscow, Nizhnii Novgorod, and Sverdlovsk—have roles which stand out from the generality of regions, and leading members of their elites—Yury Luzhkov (the mayor of Moscow), Boris Nemtsov (formerly governor of Nizhnii Novgorod and first deputy prime minister), and Eduard Rossel (governor of Sverdlovsk)—are prominent figures on the national political stage. In the spring of 1997, a number of other donor regions were involved in something of an "economic revolt" against the federal government. The contrast between regional "winners" and "losers" may be less significant than the connection between them.

Kathryn Stoner-Weiss has argued that the concentrated economic structure of donor regions such as Tiumen and Nizhnii Novgorod engenders close cooperation between economic and political elites and hence more effective regional government than in recipient regions such as Iaroslavl' and Saratov, where more diversified economies and competing economic interests express themselves in ingrained political conflict between city and oblast or between legislature and executive.[37] In the recipient regions, then, economic diversity appears as a barrier to development in the form of inter-elite rivalry. However, donor regions like the YaNAO and the KhMAO were developed as one-sided raw material appendages. Here, lack of diversity extended to such basic elements of infrastructure as housing, transport, and, ironically, domestic supplies of natural gas.[38] The emphasis on economic concentration in such regions is now all the greater given the need for foreign currency earnings. These earnings do not fuel development, although the case for diversification in such regions is well established.[39]

If diversity is a barrier to development in the recipient regions, then concentration is a barrier to development in the exporting regions. The crucial reason for the prominence of the raw material and processed goods exporting regions is not their spectacular performance in a generally healthy economy but the catastrophic decline in other sectors. Thus, in Tiumen Oblast, gas production fell from 557.16 billion cubic meters in 1993 to 554.5 in 1995,

Table 6.1 Industrial Structure of Tiumen Oblast, 1994

Industry	Whole Oblast	KhMAO	YaNAO	South
All	100	100	100	100
Electricity supply	10.5	12.9	0.1	27.2
Oil extraction	60.2	78.3	33.8	0.1
Gas	21.5	5.7	64.8	0
Chemicals and petrochemicals	1.1	0	0	14.2
Machine building and metals	1.4	0.1	0	17.7
Timber and woodworking	1.2	1.1	0.1	6.1
Production of building materials	1.3	1.1	0.7	5
Light industry	0.2	0	0	3.1
Food	2.1	0.8	0.5	20

Columns in percentages.

while oil production fell from 224.69 million tons to 201.5 over the same period under the impact of non-payment, reductions in investment, and increases in tax and excise duties (the crisis also manifested itself in a lowering of "ecological security" and an increase in industrial accidents, twenty-two fatalities resulting in 1993 alone, with a consequent "heightening of social tension").[40] In 1995 alone, exports of oil and oil products from Tiumen Oblast fell by 10 percent.[41] These two kinds of region are merely different sides of the same coin of economic decline. Russia has become heavily dependent on exports from a handful of regions, and the latter have derived some benefit from this but only at the cost of general economic development in all the regions. The one-sided development of Tiumen makes it all the more dependent on the dominant oil and gas companies, despite its apparently advantageous position in terms of reserves.

CONCLUSIONS

I have argued that the fragmentation of Tiumen Oblast is a special case of the breakdown in the traditional elite chain of command, which has generally expressed itself in regional assertiveness against the authorities in Moscow. Within the fragments, there has been a continuity of elites. In

Soviet times, the oblast elite was very much subordinate to the oil and gas ministries and was much more responsive to pressure from above than to the need for horizontal (i.e., regional) coordination, particularly when it came to the provision of infrastructure.[42] Post-Soviet federalization has, paradoxically perhaps, helped to strengthen the vertical economic links of the okrug elites at the expense of their horizontal ties across the region. The rivalry between the okrugs and the oblast over oil and gas revenue has aligned the former with the big oil and gas concerns that emerged from the old ministries, while all three have looked for support in the central political institutions. In the summer of 1998, a time of rising political and industrial as well as regional opposition to the central government, the KhMAO leadership seemed, on the contrary, to be firming up its relationship with the government by bringing its charter and laws into compliance with federal legislation.[43]

The power of the central powers may be expected to weaken. In *Izvestiia*, shortly before the dismissal of the Kirienko government, Aleksandr Bobin argued that the Russian Federation was disintegrating into a kind of feudal order, its constituent parts increasingly under the sway of despotic regional "princes and boyars." He stressed that all other existing federal states were based on a single economic, social, and legal space in which the constituent parts were not sovereign, did not have the right of secession, did not dispose of independent leadership, and did not have the right to hinder the application of federal laws. Bobin traced the regional leaders' continuing appetite for "sovereignty" ("that is, for power and property") back to what he saw as the founding slogan of "our new federalism," Yeltsin's well-known exhortation of August 1990: "Take as much sovereignty as you can get." He cited, by way of example, a number of regions and republics that had flouted federal authority on race and nationalities, economic policy, foreign policy, sovereignty, and secession.

The center's existing policy (restated by then Prime Minister Kirienko)[44] of making power-sharing treaties and agreements with individual regions was of doubtful value in Bobin's eyes: these treaties and agreements reinforced the asymmetry of the Russian Federation and gave its parts a basis for their pretensions to equality with the center. Indeed, they rather typified its weaknesses. The Federation Council, far from synthesizing the interests of the Federation as a whole with those of the regions, had steadfastly refused to introduce general rules for the federal game, while, significantly, also refusing to limit regional leaders to two terms of office. There was a danger, according to Bobin, of an increasingly explosive mixture of remnants of unitary government with the beginnings of confederation. Hence, various "exotic" ideas such as, on the one hand, abolishing the ethnically linked republics and autonomous okrugs and returning to a unitary state based exclusively on large administrative *guberniias*, and, on the other, introducing a three-layer structure consisting of a unitary (European) Russian republic, a federation of large, outlying territories, and a confederation including, for example, Chechnya, Tatarstan, and Belarus.[45]

Considered in its narrow sense, the economic crisis that occurred in Russia in 1998 could be seen as a stimulus for even greater fragmentation within Tiumen Oblast, on the basis that people tend to fight harder for reduced rations than for generous ones. This would strengthen their attachments to the oil companies, to Gazprom, and to central government. However, the Kirienko government, despite a certain regional flavor, may have had a weaker hold on the general run of regions than its predecessor did, while the governors may be on the way to becoming the focus of a more effective "party of power."[46]

The Kirienko government put pressure on the regional leaders to cut spending and increase the flow of funds into the federal budget.[47] Although the IMF-backed austerity program involved replacing payments in kind by cash (especially, though not exclusively, when it came to the payment of federal taxes), this did not stop the YaNAO and the Chuvash Republic from signing a barter trade agreement in June.[48] Political developments, in other words, may incline the Tiumen elites away from the government and the presidential administration. Three pro-Yeltsin governors were voted out in May 1998.[49] With Duma elections in 1999 and a presidential election with no obvious front-runner in the year 2000, there is uncertainty not only about the nature of the regime but about its survival. (Prior to his abortive attempt to regain the prime ministership in the summer of 1998, Viktor Chernomyrdin intended to stand in a September 1998 by-election for the State Duma in a YaNAO constituency and was expected to win and to assume the Duma leadership of Our Home is Russia).[50]

It may be that the restructuring of the oil and gas industries, and particularly the introduction of a more transparent pricing system by Gazprom, will give the three Tiumen elites more room for maneuver. However, this hope was also expressed in at least one of the okrugs at an earlier stage of reorganization without, it seems, very much in the way of results.[51] Despite their greater access to oil and gas revenue, the okrugs have had serious budgetary difficulties, if less so than Tiumen proper. A summary of these difficulties in 1995 concluded: "Obviously, the organs of power in the territories are not prepared to undertake additional expenditure, but, on the other hand, they cannot fail to do so on account of the danger of the growth of social tension in the territory."[52]

The Russian regions were not short of expressions of "social tension" in the spring and summer of 1998. In the "railway war," miners' blockade camps became a focus for so many other workers protesting about arrears of pay that one report described the events as "a full-fledged social meltdown."[53] In general, governors seem to have promoted the peaceful resolution of such

disputes. The repeated emphasis on avoiding the use of force may be a con-
fession of weakness.[54] Local and regional authorities are often in the firing
line.[55] This may fuel the increasingly hostile attitude taken by governors
toward not only central government but also toward big enterprises, public
and private. Thus, newly elected Krasnoiarsk governor Aleksandr Lebed
intervened to secure three months' back pay from the top regional railway
official, Cheliabinsk governor Petr Sumin backed the regional United Electrical Systems subsidiary in a tax dispute, and the Saratov Oblast administration, headed by Dmitrii Aiatskov, responded to a Gazprom threat to cut off
non-payers (as it had in neighboring Volgograd) with a threat to shut down
a major pumping station, virtually halting gas exports to Western Europe, on
account of Gazprom's own debts.[56]

Tiumen Oblast has not been a hot spot of protest. The Russian Oil, Gas
and Construction Workers' Union only threatened a strike in June. "The market crisis in South-East Asia and the collapse in oil prices have weakened the
oil companies," said the union's leader, Lev Mironov. "Now, even big companies are unable to pay workers' wages on time." The strike was averted,
but Mironov claimed that mounting arrears of pay were pushing Gazprom
workers to "the brink of a social explosion." Although Mironov himself
seems to be as concerned about pressing the interests of the employers on
the government as about the interests of the workers, confrontation in Tiumen Oblast seems possible. In the light of the government's tax collection
drive, Russian oil producers are considering major job cuts. Sibneft has
already announced a targeted 75 percent workforce reduction by the year
2008. LUKoil and YuKOS have announced major cuts in administrative and
social spending on facilities such as hospitals, housing, and farms. This
would have a catastrophic impact on the "company towns" of Western
Siberia.[57]

No government in Russia could survive without a close and harmonious
relationship with its major raw material-producing region. The okrug
authorities would probably be in a better position to cope with serious
industrial trouble than many of their counterparts in other regions. However,
they are also more closely aligned with Moscow than are the oblast authorities in Tiumen proper, who could raise a regionalist standard with renewed
vigor. Roketskii has, in the past, given his support to a strike of oil workers,
and a similar tactic has been mentioned as one of the options open to the
KhMAO leadership.[58] In the last analysis, many elite decisions now depend
on how ordinary Russians react to the economic and political crises.

Two issues have featured prominently in the aftermath of the crises of
1998. One is the aligning of forces in the run-up to the Duma and presidential elections. At first sight, it seems that the assertiveness of the regional
leaders has risen to unprecedented heights. The Federation Council has
defied Yeltsin by twice rejecting the resignation of the Prosecutor General,

Yurii Skuratov. At the same time, regional electoral blocs have appeared, especially All Russia (Vsia Rossiia), oriented on the presidential ambitions of Yurii Luzhkov, the mayor of Moscow. One of these blocs, Russia's Voice (Golos Rossii), includes Yurii Neelov, the YaNAO governor, and is said to have the support of Gazprom. Like LUKoil, Gazprom has been strengthening its regional ties, partly by means of the new blocs, in order to create a party of exporters. The other issue is the production-sharing legislation that finally went through the State Duma at the end of 1998 after long delays. The legislation is designed to boost foreign investment in development projects, especially in oil, where even the biggest Russian companies are hard-pressed by lack of funds. By early 1999, however, three oil fields had been cut from the list of projects since the KhMAO and the Tiumen Oblast authorities could not agree on who had jurisdiction over them. The KhMAO initially approved eight oil projects but reversed this decision when another project, the Uvatskii oil field, 80 percent of which lies inside the okrug, was added without consultation. The Uvatskii project is expected to generate $2.67 billion in overall tax revenue. Powerful interests may now wish to tighten the national grip on this important source of earnings. In May 1999, for example, the State Duma, the Fuel and Energy Ministry, and leading oil and gas companies set up a coordination council to oversee the implementation of the production-sharing law. It will be interesting to see how the political leadership of the KhMAO chooses between (or reconciles) its regional interests and its national interests.

NOTES

1. V. Kryukov et al., *Neftegazovye territorii: kak rasporiadit'sya bogatstvom? Tekushchie problemy i formirovanie uslovii dolgovremennogo ustoichivogo sotsial'no-ekonomicheskogo razvitiia* (Tiumen: "Pravovaia Ekonomika"/Novosibirsk:IEiOPP SO RAN, 1995), p. 102; Marta-Lisa Magnusson, "Den russiske regionalisering: center-periferi konflikt pa flere niveauer," *Vindue mod ost*, no. 33 (December 1995), p. 27; Nikolai Vakhtin, *Native Peoples of the Russian Far North* (London: Minority Rights Group, 1992), pp. 14–23; National News Service, "Obshchestvenno-politicheskie protsessy," http://www.nns.ru/regiony/tyumen5.html, 1995, last accessed 10 August 1998. The remainder of Tiumen Oblast is referred to as "Tiumen proper," or simply as "the south."

2. The main sources for these biographies are National News Service, "Krupnye politiki i biznesmeny oblasti," http://www.nns.ru/regiony/tyumen6.html, 1995, last accessed 3 August 1998; the Tiumen Oblast Administration, "Gubernator Tiumenskoi oblasti," http://www.sibtel.ru/Admin/gubern.html, last accessed 6 August 1998; Martin McCauley, ed., *Longman Biographical Directory of Decision Makers in Russia and the Successor States* (Harlow, U.K.: Longman, 1993). Additional sources include "Net mesta teplee Sibiri," a full-page interview with Tiumen governor Roketskii, in

Obshchaia gazeta, 25 September–1 October 1997; and a round table discussion with KhMAO governor Filipenko, in Institute of East-West Studies, *Russian Regional Report*, vol. 2, no. 36, 23 October 1997 (referred to below as *RRR* with date).

3. Comparisons with Soviet era elites are based on accounts of the latter in: Peter Rutland, *The Politics of Economic Stagnation in the Soviet Union: The Role of Local Party Organs in Economic Management* (Cambridge: Cambridge University Press, 1993); Thane Gustafson, *Crisis amid Plenty: The Politics of Soviet Energy under Brezhnev and Gorbachev* (Princeton: Princeton University Press, 1989).

4. Olga Kryshtanovskaia and Stephen White, "From Soviet *Nomenklatura* to Russian Elite," *Europe-Asia Studies*, vol. 48, no. 5 (1996), p. 729. For a more recent example of the same general approach, see Donald J. Jensen, *How Russia Is Ruled—1998* (Radio Free Europe/Radio Liberty, 1998), http://www.rferl.org/nca/special/ruwhorules/index.html, updated 28 August 1998, last accessed 8 September 1998, especially part 3. "Continuity of Elites," http:// www.rferl.org/nca/special/ruwhorules/elites-3.html.

5. James Hughes, "Sub-National Elites and Post-Communist Transformation in Russia: A Reply to Kryshtanovskaia and White," *Europe-Asia Studies*, vol. 49, no. 6 (1997), pp. 1017–1036.

6. *RRR*, 5 June 1997.

7. National News Service, "Ekonomicheskoe polozhenie Tiumenskoi oblasti," http://www.nns.ru/regiony/tyumen3.html, 1995, last accessed 9 August 1998. According to the *Open Media Research Institute (OMRI) Russian Regional Report*, 9 October 1996, the KhMAO produced only 53 percent of Russia's oil.

8. *RRR*, 17 July 1997.

9. Kryukov et al., *Neftegazovye territorii*, p. 112.

10. *Izvestiia*, 8 October 1996; Galina Kovaliova, "Siberia As a Buyer on the World Market" (summary), http://ieie.nsc.m/br/4_kovsum.htm, last accessed 4 August 1998.

11. Kryukov et al, *Neftegazovye territorii*, p. 202; V. A. Kryukov, "The Administrative Regions of Western Siberia and the Oil and Gas Sector: In Search of a New Relationship," (London, photocopy, February 1996), pp. 6–7.

12. National News Service, "Protivorechiia mezhdu interesami oblasti, AO i neftianykh VIK," http://www.nns.ru/regiony/tyumen321.html, 1995, last accessed 10 August 1998; NUPI Center for Russian Studies Database, http://www.nupi.no/cgi-win/Russland/krono.exe/284, 13 November 1996, last accessed 6 August 1998.

13. Valery Kryukov and Arild Moe, *The New Russian Corporatism? A Case Study of Gazprom*, (London: RIIA, 1996), p. 32.

14. National News Service, "Finansy, denezhnoe obrashchenie, privatizatsiia," http://www.nns.ru/regiony/tyumen34.html, 1995, last accessed 10 August 1998.

15. *OMRI Russian Regional Report*, 9 October 1996.

16. V. Naumova, "Vladimir Kolunin: 'Yamal—samostoyatel'naia territoriia unikal'noi oblasti," *Tiumenskie izvestiia*, 22 December 1995; Sergei Sobianin, "Kto snimaet slivki s tiumenskoi nefti?" *Russkaya Aziia*, 17 January 1996.

17. *OMRI Daily Digest*, part 1, 16 December 1996; the text of the draft law was published in *Tiumenskie izvestiia*, 21 December 1995, p. 6.

18. Dmitrii Kamyshev and Vladimir Shpak, "'Pravovoi razboi' bez zaseneniia v protokol," *Segodnia*, 26 June 1997; NUPI Center for Russian Studies Database,

http://www.nupi.no/cgi-win/Russland/krono.exe/807, 17 July 1997, last accessed 6 August 1998.

19. Valentin Samoilik, "Administrativnyi soviet prinimaet sotsial'ny programmy. I ne tol'ko," *Sibirskii posad*, 2–9 February 1996. The text of the treaty was published in *Sibirskii posad*, 29 September–6 October 1995, p. 4, and in *Tiumenskie izvestiia*, 21 December 1995, p. 5.

20. Sergei Leskov, "Ostorozhno: vo vlast' idet Atroshenko," *Izvestiia*, 10 January 1997; see also Robert Orttung, "Tiumen re-elects Roketsky," *OMRI Russian Regional Report*, 15 January 1997.

21. Sergei Mulin, "Leonid Roketskii protiv popytki razdelit' oblast'," *Nezavisimaia gazeta*, 28 September 1996.

22. Ol'ga Kryshtanovskaia, "Finansovaia oligarkhiia v Rossii," *Izvestiia*, 10 January 1996.

23. This section is based on the distinction between social structure and political regime made by Alex Callinicos, *The Revenge of History* (Cambridge, U.K.: Polity Press, 1991), p. 57; see also Philip Hanson, *Regions, Local Power and Economic Change in Russia* (London: RIIA, 1994), p. 15.

24. Kryukov and Moe, *New Russian Corporatism.*, p. 31.

25. Kryukov et al., *Neftegazovye territorii.*, pp. 251–253.

26. National News Service, "Finansy, denezhnoe obrashchenie, privatizatsiia," http://www.nns.ru/regiony/tyumen34.html, 1995, last accessed 10 August 1998.

27. Sobianin, "Kto snimaet slivki s tiumenskoi nefti?"

28. Darrell Slider, "Federalism, Discord, and Accommodation: Intergovernmental Relations in Post-Soviet Russia," in *Local Power and Post-Soviet Politics*, ed. Theodore H. Friedgut and Jeffrey W. Hahn (Armonk , N.Y.: M. E. Sharpe, 1994), p. 252.

29. Sobianin, "Kto snimaet slivki s tiumenskoi nefti?"

30. David Cameron Wilson, *CIS and East European Energy Databook 1995*, Tadcaster, U.K.: Eastern Bloc Research Ltd., p. 25.

31. Kriukov and Moe, *New Russian Corporatism.*, p. 15.

32. Kryukov, "Administrative Regions."

33. *RRR*, 30 April 1997.

34. Peter Rutland, "Russia's Inside-Out Economy," paper presented at the British Association for Slavonic and East European Studies conference, 13 April 1997, pp. 3–4.

35. A 1994 list also included Moscow and Ul'ianovsk oblasts (Hanson, *Regions, Local Power and Economic Change in* Russia., p. 26); a 1995 list added the republics of Bashkortostan and Tatarstan, plus Lipetsk, Samara, and Yaroslavl oblasts, but did not include the republic of Sakha, Alastair McAuley, "The Determinants of Russian Federal-Regional Fiscal Relations: Equity or Political Influence?" *Europe-Asia Studies*, vol. 49, no. 3 (1997), p. 441; a 1995 report cited fourteen donor regions (NUPI Center for Russian Studies Database, "'Donor' regions demand changes in economic policy," 20 November 1996, http://www.nupi.no/cgi.win/Russland/krono.exe/302, last accessed 6 August 1998); a 1996 list, in descending order of the size of their transfers to the center per head of their population, included KhMAO, YaNAO, Moscow, Samara, Sverdlovsk, Moscow Oblast, Perm, Irkutsk, Krasnoiarsk, Lipetsk, Bashkortostan, and Tatarstan (Aleksei Lavrov, *Mify i rify rossiiskogo biudzhetnogo federalizma*,

[Moscow: Magistr, 1997], cited in NUPI Center for Russian Studies Database, http://www.nupi.no/cgi-win/Russland/krono.exe/2162, 30 April 1998); a more recent estimate is seven (Iurii Riazhskii, "Chernomyrdin's Ears," *Moskovskii komsomolets*, 28 May 1997, translated in *Johnson's E-mail Russia List*, 30 May 1997).

36. Rutland, "Russia's Inside-Out Economy," p. 3.

37. Kathryn Stoner-Weiss, *Local Heroes: The Political Economy of Russian Regional Governance* (Princeton: Princeton University Press, 1997), pp. 164–191.

38. Veronika Naumova, "Vladimir Kolunin: 'Iamal-samostoyatel'naia territoriia unikal'noi oblasti,'" *Tiumenskie izvestiia*, 23 December 1995.

39. Gustafson, *Crisis amid Plenty*, p. 94; Rutland, *Politics of Economic Stagnation*, pp. 123–141; Kryukov et al., *Neftegazovye territorii*, pp. 112–115.

40. National News Service, "Predpriiatiia toplivo-energeticheskogo kompleksa," http://www.nns.ru/regiony/tyumen32.html, 1995, last accessed 10 August 1998.

41. National News Service, "Finansy, denezhnoe obrashchenie, privatizatsiia," http://www.nns.ru/regiony/tyumen34.html, 1995, last accessed 10 August 1998.

42. Gustafson, *Crisis amid Plenty*, p. 306.

43. *RRR*, 14 May, 25 June, 1998.

44. NUPI Center for Russian Studies Database, http://www.nupi.no/cgi-win/Russland/krono.exe/2162, 30 April 1998, last accessed 6 August 1998; as of June 1998, there were forty-six such agreements out of a total of eighty-nine regions (*RRR*, 18 June 1998).

45. Aleksandr Bobin, "Federalizm v krizise. Pora razminirovat," *Izvestiia*, 4 August 1998.

46. *RRR*, 14 and 21 May 1998.

47. *RRR*, 14 May 14, 11 June 1998; the inducements include the transfer of federal property to the regions, and it looks as if Kemerovo governor Aman Tuleev is already bargaining on this basis; see *RRR*, 6 August 1998.

48. *RRR*, 18 June 1998.

49. *RRR*, 21 May 1998.

50. NUPI Center for Russian Studies Chronology of Events, "Chernomyrdin Registered for Duma Race," 9 July 1998, http://www.nupi.no/cgi-win/Russland/krono.exe/2426, last accessed 13 August 1998.

51. Evgenii Kibalov, "Kto i kak budet 'igrat' muzyku' na rynke oligopolistov?" *Russkaia Aziia*, 31 August 1994.

52. Kryukov et al., *Neftegazovye territorii*, p. 219.

53. Matt Taibi, "The People Go Pitchfork," *the eXile*, 14–18 June 1998.

54. See, for example, reports on the Sakhalin and Cheliabinsk miners' strikes in *RRR*, 6 August 1998; "Bad Fall Ahead," *Moscow News*, 30 July–5 August 1998.

55. "Tver Local Government Executives under Fire," *RRR*, 2 July 1998.

56. *RRR*, 18 June, 2 July, 6 August 1998.

57. ICEM Eastern European Regional Conference, 3–4 June 1998, Moscow, "Globalization of the Oil and Gas Industries and the Eastern European Region: Trade Union Challenges and Opportunities;" Pay Us Our Wages Cybercampaign, August 1998, http://www.icem.org/campaigns/no_pay_cc/conf9806.html, last accessed 13 August 1998.

58. McCauley, ed., *Biographical Directory*; Kibalov, "Kto i kak buet."

Part 3

International and Foreign Policy Implications

7

Oil, Politics, and Foreign Policy

Peter Rutland

The goal of this chapter is to examine the role of energy factors in Russian foreign policy since 1991. Oil is both an end in itself (for the wealth it brings) and a means to an end (the projection of Russian power and influence). Energy interests have pulled Russian policy in different directions at different times, and often in different directions at the same time. No single model can capture these conflicting and confusing pressures and trends. Studying the role of oil in Russian foreign policy is like trying to assemble a jigsaw puzzle where the pieces from five different puzzles have been mixed together, and where one has no picture of what the completed puzzle is supposed to look like.

The first half of the chapter outlines Russian energy policy toward the various neighboring states. The second section reviews the available conceptual frameworks for tackling the problem. Images of what is driving Russian policy range across the full gamut. Some posit that policy is driven by a conspiracy of elite interests, others that there is no discernible policy at all. Some of these paradigms rely on universal economic theories, and some on the logic of geopolitics. Few of the authors advancing these competing paradigms spend much time on the economics of energy per se.

A PLETHORA OF GEOPOLITICAL PROBLEMS

Russia's energy policy faces a variety of challenges, each point of the compass bringing with it a different set of problems. Russia's huge land mass and complex historical legacy mean that it is impossible to reduce the politics of energy in Russia to a single or simple formula. To the west, it faces the challenge of securing transport routes across a zone of somewhat unstable and/or potentially hostile states that emerged from the collapse of the Soviet Union. To the south, there is the challenge of winning a share in the oil riches of the Caspian basin. To the east, the fact that most of the energy deposits lie east of the Urals provides a strong incentive for Russia to sell her resources to the energy-dependent economies of East Asia, although this will require the development of a new and expensive export infrastructure to carry them across Siberia.

However, it is important not to exaggerate these geographical challenges. First, one must remember that elsewhere in the world it is not at all unusual to find oil and gas fields straddling political fault lines. Russia's relations with the Baltic states, Belarus, and Ukraine may be testy and occasionally bitter, but they are much more stable and predictable than the explosive geopolitics of zones like the Caucasus and the Persian Gulf, which repeatedly erupt into armed conflict. Second, like many economic questions, Russia's geographical challenges boil down to problems of time and money. In order to circumvent geopolitical problem zones, new pipelines can be laid, and new port terminals developed, although this will take a few years and billions of dollars of investment.

Whether Moscow will press ahead with projects to develop new alternative transport outlets for its energy depends upon a mixture of political and economic considerations. Russia's motive is not simply to guarantee the cheap and secure shipment of energy to global markets. There are elements in Russia which are also keen to use the energy factor to reestablish a sphere of influence in the "near abroad." The fact that pipelines cross other countries has advantages as well as disadvantages for Russia, since it creates a pattern of mutual dependency. Russia's Western neighbors are all heavily dependent on energy imports, and need the revenue from energy transshipments just as much as Russia needs to use the existing export infrastructure.

Similarly, Russia has a somewhat ambivalent attitude toward the energy-rich countries of the Caspian Sea basin. On one hand, those countries are competitors, who can flood the region with additional supplies, and who seem keen to bring in foreign multinationals and the political ties that come with them. On the other side, Russia very much wants to share in the region's energy development projects, whether in terms of supplying management and technology or in providing export routes. Russia has important ties with other countries adjacent to the region (China, Iran, and Turkey) and cooperation rather than confrontation is likely to be a winning strategy both for Russian national interests and for Russian petroleum companies.

In the Far East, the geography generally works to Russia's advantage. Although distances are long and the terrain difficult, Russia is adjacent to Japan and China—two of the largest markets for energy in the twenty-first century. Russia already exports electricity to the giant Erdamet copper smelter in Mongolia. Relations with China are warm, and the demarcation of the mutual border is nearly completed—despite the patriotic rhetoric of Yevgennii Nazdratenko, the governor of Primorskii Krai, protesting the "concessions" to China. Russo-Japanese relations also seem to be improving. South Korea, which now has no political quarrels with Russia, is also keen to invest in Siberian energy projects, such as a 3,000-mile gas pipeline from the Kovytkin field in Irkutsk to China and on to South Korea. Despite the East Asian economic crash, China is reportedly keen to proceed with the scheme, in which Sidanko will be the leading Russian partner.[1]

The Primacy of Economics

Looking back at the trajectory of Russian policy toward the newly independent states since 1991, it is remarkable to what extent political and military considerations have taken a backseat to economic concerns. The much-feared presence of a 20-million strong Russian diaspora in the "near abroad" has had a negligible impact on Russian foreign policy, with the partial exception of relations with Estonia and Latvia. The division of the military assets of the Soviet army went more smoothly than anyone would have expected—most notably, the withdrawal of nuclear weapons from non-Russian territory. The lingering dispute over the division of the Black Sea is more an exercise in historical symbolism than a matter vital to the security concerns of either Russia or Ukraine.

Energy policy quickly emerged as perhaps the major area of contention between Russia and its neighbors. The issues include: the problem of debts for Russian energy deliveries; conditions for Russian exports across the Western republics; conditions for Caspian basin exports across Russia; and Russia's role in the development of Caspian basin energy fields. These problems are examined first with regard to Ukraine and Belarus, and then to central Asia and Azerbaijan.

The Western Frontier

One of the first problems to emerge after 1991 in Russia's relations with the "near abroad" was that of the energy debts of the Commonwealth of Independent States (CIS) countries. All the non-Russian republics save Turkmenistan were net energy importers, and in the Soviet era, the Russian Republic had subsidized the non-Russian republics to about 5 percent of Russian GDP, mainly through the delivery of energy at less than world market prices.[2] This situation continued through inertia into 1992, when interstate trade was based on barter deals negotiated at governmental level. These deals were based on prices that were far removed from prevailing world market levels. Russian oil and gas were being sold to CIS customers at 20 percent of what they would fetch on world markets. Moreover, because of lack of money CIS customers usually fell behind even on these reduced payments. By the end of 1994 Russia had issued a total of $5.9 billion credits to CIS countries, of which $2.8 billion was for energy deliveries.[3]

In an effort to stem the leakage, in April 1993 Russia announced that it would switch to world market pricing for energy from September 1993.[4] The Russian Central Bank refused to continue issuing "technical credits" to cover the trade debts that each country ran up with Moscow. They also refused to ship new (1993 minted) rubles to the other states, and in July Russia pulled the plug on the ruble zone by withdrawing the old rubles from circulation.[5] Meanwhile, Russian companies began insisting on payment up front for future energy deliveries to CIS customers. The existing stock of debt, which had built up in 1992–93, gave Russia potential leverage over the CIS debtor nations. Most of the CIS countries continued to run up debts for Russian energy deliveries (especially gas), despite the fact that Russia charges them less than the world price. (The average oil price paid by CIS clients in 1996 was $80 a ton compared to $120 for other clients.)[6] CIS country debts for energy supplies alone rose from 1.6 trillion rubles at the beginning of 1993 to 13.9 trillion rubles ($3 billion) by August 1995, of which 11.8 trillion was for gas, 1.8 trillion for electricity, and 330 billion for oil.[7] By February 1996 Gazprom was owed $1.1 billion by Ukraine, $910 million by Belarus, and $333 million by Moldova.[8]

Belarus and Ukraine are both heavily dependent on Russia for energy supplies. They each have small oil fields which meet about 10 percent of their oil needs. Ukraine has gas fields which cover 20 percent of annual consumption, and in 1993–94 was covering 20 percent of its consumption with gas purchased from Turkmenistan. (The way the deal worked was via a gas "swap," a standard international practice. Turkmenistan supplied gas to the Russian network and Russia pumped its own gas to Ukraine. No gas actually traveled from Ashgabad to Kyiv.) Ukraine has coal and nuclear power, so it can meet its own electricity needs, while Belarus must import most of its electric power from Lithuania and Russia. Still, Ukraine is struggling to generate sufficient export earnings to pay its bills for energy and other imports, and oil purchases alone account for 50 percent of Ukraine's import bill. In 1996 Ukraine's exports reached $14.1 billion, but its imports stood at $18.2 billion.[9]

Complicating the picture of debt recovery is Russia's reliance on existing pipelines crossing Belarus and Ukraine to export her oil and gas to Europe. Most of the export routes laid down during the Soviet period traversed non-Russian republics. The natural gas export pipeline crosses Ukraine, while the oil pipelines to Europe cross Belarus and Ukraine, and much of Russia's oil is shipped through ports in the now independent Baltic countries. Only 15 percent (35 million tons) of Russia's oil exports are currently shipped from Russian port terminals.[10]

Belarus and Ukraine complain that Russia is not paying them enough for the right to use the transit pipelines, and is overcharging them for the oil and gas they buy for their own consumption.[11] This argument now seems to be an annual ritual, breaking out in January, when the new year's tariff agreement can no longer be delayed. The typical pattern is that Russia reduces the supplies for a few days, after which a compromise is reached. From Russia's point of view, oil is less of a problem than gas, since oil deliveries are closely monitored and can be cut in the event of non-payment. As a result neither Belarus nor Ukraine has accumulated significant new debts for oil deliveries. Natural gas poses a different problem, since it cannot be cut off entirely for technical reasons (it may blow up when it is turned on again). Curiously, although Gazprom president Rem Vyakhirev periodically complains that local Ukrainian utilities are stealing gas, Gazprom has not made any effort to install meter technology or to separate the export pipeline from the Ukrainian grid. Thus nobody seems to know exactly how much gas Ukraine is using. There may be a method to this apparent madness. Certainly, it is not in Gazprom's short-term interest to disrupt the status quo; both Gazprom and the Russian government desperately need the monthly revenues from gas sales in Europe. The deal for 1997 was that Ukraine would obtain (free of charge) 30 billion of the 53 billion cubic meters of gas it will import from Russia in lieu of transit fees for the 110 billion cubic meters of gas that will cross the country from Russia to Europe.[12] Ukraine earned $86 million in transit fees from oil flowing through the Druzhba pipeline in 1996. Scrutiny of the numbers suggests that Russia seems to be charging a reasonable price for its energy and paying a reasonable price by way of transit fees.[13]

In 1993–1995 the IMF and the United States stepped in with loans to help Ukraine and Belarus cover their arrears, but this only served to delay the problem for another year or two. It was initially thought that U.S. involvement would "trilateralize" the problem and help Ukraine strike a better deal, but as the years passed and Ukrainian economic reform remained deadlocked the United States showed dwindling enthusiasm for this line of action.

Russia has tried to use this energy dependency to win various political and economic concessions from its neighbors. Gazprom has repeatedly pressed the ex-Soviet republics to pay off their gas debts with equity in energy installations. Ukraine has rebuffed this suggestion, although Moldova and Kyrgyzstan have taken up the offer, and in December 1996 Belarusian president Alyaksandr Lukashenka agreed to allow LUKoil and YuKOS to take majority ownership in the Mazyr and Novopolotsk refineries.[14] In September 1993, Yeltsin proposed to Ukrainian president Leonid Kravchuk that Ukraine give up its part of the Black Sea fleet in return for cancellation of Ukraine's energy debts.[15] Given the mutuality of the dependency, however, Russia's ability to use the energy weapon to extract major concessions from the debtor states is limited.[16] Since August 1993 Gazprom has periodically threatened to cut off supplies to the CIS states, but such threats are not really credible because a complete shutdown would cause a political scandal and would harm Russian firms that are dependent on trade with these countries. For example, Russia tried to pressure Kazakhstan to stop leasing their chromium deposits to Japanese companies, by threatening to cut off electricity supplies to northern Kazakhstan.[17] Liberal deputy prime minister Anatolii Chubais opposed this move, fearing that the Russian budget would be called upon to subsidize the Kazakh plants. Kazakhstan ignored the threats from Moscow, and pressed ahead with its program to privatize its metals and energy industries to Western firms despite vociferous Russian objections.[18] Even the Baltic states are not immune to Russian encroachment, however. In 1996, Gazprom agreed with a German consortium (Ruhrgas and Preussen Elektra) that each side would buy a 16 percent stake in Latvijas Gaze for $51 million each plus a promise of $55 million investment.[19]

Strategies for dealing with the energy dependency on Russia have varied. While Belarusian leader Alyaksandr Lukashenka chose to embrace Russia and offer political fealty in return for debt cancellation, Ukraine has moved in the opposite direction, seeking alternative sources of supply and trying to avoid bargaining with Moscow. Lukashenka has perfected the art of the "zero option" deal. In 1993 Belarus agreed to waive its rights to Soviet assets in return for cancellation of its energy debts. By 1996 Belarusian debts had risen once again, to $1.2 billion (including $800 million for energy deliveries). In February of that year Lukashenka pulled off a second "zero option" deal, under which energy debts to Russia were wiped out in return for Belarus withdrawing claims on Russia stemming from the stationing of Russian troops on Belarusian territory and compensation for dismantled nuclear facilities. Belarus's ailing and unreformed economy is chronically unable to meet its energy bills: by mid-1997 the Belarusian debt to Gazprom had once again reached $200 million.[20]

Although both Ukraine and Russia profess their dissatisfaction with the current state of affairs in their energy relations, they recognize their mutual dependency for the next few years at least. An Italian energy executive, discussing problems with shipping natural gas across Ukraine, described Russo-Ukrainian relations as "a Catholic marriage, where the partners argue all the time but know they will never divorce." Ukrainian nationalists would not accept the "Catholic marriage" analogy: they consider the 1991 Belavezha accords to represent a decisive divorce. The Ukrainian elite seems divided over the extent to which Russia can be regarded as a reliable partner for business and political dealings.[21] Only a minority want to adopt a confrontational stance with Russia: the centrist position, as espoused by President Leonid Kuchma, is to seek to cooperate with Moscow while looking for alternative solutions. (Ukrainian public opinion is more favorably inclined toward cooperation with Russia than is elite opinion.)[22]

Ukrainian nationalist politicians are pressing the government to speed up the development of a new port at Odessa in order to ship oil from the Caucasus (from Georgian ports) once it comes on stream. The most bizarre example of this line of thinking is a proposal to build a *south-north* pipeline across Turkey to bring Persian Gulf oil to the Black Sea (bizarre because Turkey is also pressing ahead with a plan to build a *north-south* pipeline across the same route to ferry Caspian Sea oil to the Mediterranean!). These alternatives are going to be much more expensive than Russian oil and gas, and if Ukraine has problems paying off its Russian suppliers, how can it hope to pay for more costly supplies? In the meantime, Ukraine has been trying to diversify its energy imports by buying oil and gas from Kazakhstan and Turkmenistan, in order to introduce some price competition to Russian suppliers, and also in the hope that the central Asians will be willing to accept barter deliveries in lieu of cash. Ukraine imported 5 million tons of oil from Kazakhstan in 1998, more than double the 2.3 million tons planned for 1997, which was in turn one-third more than the amount purchased in 1996.[23] (In 1997 Ukraine bought about 6 million tons from Russia.) Kazakhstan accepted food and steel goods in partial payment. However, one should recall that Ukraine tried to diversify its gas supplies in 1993 by buying from Turkmenistan, but ran up unpaid bills of $1.1 billion, which caused Turkmenistan to stop deliveries.[24] (Since 1994 Gazprom has refused to allow Turkmenistan to negotiate gas deliveries with any other European customers.) Neither Kazakh oil nor Turkmen gas are really strategic alternatives to Russian supplies, since they are currently shipped through the Russian domestic pipe network and thus potentially hostage to changes in Russian quota and transit tariff policies. The alternative supply argument only really makes sense if one expects Russia to exert crude political blackmail, threatening to cut off supplies unless exorbitant prices are paid, or if one expects civil disorder in Russia and hence a breakdown in supplies. These are possible but unlikely developments, and it is doubtful whether Ukraine is rich enough to be able to insure itself against such risks.

For its part, in 1996 Russia's Gazprom began work on a new $3.5 billion pipeline, which will carry gas from the Yamal field in northern Siberia across Belarus to Poland and Germany. This is the first new pipeline, oil or gas, to be built by Russia for fifteen years. Yamal, with 70 billion cubic meters capacity, will partly reduce Russia's dependency on the Ukrainian line—but even when Yamal comes on stream, Russia will not want to jeopardize the exports flowing across Ukraine.[25]

Further north, Surgutneftegaz won permission to build three new oil-handling facilities in the Leningrad Oblast, on the shores of the Gulf of Finland, which are intended to reduce the company's reliance on the costly ports in the Baltic republics. The new Primorsk port, with a capacity of 45 million tons, could generate fees of $1.5 billion a year.[26] LUKoil is building another terminal in the Arctic port of Murmansk, and for that reason turned down an offer from Lithuania to help finance the reconstruction of the Klaipeda terminal in return for a 10 percent equity share.[27] YuKOS, however, said they were interested in the Klaipeda project.

The Southern Frontier

The energy environment that Russia faces on its southern frontier is quite different. The vast mineral resources of Kazakhstan and the Caspian Sea hold out the prospect of a future cornucopia for central Asia.[28] Some of the more extravagant claims for the region's energy reserves may be exaggerated. Central Asia and the Caucasus probably hold about 5 percent of the world's oil and gas reserves, while Russia itself holds 20 percent.[29] Still, the energy wealth may be sufficient to ensure the economic viability of the newly independent states of the region.

However, these landlocked countries are currently dependent on rail links and pipelines that cross Russian territory. Kazakhstan in particular is almost totally dependent on routes across Russia for its oil and gas exports. The two main pipelines out of the Caspian Sea basin traverse war zones in the secessionist regions of Chechnya and Abkhazia (in Georgia) and around Nagorno-Karabakh (in Azerbaijan). Apart from the question of export routes, Russian involvement in the development of the Caspian Sea fields involves complex negotiations with the other four littoral states over the legal status of the sea, and with a host of international corporations involved in development projects in the region.

Kazakhstan has been struggling since attaining independence to move out from Russia's shadow and develop its oil and gas resources. The long and largely unguarded border with Russia and the presence of a 30 percent Russian minority inside Kazakhstan mean that Kazakhstan's leaders must keep looking over their shoulders at Russian reactions. Kazakhstan was severely hit by the economic disruption caused by the Soviet collapse: oil production has actually fallen, from 21 million tons in 1991 to 15 million tons in 1995.[30] Kazakhstan's economy is still heavily interdependent with that of Russia. Oil mined in eastern Kazakhstan is processed in Russian refineries; Kazakhstan's own refineries in the east of the country import oil from Siberia. Kazakhstan exports gas from its western Karachaganak field to Russia, but must import gas from Uzbekistan and Turkmenistan for its eastern cities. Still, Kazakhstan has pressed ahead with an ambitious privatization program which has seen many energy installations leased to foreign contractors—selected from all around the globe, from Argentina to South Korea (but not from Russia). In 1997 China won a share in projects to develop the Aktyubinsk and Uzen oil fields, with combined investment projected at $5 billion.

Russia has threatened (and implemented) cuts in access to export pipelines for Kazakhstan in order to win shares in the major energy development projects. In 1995 this tactic won Russia's Gazprom a 15 percent share in the Karachaganak field, which was being developed by British Gas and the Italian Agip company. Russian obstructionism helped cause Kazak gas output to slide from 4.2 billion cubic meters in 1991 to 2.5 billion in 1995. Russian policy toward Kazakhstan is mediated, if not actually driven, by the major energy corporations: Sidanko and LUKoil compete to supply Kazakhstan's Pavlodar refinery and Transneft negotiates quotas for the pipeline network.

Kazakhstan's main hope for revival has been the giant Tengiz field, on which Chevron has now spent $800 million through the joint venture, Tengizchevroil. Chevron holds 45 percent, the Kazakh partner Tengizmunaigaz 25 percent, and Mobil 25 percent. In January 1997 LUKoil bought 5 percent in the consortium for $200 million. In 1992 the international Caspian Pipeline Consortium (CPC) was formed by Kazakhstan, Russia, and Oman to build a new 1,000-mile, $2-billion pipeline from Tengiz to Astrakhan in Russia and on to the Black Sea port of Novorossiisk, with a projected capacity of 70 million tons a year.[31] Chevron found the economics of the pipeline unattractive, and work was delayed. The CPC was restructured in 1996, cutting Chevron's share to 15 percent and virtually removing Omani participation. The Russian government now holds 24 percent, Rosneft (in a joint venture with Shell) 7.5 percent, and LUKoil (in a joint venture with ARCO) 12.5 percent.[32] Pending construction of the pipeline, Kazakhstan has been shipping some oil by tanker to Azerbaijan. In 1996 Kazakhstan took some other steps to diversify its transport options—opening rail links to China and Iran and starting modest oil exports through the latter. Kazakhstan hopes to produce 26 million tons of oil in 1997, of which 7 million will be exported through Russia, 1 million through Baku, and 1 million in a swap deal with Iran (delivered across the border in railcars).[33] Sarah Lloyd concludes that "Kazakhstan's dream of oil wealth is unlikely to become a reality for at least another five years."[34]

Azerbaijan has been able to pursue a more independent line than Kazakhstan, although in the last two years steps have been taken to bring in more Russian partners. In September 1994 Azerbaijan signed the "contract of the century" with a group of twelve leading oil companies (the Azerbaijan International Operating Consortium, or AIOC), a deal which envisions the investment of $8 billion over the next decade in developing the Azeri and Chirag offshore fields. The AIOC includes British Petroleum (BP) (17 percent), Amoco (17 percent), the State Oil Company of Azerbaijan (10 percent) and Russia's LUKoil (10 percent). In November 1995 a second consortium, the Caspian International Operating Company (CIOC), was created to develop the Karabakh offshore field. A majority (62 percent) stake in the CIOC is held by a joint venture of LUKoil and Agip, with Pennzoil holding 30 percent. A third consortium, for the Shah-Deniz field, formed in June 1996, granted 10 percent to LUKoil and 10 percent to the Iranian National Oil Company; BP and Statoil have 25 percent each.

The Caspian Sea has some 4 billion tons of proven oil reserves, and the AIOC should be producing 35 million tons a year by the year 2010. However, as J. M. Keynes noted, there is a difference between the short run and the long run. Due to the disruption caused by the Soviet collapse, Azerbaijani oil output actually fell from 15 million tons in 1991 to 9 million in 1996.[35] Only in October 1997 did the first oil from the offshore Chirag field start to come ashore at Baku, and this will be a mere 5 million tons for the next couple of years. It remains unclear how this "early oil" will be shipped to the west. The initial plan is to send half through the Russian pipeline that traverses Chechnya to Novorossiisk, and half across Georgia to Supsa. (The dual export plan was reportedly a U.S. idea.)[36] Azerbaijan's main hopes for export access lie in the building of new large capacity pipelines across Georgia, and then possibly through Turkey to the Mediterranean (obviating the need to ship the oil across the Black Sea). Developing energy resources is a risky business: the outbreak of conflict in the Caucasus, or a drop in the international oil price (which could follow the lifting of sanctions on Iraq), could undermine the attractiveness of these projects for Western corporations.

Pending the development of their oil and gas fields, the central Asians are still to a degree dependent on Russia for their economic development. Intra-CIS trade still accounted for 55 percent of the Central Asian countries' exports in 1995 (down from 72 percent in 1990).[37] Thus Russia accounted for 45 percent of Kazakhstan's $4.7 billion exports in 1995, and 48 percent of her $3.8 billion imports.[38] China's total turnover with Kazakhstan that year was only about $600 million. Some 50 percent of Uzbekistan's $6 billion trade turnover is with Russia, followed by 15 percent with Kazakhstan. (Eighty percent of Uzbekistan's export earnings are from raw cotton sales.)

There are several contentious aspects to the exploitation of the Caspian Sea basin. There are arguments over who owns the resources in the sea, over how to forge the business consortia to develop them, and over how to export the oil to the world market.

There is a serious and unresolved dispute over the legal status of the Caspian Sea itself. Moscow and Teheran wanted the sea to be treated as a lake from the point of view of international law, meaning that the exploitation of its resources beyond a coastal strip must be the joint endeavor of all the littoral states. Azerbaijan and Turkmenistan have argued that the sea should be divided up between the littoral states by extending the sovereign territory of each country outwards until it meets the others in the middle, a solution which would give them exclusive rights to the most promising offshore fields. Kazakhstan has wavered between the two positions. Turkmenistan has also shifted from its earlier pro-Azeri stance to an ambiguous position, and in July 1997 challenged Azerbaijani plans to develop the disputed Kyapaz field. Russia tried to compromise by expanding the allowed coastal strip to seventy-five kilometers, but this has not affected the Azeri-Turkmen position. Most of Azerbaijan's offshore fields, unlike those of Kazakhstan, lie more than seventy-five kilometers offshore. In a bid to appease the Russians, Azerbaijan granted LUKoil a 33 percent stake in the Karabakh field and a 10 percent stake in the Chirag and Shah-Deniz fields. Russia started to shift its position in response to Azerbaijan's willingness to grant Russian companies a share in development projects. Since April 1998, Russia has been agreeable to national subdivision of the seabed while still favoring joint management of the waters and fisheries. In part this shift was the result of a realization that contrary to prior expectations quite rich energy deposits probably lay in the northern, potentially Russian zone. Iran was still holding out for splitting the seabed into five equal portions—since the Iranian share based on coastline, the International Convention for Seabed Rights, would be only 10 percent.

Assuming that the development of the basin overcomes these problems, there is still the question of which export route to adopt. Russia, Georgia, and Iran are the most likely routes. China and Afghanistan are long-shot possibilities.

The Eastern Option

In 1997 China announced a $9.5 billion deal with Kazakhstan to build a 3,700-mile pipeline from West Kazakhstan to central China. This would be the longest pipeline in history, would have to cross desolate and difficult terrain, and would transit the politically sensitive region of Xinjiang, which has an active Muslim (Uighur) separatist movement. It is too early to say whether work on this pipeline will actually begin in the immediate future. Turkmenistan is also pondering a natural gas pipeline to China, and there is talk of both oil and gas pipelines traversing some eight hundred miles across Afghanistan to Pakistan. However, the Taliban do not strike one as the most welcoming of business partners, and the November 1997 murder of four U.S. oil executives in Pakistan does not augur well for that country as an oil export hub.

The Russian Routes

"Early oil" from the Caspian is now being pumped via the existing Russian pipelines to Novorossiisk, in accordance with a January 1996 agreement signed with the AIOC. It is thought that 200,000 tons will be pumped in 1997, rising to 1.5 million in 1998 and 5 million tons thereafter.[39] There are two pipelines in 1999—a northern route that links up with the Astrakhan-Novorossiisk line, and the more direct line across Chechnya. These existing pipelines can handle the "early oil," but a new pipeline with capacity of 40–50 million tons must be built as soon as possible. Most of the central Asians would rather not put all their export eggs in the Russian basket, but Russia is keen to see the new pipeline built across her territory.

The interdependence of oil and politics is vividly illustrated by the case of Chechnya. Many—including former Security Council secretary Aleksandr Lebed—believe that the Chechen war was started in December 1994 by financial interests keen to get a piece of the oil action bubbling up in Azerbaijan. The timing seems more than coincidental. For three years Moscow had effectively ignored Chechnya's November 1991 declaration of independence, but then it sent Russian forces into the republic just two months after the signing of the "deal of the century" in Baku. Chechnya has its own modest oil field and a large refinery (with 19-million-ton capacity), and more importantly it sits astride the main export pipeline from Azerbaijan. Somehow or other, the Chechen pipeline continued to operate through the first year of the Russian war, although the line was tapped in literally hundreds of places in order to provide fuel for backyard oil refineries. The line appears to have ceased operations sometime in 1996. The signing of the Khasavyurt treaty in August 1996 paved the way for the withdrawal of Russian forces by January 1997 and the establishment of de facto Chechen independence.

Throughout 1997 sporadic negotiations continued between Grozny and Moscow, with the latter holding out the carrot of economic cooperation but the former insisting on Russian recognition of Chechen independence. Boris Berevozski was brought into the government as deputy secretary of the Security Council, ostensibly to forge a business deal which would lure Chechnya into recognizing some sort of status within the Russian Federation. Berezovski's deal failed to materialize, although the pipeline itself was rehabilitated and oil began flowing again in December. However, exasperated by continuing terroristic incidents, in September Russian first deputy prime minister Boris Nemtsov proposed building a new $220-million oil pipeline bypassing Chechnya. (Just as in 1997 a new eighty-kilometer railway was built linking Dagestan with Rostov without crossing Chechen territory.)

Nemtsov's proposal was not broadly supported within the Russian government. The Kremlin still has not given up on the idea of keeping Chechnya within the Russian Federation, and sees the transshipment of oil across the republic as a carrot which can be used to lure it into accepting some sort of status within the Russian Federation.[40] Russia's problems with separatist violence are not confined to Chechnya. Both the Chechen and the northern pipelines transit Dagestan, where there are increasingly frequent clashes between the Chechen minority and other ethnic groups. The Lezgin minority, some one million strong, live astride the Russian-Azeri border and also have an incipient separatist movement. (Lezgin activists were charged with setting the 1994 bomb in the Baku subway.)

The Georgian Route

Haidar Aliev, president of Azerbaijan since 1993, has pursued a clear-cut and so far successful strategy to overcome Azerbaijan's diplomatic isolation. First, to develop the Caspian Sea fields he has encouraged an influx of foreign companies—from as many countries as possible, in order to dilute the Russian component and increase diplomatic leverage on Russia. Second, he has vigorously developed a political and commercial partnership with Turkey. Ankara is seen as the most loyal ally for Baku for ethnic and geopolitical reasons: it is the traditional adversary of the three countries causing problems for Azerbaijan (Armenia, Russia, and Iran). Turkey has the added advantage of being an important ally of the United States, a NATO member with U.S. aircraft monitoring the Iraqi northern no-fly zone from Turkish bases.

The size of deposits found in Azerbaijan's offshore fields has proved disappointing, however. That, together with a shortage of drilling equipment in the Caspian Sea and worries over the slump in the world oil price after the fall 1997 Asian crisis, led oil companies to push back their plans for the construction of a high-volume export pipeline. October 1998, which had been widely regarded as the deadline for announcing the route of the new pipeline, came and went with no announcement being made. Oil companies are dubious about the commercial viability of the project unless and until oil prices recover: the U.S. government has been insistent that it would encourage but not directly subsidize the construction of the pipeline.

The central symbol of the Azeri-Turkish partnership has been the new five-hundred-mile, $1 billion export pipeline from Baku to Supsa in Georgia, now under construction, and its proposed extension south to Ceyhan on Turkey's Mediterranean coast. Ending the pipeline at Supsa would mean that oil would have to be exported beyond the Black Sea by ship through the Bosphorus. In 1995 Turkey declared new limits on tankers passing through the Bosphorus, arguing that the risk of ecological disaster was too high. Russia claimed that this was a violation of the 1936 Montreux international convention guaranteeing free passage through the straits.

The proposed Supsa-Ceyhan pipeline is just as much a political as an economic project for Aliev. Aliev hopes that bringing in outside powers, from Turkey to the United States, will give him the leverage he needs to bring about a resolution of the Karabakh conflict—which remains the number one political challenge for the Azerbaijani president. To some extent, the political attractiveness of the project (for Azerbaijan) is more important than its attractiveness in terms of economic interests.

The proposed Turkish pipeline skirts several conflict zones—in Armenia, Georgia, and inside Turkey itself (the rebellious provinces of Kurdistan). The main question mark over the viability of the southern route is the stand-off over Nagorno-Karabakh. Renewed conflict over Karabakh could trigger a full-scale war between Armenia and Azerbaijan, or could involve attacks on the pipeline which passes close to Armenian-held territory.

The Karabakh problem surfaced in 1988, when fighting broke out for con-trol over that Armenian enclave inside Azerbaijan. The conflict saw pogroms and the flight of one million refugees from the two countries, and was sup-pressed by Soviet troops. Open fighting broke out again in 1992, and the 125,000 Karabakh Armenians, aided by volunteers from Armenia and the covert delivery of $1 billion worth of Russian military hardware, were able to drive back Azeri forces and occupy six additional districts, amounting to over 10 percent of Azerbaijani territory. Karabakh proclaimed itself an inde-pendent republic, but it has not been recognized by any country. A shaky truce has held since 1994. Azerbaijan and Turkey have maintained a block-ade of Armenia since 1992 pending resolution of the Karabakh situation. The Armenians are reluctant to give up the additional conquered territory around Karabakh because in the south it provides the sole land bridge between Karabakh and Armenia. In the north it overlooks the main road, rail, and pipeline links between Baku and Georgia, and the risk of Armen-ian terrorist attacks on the Azeri-Georgian pipeline are obvious—not least because Azerbaijan is likely to use some of its oil revenues to re-equip its army and possible try to retake Karabakh by force at some point in the future. Robert Kocharian, the former president of Karabakh who was appointed prime minister of Armenia itself in March 1997, was reportedly fond of saying "no peace, no oil."

Due to the large Armenian diaspora in the United States, American policy has generally favored the Armenian side. The 1992 Freedom Support Act (section 907) introduced a ban on aid to Azerbaijan unless it revokes its blockade of Armenia. However, a powerful pro-Baku lobby has now emerged in the United States, fueled by a combination of oil corporation dollars and ex–Cold War Warriors who would like to see a band of inde-pendent and economically robust states emerge between Russia and Iran.[41] Russia, meanwhile, seems to be firm in its historic alliance with Armenia, signing a new security treaty in August 1997. However, at no point has Rus-sia endorsed the idea of Karabakh independence, since it adheres to the principle that all the post-Soviet borders are final.

In October 1997 there seemed to the prospect of a breakthrough in the Karabakh deadlock at the Council of Europe heads of state meeting.[42] Pres-idents Yeltsin and Chirac persuaded Armenia's Ter-Petrosyan to move ahead with negotiations for a "step-by-step" solution, under which a deci-sion on Karabakh's status would be postponed, while in the meantime

Armenian forces withdraw from the occupied districts around Karabakh, refugees are allowed to go home, and Azerbaijan lifts its blockade of Armenia. Ter-Petrosyan said on 26 September 1997 that Armenia must be ready to make "serious concessions" if it is to become a "normal country" and if Karabakh is to avoid the fate of the Krajina Serbs—driven out of Croatia in 1995 while the international community, exasperated by Serbia's uncompromising stance, did nothing to stop the ethnic cleansing. Ter-Petrosyan's willingness to compromise cost him the Armenian presidency. He lost the support of his defense and security establishment and was forced to resign in February 1998. He was replaced as president by Robert Kocharian, formerly the head of the self-declared Republic of Nagorno-Karabakh.

Georgia has secessionist problems of its own. It lost control of the provinces of South Ossetia and Abkhazia in 1992, causing four hundred thousand refugees to flee into the remainder of Georgia. Bitter fighting continued in Abkhazia for another year, with Russian forces supporting the numerically outnumbered Abkhaz forces. (Russian assistance explains how 125,000 Abkhaz could defeat the army of Georgia, a nation of 7 million.) Russian peacekeepers are still in place in the two regions, and Russia has forced various concessions from Georgia in return for promises to help bring the conflicts to an end. Georgia reluctantly joined the CIS in 1993 and signed an agreement allowing Russia to keep four military bases on Georgian territory: Russian troops also police the Georgian border with Turkey (and with Chechnya). Tbilisi has got little from Russia in return: even promises to facilitate the return of Georgian refugees to Abkhazia have not been implemented. There may also be trouble brewing in the southern Georgian province of Javakhetiya, which sits astride the proposed Ceyhan pipeline route, and where 55 percent of the 230,000 population are ethnic Armenians.[43]

It seems clear that the Russian military has been fishing in troubled waters in Georgia, manipulating its peacekeeping role to maintain instability in the region. Many Georgians are exasperated with this state of affairs, and hope that more countries—such as Ukraine—can be persuaded to become involved in peacekeeping operations, possibly in Karabakh and Moldova as well as inside Georgia.

Hopes that Turkey would enter the area as a power capable of deflecting Russian influence have not yet been realized, in part because of the ongoing struggle within Turkey between secularist and Islamic forces. Also, Russian relations with Turkey remain good, and during a December 1997 visit Chernomyrdin signed off on a deal to build a gas pipeline across the floor of the Black Sea, to boost Russian gas supplies to Turkey from 6 billion to 30 billion cubic meters per year by 2010. (Currently Turkey buys Russian gas via a small pipeline across Bulgaria.)

Overall, the geography and conflictual geopolitics of the region mean that Russia still plays a pivotal role as the dominant power in the region. Energy specialist Robert Ebel concludes that, in the Caspian region, "There can be no game unless Russia is invited to play."[44]

Iran

The potential involvement of Iran in the export of Caspian basin resources is yet another complicating factor. Iran is generally cool toward Azerbaijan because of the presence of a 10-million-strong Azeri minority in Western Iran, with possible irredentist aspirations, and toward Turkey. Presumably operating on the principle that my enemies' enemy is my friend, Iran has developed a good relationship with Armenia, and provides the primary land transport route to that country. Iran has sided with Russia in the dispute over the legal status of the Caspian Sea, and is buying Russian technology to equip the Bushehr nuclear reactor.

In 1996 the U.S. Congress passed the Iran and Libya Sanctions Act, calling for the imposition of sanctions on foreign firms that invest more than $20 million in Iranian energy industries. There are currently three central Asian projects that involve Iran. Turkmenistan plans to build a pipeline to export natural gas across Iran to Turkey. The $2.5-billion project will involve a two-hundred-kilometer pipeline from Korpedzhe to Kurdkui to link Turkmenistan's gas field to the Iranian network, enabling Turkmenistan to export 3 billion cubic meters annually, rising to 8 billion by the year 2006. Second, the Chinese-Kazak deal mentioned above also envisions some transshipment across Iran. The focus of attention in the United States, however, is a $2-billion Franco-Russian deal to develop an Iranian offshore gas field.[45] The latter is the most likely target for U.S. sanctions, since it involves the direct development of Iranian resources. The partners in the plan include Russia's Gazprom, Total of France, and Malaysia's Petronas. The whole question of U.S. efforts to impose legal sanctions on foreign companies (extra-territoriality) is a bone of contention between Washington and the European Union, mainly because of the earlier Helms-Burton Act, which extended sanctions to foreign companies investing in Cuba. News of the Iranian gas deal leaked just as Gazprom was preparing to raise $2 billion on the international bond market. This was ostensibly to fund its Yamal pipeline, and not the Iranian project, but it was nevertheless "money that will go right into the company's coffers just as it is preparing to write the Iranians a fat check."[46] Gazprom preemptively rejected a $750-million U.S. Eximbank loan that had been agreed in 1994.[47] Gazprom chairman, Rem Vyakhirev, said: "The whole world trusts us. . . . Why should we put up with idiotic conditions?"

Strong ties with Iran seem to be a policy that unites most of the various actors who shape Russian foreign policy. The military lobby can hope to sell arms to Iran, and see it as a handy counterweight to U.S. influence in the region. The Russian atomic energy ministry is building a nuclear reactor at Bushehr and looks forward to business worth more than $1 billion a year. Oil and gas companies can also look forward to lucrative contracts in rehabilitating Iran's ailing oil industry infrastructure. LUKoil, because of its heavy involvement in Azeri offshore projects, is thought to be wary of the pro-Iran policy.

COMPETING PARADIGMS

What patterns emerge from this complex web of geopolitical commitments and contentions? Most discussion of the energy-foreign policy nexus can be grouped into one or other of the following schools of thought. Some observers believe Russian policy is responding to the logic of an unfolding economic model: perhaps energy-dependency, perhaps liberalization, possibly a looting of the national treasury by a narrow group. Others see it as an ephiphenomenon of geopolitical necessity. Alternatively, policy may be tossed from one side to another in response to pressure from competing groups, none of them capable of providing it with a clear direction.

The Kuwaitization Model

According to this broad school, Russia's vast endowment in natural resources means that its comparative advantage in the international division of labor lies in the exploitation of its energy fields. The boom in Russian exports since 1993 has been driven by sales of oil and gas, and by sales of other minerals such as steel and aluminum whose processing is dependent on cheap energy.

Proponents of "Kuwaitization" argue that an energy boom is the best hope (perhaps the only hope) for Russia's economic renaissance, especially if contracts for pipe and machinery are placed with Russian engineering plants rather than Western suppliers. Opponents, whose ranks include Moscow mayor Yurii Luzhkov, argue that such a strategy will condemn Russia to subordinate status as a "raw materials appendage" of Western multinational corporations, who will deny Russia a fair share of the proceeds and will not allow Russian engineering plants to pick up supply contracts.[48] For the patriotic opponents of Kuwaitization, production-sharing agreements are an infringement of Russian sovereignty, something which Iran and Saudi Arabia have refused to deal with since the 1970s. Hence the Duma's glacially slow adoption of PSA legislation and subsequent project authorization, in heroic defense of Russia's "economic security."

The Kuwaitization model implies that Russia is a passive victim of international economic forces. However, foreign investors have been very slow to penetrate the domestic energy industry. Instead, domestically based corporations have emerged as powerful forces, subsidizing regional authorities and providing some 40 percent of federal government revenues.[49] Accordingly, this paradigm, shorn of its negative political rhetoric, in fact implies that Russia's oil and gas corporations will play a dominant role in determining Russia's general policy toward the "near abroad," seeking to keep out potential competition from Caspian Sea fields and/or to maneuver themselves into a share in those projects.

The Liberalization Model

For the Gaidar school, the overwhelming priority in 1992 was to unleash market forces and remove state restrictions on economic activity. Any efforts by the state to "pick winners" and run an industrial policy would merely allow the old vested interests of the command economy to creep in through the back door, and would be a waste of resources. The government's goals were to be focused on the mantra of "liberalization, stabilization, and privatization," and success in these measures would be in the general interest of Russian society. The policy was delayed and distorted by opposition from entrenched interests, but supported by international financial institutions, which often made new loans conditional on progress in these three areas.

Despite being unpopular with the general population, and having few discernible bases of support within political and economic elites, the Yeltsin-backed governments of Gaidar and later Chubais were able to ram through most of the liberal agenda.[50] Landmarks in the policy included the removal of oil export quotas in 1995 and the introduction of the loans-for-shares scheme in the fall of 1995, which was a way of transferring some of the major oil companies into private ownership in the absence of Duma legislation authorizing the second wave of cash privatization. Despite the extensive liberalization, there is still plenty of scope for bargaining with government agencies. Although oil export quotas were formally abolished, at IMF insistence, in 1996, companies are still only allowed to export an average of 27 percent of their oil production, and the criteria for awarding access to pipelines are still rather opaque (with Rosneft allowed to export 52 percent of its oil).[51] Tax arrears are another bone of contention. Oil and gas enterprises owe some 19 trillion rubles to the federal budget as of late 1997—but in turn are owed more than 100 trillion rubles by their customers, leaving plenty of scope for bargaining over offsets.[52]

The defenders of liberalization argue that market reform offers the best hope—the only hope—of economic revival in Russia. They note that Russian consumers seem to prefer the full shelves (even with thinner wallets) of the market economy to the economics of shortage which prevailed prior to 1992. Ordinary Russians relish the opportunity to purchase imported goods, and the freedom to change rubles into dollars. At international level, liberalization has won Russia membership (of a sort) in the exclusive G7 club and the prospect of entry into the World Trade Organization. The considerable progress toward liberal, market policies implies that contrary to the Kuwaitization model Russian policy has not been captured by a single powerful group of interests.

The Rent-Seeking Model

A cynical position is to argue that the Russian oil and gas industry is a classic example of the triumph of rent-seeking over profit-seeking.[53] A narrow circle of elites were fortuitously positioned by the Soviet collapse to loot Russia's energy resources, and they will continue to do so until the cookie jar is empty. The oil and gas industry had been built up under central planning, with decades of costly investment. The Soviet collapse shattered the planning system that channeled resources into the sector, but left the infrastructure intact—and left a small number of managerial and political elites with the opportunity to divert the proceeds from oil and gas exports without having to worry about ensuring the renewal of the production infrastructure.

Rent-seeking involves the exploitation of a monopolistic position, and is contrasted with profit-seeking, which involves the pursuit of wealth in a competitive market environment. The Russian rentier elite enjoys a monopoly in terms of its political access to the oil industry infrastructure and its consequent ability to skim revenues from oil and gas exports.

The rent-seeking model implies that the current situation is transitory. Sooner or later the infrastructure will decay, production will fall below the point at which domestic and foreign consumers can be satisfied, and the available rents will start to evaporate. At that juncture the elite will/should shift over to a nationally managed policy for development of the energy sector (Kuwaitization) or will be obliged to open up to market forces, including access for new owners.

The "Russian Bear" Paradigm

Some argue that behind the apparent chaos of governmental decision-making one can discern the inexorable logic of national interests.[54] Russia is still a great power, with geopolitical interests stretching at least across the "near abroad." However, Russia's military forces are in disarray, and the international community will not allow Russia to use military force to rebuild its sphere of influence. If Russia can no longer rely on military means to project its power, it must thus turn to economic levers of control. Hence the widely cited May 1996 theses on Russian policy toward the "near abroad," published by the non-governmental Moscow-based Council on Foreign and Defense Policy, urged that Russia should avoid military methods and should instead use its economic muscle to become the "natural" center of the CIS.[55]

In this context, Russia's energy corporations are seen as a surrogate for Russia's deep-rooted national interests. Russia is energy rich, while its Western neighbors are energy poor, and its eastern neighbors are dependent on Russian goodwill for the easiest access to international markets. Russia is seen as exploiting the energy debts of those countries to extract political concessions and perhaps acquire equity shares in their energy industries. In response, the newly independent countries engage in efforts to develop alternative energy supplies, and to find alternative routes to world markets, which are seen as vital to ensuring the real sovereignty of the newly independent states. Some commentators who see matters from this geopolitical perspective point to the emergence in 1997 of a GUAM axis (Georgia-Ukraine-Azerbaijan-Moldova), uniting the southern tier of countries in their mutual determination to check Moscow's erratic policies.[56]

The Pluralism School

A fifth approach is to look at Russian policy-making as an open-ended process in which rival groups compete to influence policies as they flow through the decision-making procedure. In this "garbage can" paradigm, the dominant picture is one of fragmentation and confusion, since the tightly integrated decision-making process of the Soviet era has given way to a chaotic free-for-all.

With the dissolution of central authority, no clear decision-making procedure can be discerned at all.[57] There is no clear division of power between the Duma and the executive branch. Sometimes the executive branch chooses to implement policy by decree and ignores the legislature. At other times, the government defers to the Duma and seeks a legislative framework for its actions. The policies emanating from the governmental machinery are often at odds with decrees coming out of the presidential apparatus. Government policy itself can be rather schizophrenic, with the eight deputy prime ministers espousing a broad range of agendas. New agencies such as the Security Council and Defense Council have been created, but they have had little success in imposing order on the situation. Foreign policy toward the CIS often seems to have been driven by independent actors on the ground—from military commanders in the Caucasus and Trans-Dniester to energy corporations like Gazprom and LUKoil. (For example, nobody has admitted responsibility for the transfer of $1 billion worth of weapons to Armenia.) Adding to the confusion has been the decentralization of power from Moscow to the regions. The newly empowered presidents and governors of Russia's regions have considerable leeway to try to run their own foreign policy, from attracting foreign investors to managing relations with neighboring states.[58]

This all amounts to pluralism run amok, where the "decision-making process" seems to be reinvented for each decision. In order to understand policy, whether it be the decision to build the Primorsk oil terminal on the Baltic coast, or the decision to build a new pipeline around Chechnya, one must construct a separate model for each issue, listing the interests for and against *and* the institutions through which they try to operate.

The Policy Process

There do seem to be some regularities in the policy process. For example, the Foreign Ministry seems able to exercise more control over policy toward the "far abroad" than toward the CIS. Russian policy toward China, Iraqi sanctions, or NATO expansion is clearly espoused and skillfully pursued, and correspondingly seems to enjoy a fairly high degree of consensus among Russian elites and (to the extent that they care) the Russian public at large. The same can not be said for virtually any aspect of policy toward the CIS. This is presumably a reflection of the historical continuity of the foreign policy-making apparatus vis-à-vis the outside world, and of the need to create institutions (and policies) from scratch to deal with the CIS. Foreign policy toward the "far abroad" becomes somewhat more contentious when one moves from the political to the economic arena. Issues such as IMF lending or access for foreign investors generate considerable controversy.

The government has had some successes in enforcing a single policy toward the CIS—in stubbornly pushing ahead with trade liberalization and the introduction of the "ruble corridor" in the summer of 1993, for example—which, it should be noted, occurred during a period when Yeltsin was in the ascendant and heading for a showdown with the Duma. Since then, some of the fiercest "under the carpet" arguments between rival factions of Russia's ruling elite have taken place over policy toward the "near abroad." The energy lobby pushed for the Russian state to take over responsibility for all the CIS debts, past, present, and future, and generally favored cutting back on deliveries to CIS countries unable to pay for them. However, people like First Deputy Prime Minister Oleg Soskovets, a product of the metallurgy lobby, believed that it was important to preserve Russia's market share in the CIS, even if it meant selling energy to CIS members at less than world prices (and selling to customers who could not pay), both for political reasons and because many Russian manufacturing plants were dependent on supplies from Ukraine and Kazakhstan (and vice versa). Overall, however, "with regard to the CIS, Russia seems to be in a state of confusion and helplessness."[59] It has been singularly unsuccessful in mobilizing support from CIS countries in its diplomatic initiatives—most notably, in its failure to prevent NATO expansion.

Clearly, the energy corporations play a large if not dominant role in shaping Russian foreign policy toward the "near abroad." As an outsider, one can only guess exactly how this works in practice. It does not look as if there is any organized, structured process through which policy is formulated. Rather, it seems to be driven by the same process of informal bargaining that has come to dominate most of Russian domestic policy-making. It is hard to say where domestic politics ends and "foreign policy" begins. The deals and favors which oil companies trade with government officials with respect to foreign projects are seamlessly connected to the same process in the domestic arena. Bargaining ranges over a broad gamut of activities: from sweetheart privatization deals to export pipeline quotas; from tax arrear waivers to "goods credits" (*tovarnye kredity*) for farmers. The bargaining spills over into the political realm: the same corporations bankroll political campaigns and fund newspapers that energetically engage in mudslinging against hostile politicians.

Several general rules of the game seem to have emerged in recent years. First, there are strong elements of continuity. The vested interests resist efforts to disrupt the status quo, and have to be given something in order to induce them to accept a policy change. Note for example Gazprom's success in beating off the reformist challenge from First Deputy Prime Minister Boris Nemtsov, who took office in March 1997 with a pledge to break up the utility monopolies and introduce competitive pricing. Gazprom president Vyakhirev was explicit in rejecting Nemtsov's suggestions for political and not economic reasons: "We are not simply producing and selling gas. We are pursuing a popular, socially-oriented policy whose significance goes beyond narrow economic calculation."[60]

Second, the process of privatizing the remaining state-owned oil corporations, both in the 1995 loans-for-shares scheme and in the 1997 cash auctions, suggests that the good old Soviet principle of "an earring for each sister" still holds sway. That is, favors and special projects should be doled out in turn to the rival consortia. It was the feeling that this understanding was being violated—in favor of Vladimir Potanin's Oneksimbank (which controls Sidanko)—that triggered the bankers' attack on Chubais in 1998, an assault that later culminated in the removal of nearly all the Chubais appointees from the government.

Third, as the market economy takes root in Russia the autonomy of these companies vis-à-vis the government will tend to increase. The ability of these companies to access world capital markets means they are less dependent on financial support from the Russian government (in the form of allotted shares in World Bank financing for example).[61]

REFLECTIONS

Overall, Russia's foreign policy toward the "near abroad" is opportunistic rather than strategic, and is negative (blocking initiatives, stalling progress) rather than positive (creating new openings and developing new projects). Russia is not the source of the poverty and strife which has gripped much of the newly independent countries, but it is not doing much to alleviate the situation. Though weakened, Russia still has a broad variety of legal, political, military, and economic tools that it can and does deploy to advance its interests. The Russian energy corporations seem to play a dominant role in formulating and actually implementing Russian foreign policy in many crucial respects.

In this situation one can see the *potential* for the emergence of a neoimperialist strategy that suits both the oil companies and the "power ministries" who claim to speak for Russia's national security interests. In this scenario, in the future, Russian energy corporations and associated financial groups will move into the countries of the "near abroad" and gain political influence using the same tactics of financial manipulation that they have been perfecting inside Russia itself. Some countries are more vulnerable to this tactic than others. Such a neoimperialist strategy would receive broad support across the political spectrum in Russia. Even the liberal Boris Nemtsov suggested, shortly before his appointment to the government, that the solution to the Black Sea Fleet dispute lay in Russian businesses buying up property in Sevastopol since "Historical justice should be restored by capitalist methods."[62]

So far, however, most of the newly independent states have been quite successful at resisting these advances. Despite severe economic problems Kazakhstan and Ukraine seem more, not less, independent than they were five years ago. Even Belarus, in its own way, is pursuing an independent political path. Moreover, the "neoimperialist" strategy may generate countervailing tendencies. As Russia follows such a policy, it will find its relations shifting into a more positive direction, as Russian companies acquire a direct stake in the successful development of these neighboring economies, and cooperative rather than confrontational strategies will look more attractive.

Trends in 1997–1999 merely served to underline the impasse into which Russian energy policy had fallen after the collapse of the Soviet Union. Banking and energy interests continued to vie for control over an incompetent and ineffective government that proved unable to come up with a policy package that could attract foreign investors and revive energy production.

The 40 percent fall in the world oil price in 1997–98 undercut the profitability of Russian oil and gas companies and made them more dependent on waivers of tax arrears and other favors from the Russian government. Yeltsin's abrupt dismissal of Prime Minister Viktor Chernomyrdin in March 1998 removed their main protector in the corridors of power. However, the banking interests who were the energy lobby's main rival were engaged in a series of ugly conflicts among themselves as they struggled for favor in the privatization of the remaining assets in state hands—including the Rosneft oil company. The reformist government of Sergei Kirienko, who replaced

Chernomyrdin, proved ineffectual, and triggered the dramatic financial collapse of August 1998, which emptied the coffers of the leading Russian oligarchs and weakened their influence vis-à-vis state officials at national and regional levels. The radical devaluation of the ruble should serve to restore the profitability of the oil companies.

Unless and until Russia's political stalemate is resolved and an effective government is installed—something that will not happen before the June 2000 presidential elections, if then—one can expect the country to continue squandering its potential mineral wealth in a mess of political infighting and sleazy deal-making.

NOTES

1. *Izvestiia*, 27 December 1997.

2. Projecting back using world prices, IMF officials estimate that the implicit subsidy was about $18 billion in 1991, falling to $4 billion in 1992. B. V. Christensen, *The Russian Federation in Transition: External Developments* (Washington, D.C.: IMF Occasional Paper no. 111, February 1994) no. 111, p. 22; see also *Financial Relations among Countries of the Former Soviet Union* (Washington, D.C.: IMF Economic Reviews, February 1994), no. 1; S. Brown and M. Belkindas, "Who's Feeding Whom?" in *The Former Soviet Union in Transition* (Washington D.C.: Joint Economic Committee, 1993), pp. 163–182.

3. *Ekonomika i zhizn*, no. 17, April 1995, pp. 34–35.

4. B. Sidorov, "Dvustoronnie soglasheniya pomogut preodolet' torgovye problemy" ["Bilateral Agreements Will Help Overcome Trade Problems"], *Finansovye izvestiia*, 24 April 1993.

5. Ye. Vasil'chukh, "Obmen deneg" ["Money Exchange"], *Finansovye izvestiia*, 24 July 1993.

6. Itar-Tass, 10 November 1996.

7. *Russian Economic Trends*, vol. 4, no. 4 (February 1996), Working Center for Economic Reform, Government of the Russian Federation, table 77.

8. *Delovoi vtornik*, 20 February 1996, p. 1; Interfax, 19 March 1996.

9. *Ukrainian Economic Trends* (Kyiv: European Center for Macroeconomic Analysis of Ukraine, January 1997), p. 62.

10. V. Ilin, "Those Who Lost in the Baltic Seek a Northern Route," *Delovoi mir*, 30 April 1997, p. 1.

11. Ustina Markus, "Energy Crisis Spurs Ukraine and Belarus to Seek Help Abroad," *Transition* (OMRI), vol. 2, no. 9, 3 May 1996, pp. 14–18.

12. Interfax, 1 July 1997; *Delovoi mir*, 11–14 July 1997, p. 2.

13. Reuters, 20 January 1997; Interfax, 1 July 1997.

14. Denis Kirillov, "Rossiiskie neftyaniki vystupayut za ekonomicheskuyu integratsiyu s Belorusiei" ["Russian Oilmen Favor Economic Integration with Belarus"], *Finansovye izvestiia*, 8 April 1997, p. 2. LUKoil plans to invest $500 million to boost capacity from 7 million to 25 million tons: costs are half those of Russian refineries.

15. Markus, "Energy Crisis," p. 14.

16. Interview with Andranik Migranian in *Argumenty i fakty*, 23 June 1997, p. 3.

17. Vladimir Kucherenko, "By Developing Cooperation Russia Can Regain the CIS Market," *Rossiiskaya gazeta*, 26 September 1995.

18. *Rossiiskaya gazeta*, 26 September 1995, p. 1; Vladimir Kiselev, "They Will Not Get Down on Their Knees Anymore," *Obshchaya gazeta*, 22–28 May 1997.

19. DPA, 2 April 1997.

20. Russian Public Television (ORT), 18 July 1997.

21. Terrence Hoffman, Stephen Shenfield, and Dominique Arel, *Integration and Disintegration in the Former Soviet Union*, (Watson Institute, Brown University, occasional paper no. 30, 1997).

22. Polling data cited by Dominique Arel, "Does Culture Matter?" Paper presented at American Association for the Advancement of Slavic Studies, Seattle, Wash., 20 November 1997.

23. Jamestown *Monitor*, 17 October 1997.

24. Interfax, 7 May 1997.

25. Gazprom produced 601 billion cubic meters in 1996, 128 billion of which were exported outside the CIS, and another 80 sold inside the CIS. Reuters, 24 April 1997.

26. See Ilin, "Those Who Lost," Agence France Presse, 22 March 1997.

27. *OMRI Daily Digest*, 1 October 1996.

28. John Roberts, *Caspian Pipelines* (London: Royal Institute of International Affairs, 1996); Rajan Menon, *Treacherous Terrain: The Political and Security Dimensions of Energy Development in the Caspian Sea Zone* (Washington, D.C.: National Bureau of Asian Research, December 1997).

29. John Mitchell, *The New Geopolitics of Energy* (London: Royal Institute of International Affairs, 1996), p.63.

30. Sarah Lloyd, "Pipelines to Prosperity?" *International Spectator* (Rome), vol. 32, no. 1 (January 1997), pp. 53–70.

31. Interfax, 5 June 1997. For half the distance the existing line will be rebuilt, and for the remainder a parallel line will be built.

32. Rustam Narzikulov, "Perevorot v KTK" ["Coup in CPC"], *Nezavisimaya gazeta*, 17 December 1996.

33. *Nezavisimaya gazeta*, 9 April 1997.

34. Lloyd, "Pipelines," p. 62.

35. *Obshchaya gazeta*, 9 March 1997.

36. Robert Ebel, "Geopolitics and Pipelines," *Analysis of Current Events*, February 1997, pp. 1–3.

37. Yevgenniya Pis'mennaya, "Integratsiya SNG" ["CIS Integration"], *Finansovye izvestiia*, 21 January 1997.

38. *Kazakstan Country Report*, Informed Business Services, November 1997.

39. Itar-Tass, 27 March 1997.

40. Aleksei Chichkin, "Oil and the Chechen War," *Vek*, 16–22 February, 1996, p. 7; Igor Rotar, "Will Caspian Oil Flow over the 'Northern Variant'?" *Prism* (Jamestown Foundation), vol. 3, no. 12, part 3, 25 July 1997.

41. "Caspian Caviar," *Washington Times*, 28 July 1997; Ariel Cohen, "US policy in the Caucasus and Central Asia," Heritage Foundation Backgrounder, 24 July 1997; Thomas Goltz, "Catch 907 in the Caucasus," *National Interest*, no. 48 (summer 1997).

42. Emil Danielyan, "Nagorno-Karabakh: Imminent Breakthrough or Another Stalemate?" *Prism* (Jamestown Foundation), vol. 3, no. 18, 7 November 1997.

43. Ugur Akinci, "Javakhetia: The Bottleneck of Baku-Ceyhan Pipeline," *Silk Road*, vol. 1, no. 2 (December 1997).

44. Ebel, "Geopolitics," p. 3.

45. Sonia Winter, "US Questions Turkmen Gas Pipeline via Iran," *RFE/RL*, 16 October 1997.

46. *New York Times*, 16 October 1997; Jamestown *Monitor*, 2 and 17 October 1997.

47. The Eximbank has lent $135 million to Gazprom and $525 million to the Russian oil industry, with another $900 million lined up for the latter. *Journal of Commerce*, 18 April 1997.

48. Yurii Yeremenko, "Bessmyslennost eksporta dlya Rossii" ["Senseless Exports for Russia"], *Ekonomicheskaya gazeta*, no. 33 (August 1996); Oleg Cherkovets, "Bananovaya sudba" ["Banana Fate"], *Sovetskaya Rossiya*, 6 January 1996.

49. Konstantin Baskaev, "Rossiiskii TEK vykhodit na avanstsenu borby s neplatezhami" ["Russian Energy Complex at Center of Struggle with Arrears"], *Finansovye izvestiia*, 13 March 1997. Oil alone accounts for 20 percent: Itar-Tass, 14 September 1997.

50. Oleg Davydov, "Period liberalizatsii vneshnei torgovli zavershen" ["The Period of Trade Liberalization Is Completed"], *Segodnia*, 6 June 1996.

51. *Kommersant-Daily*, 17 October 1997.

52. *Finansovaya Rossia*, 9 October 1997.

53. Anders Aslund, "Reform versus 'Rent Seeking' in Russia's Economic Transformation," *Transition* (OMRI), vol. 2, no. 2, 26 January 1996, pp. 12–16.

54. William Odom and Robert Dujarric, *Commonwealth or Empire? Russia, Central Asia and the Transcaucasus* (Indianapolis: Hudson Institute, 1995).

55. "Vozroditsya li Soyuz?" ["Will the Union Be Reborn?"] *Nezavisimaya gazeta*, 23 May 1996, abridged translation published in *Transition*, vol. 2, no. 15, 26 July 1996, pp. 32–35.

56. Vadim Dubnov, "Gifts from Aliev," *Itogi*, no. 28, 15 July 1997, pp. 22–23. Some people, such as Andranik Migranian, even place Uzbekistan in this alliance. "SNG nachalo ili konets istorii?" ["CIS: The Beginning or the End of the Story?"] *Nezavisimaya gazeta*, 26 March 1997.

57. Neil Malcolm et al., eds., *Internal Factors in Russian Foreign Policy* (New York: Oxford University Press, 1996).

58. Foreign Ministry legal official Yakov Ostrovskii noted that many governors had signed agreements with foreign countries that "are not always in full compliance with Russia's legislation and international obligations, its political and economic interests." Interfax, 16 June 1995.

59. Aleksandr Bovin, "Rossiya vozvrashaetsya v mirovuyu politiku" ["Russia Returns to World Politics"], *Izvestiia*, 26 December 1997.

60. Rem Vyakhirev, "Ya tak prosto ne sdamsya" ["I Will Not Give Up That Easily"], *Nezavisimaya gazeta*, 25 March 1997.

61. LUKoil has raised $420 million through selling bonds over the past two years, and plans to raise another $780 million through global depositary receipts. *Bloomberg News*, 8 April 1997.

62. *Kommersant-Daily*, 18 February 1997.

8

Russian Interference in the Caspian Sea Region: Diplomacy Adrift

Jean-Christophe Peuch

After the collapse of the Soviet Union in late 1991, Russia lost control over a territory approximately equivalent to a quarter of its former empire. Although it has been facing deep economic crisis, Moscow still sees itself as a superpower and "one of the centers of the multi-polar world that is taking shape."[1] Surprisingly enough, while most of the Western countries support their private oil companies competing in the Caspian basin, Russia does not seem to pay much attention to the enormous economic potential represented by the considerable hydrocarbon reserves of the sea. Looking retrospectively at Moscow's diplomacy toward the Caspian states, it is striking to see how regularly the interests of Russian oil companies have clashed with those of the Foreign Ministry, for which development of the oil sector is not a top priority.

Unlike other countries where diplomats lobby foreign governments on behalf of companies willing to expand their activities abroad, Russia's private corporations have to submit to what the political leadership sees as its national interests (provided that it has a clear notion of what they should be). As one U.S. State Department official put it, "Russia has still to define what its national interests are."[2]

The aim of this chapter is to show how the Kremlin, despite its tactical alliances, is lacking a coherent long-term strategy in the Caspian region. As a result, it has so far prevented its own private oil and gas corporations from developing business in the area and could, sooner or later, be left out of the "Great game" that is taking place around the Caspian Sea.

THE SOVIET LEGACY

The main trends of Russia's foreign policy are rooted in the military doctrine adopted in 1993. Although it claimed that Moscow no longer regarded any state as its enemy, this policy document defined the former frontiers of the Soviet Union as a continuing zone of security for Russia. Recently, the English-language journal of the Russian Foreign ministry stated that the external borders of central Asian states were also "a southern border of Russia."[3]

For the Kremlin, the creation of the Commonwealth of Independent States (CIS) was essentially meant to help maintain Russia's hegemony over its immediate neighbors. During 1992–93, Moscow launched an aggressive policy of interference in its neighbors' domestic affairs and supported separatist movements in some of Russia's borderlands. In the view of the Russian strategists, this policy was considered a means to weaken those countries that were still reluctant to join the CIS.[4] Russia's support of those separatist movements varied according to political developments in the targeted countries and their geostrategic environment. If Moscow no longer supports breakaway regions within the CIS, internationally legitimized peacekeeping operations have justified the continuous presence of Russian troops in most of its former satellites.[5]

Moscow's foreign policy toward the oil-rich riparian states of the Caspian Sea originates in the same strategy of destabilization. Since 1991 the biggest Western oil companies have started a lucrative collaboration with Azerbaijan, Kazakhstan, and Turkmenistan. Russia alone seems to be left out of this oil boom. Not only are most of the production-sharing agreements (PSAs) initialed during the past few years by Moscow and foreign companies in a state of stalemate, but the progress of Russian oil producers in the Caspian area—with the notable exception of LUKoil, the country's biggest—remains below what one could have expected. In an interview on Chinese television, the then Russian first deputy prime minister Boris Nemtsov acknowledged in late 1997 that his country had missed an opportunity and allowed the United States to take the lead in joint exploration of the Caspian Sea area with Azerbaijan.[6] Other Russian commentators, including the authors of an anonymous foreign policy paper published in March 1997, argue that their country has suffered a overwhelming defeat since in 1994 a Western consortium won a multibillion-dollar contract, known as the "deal of the century," to develop oil deposits off Azerbaijan.[7]

Surprisingly enough, the Kremlin does not seem to be very concerned about the economic potential represented by the large oil and gas reserves of the Caspian Sea. More important, to Moscow, is the fact that these large deposits have lured Western businessmen into a region it tries to keep under its own influence and which was, traditionally, a zone of Russian expansion. Consequently, the presence of American and European major corporations around the Caspian Sea is seen by the Kremlin not as potential competition to Russian oil companies but as a strategic threat which should be put at the same level as "western cultural and ideological expansion in Russia."[8] Western countries, the United States especially, claim that Transcaucasia and central Asia are regions of vital interest to them and that those regions' hydrocarbon reserves are essential to assuring the world's energy future. Moscow understands these policy statements as a direct threat to its security and an endeavor to infringe upon what it considers its legitimate rights over the former Soviet Empire. As one Russian diplomat stated in 1997, "Russia is obliged to take appropriate actions to oppose attempts to elbow it out and to lock it within its own borders."[9] The problem is that if Russia could ever afford imperial engagements, that capacity no longer exists. Moscow clearly lacks the economic potential, which would be the essential prerequisite to exerting political control over its former marches. Therefore Kremlin policymakers insidiously try, wherever they consider it feasible, to put obstacles in the way of Western industrial projects around the Caspian Sea and of the expanding cooperation between foreign companies and the former Soviet republics of Transcaucasia and central Asia.

SHORT-TERM VICTORIES, LONG-TERM DEFEATS

From the very beginning of the development of the Caspian basin, Russia has developed a diplomacy of short-term objectives based on a system of fragile tactical alliances and failed to implement a long-term strategy. Relations between Russia and Azerbaijan provide a perfect example of the Kremlin's shortsighted foreign policy.

In Moscow's view, Baku holds a key position in the Caspian basin, not only because it is the country with the most developed cooperation with Western companies, but also because the Kremlin fears that the emergence of a strong Shiite Muslim Azerbaijan, contiguous to Turkey, might profit Ankara and, consequently, diminish Russia's already ailing influence in the Caspian region.

There is little doubt left about Moscow's involvement in the ousting of the pro-Turkish, anti-Russian regime of President Abulfaz Elchibey in June 1993.[10] Led by Suret Huseinov, a former businessman who was at the time a colonel in the Azerbaijani national army, a military coup accidentally brought back ex-Soviet Politburo member and former first secretary of the Republic of Azerbaijan, Heydar Aliyev, to power.[11] According to former Azeri Parliament speaker, Rasul Guliyev, Moscow's initial plans envisaged the return to power of Ayaz Mutalibov, the head of state ousted by Elchibey in 1992. Aliyev reportedly failed to keep his promises to share power and eventually became the sole ruler of Azerbaijan, forcing Mutalibov to stay in Russia.[12]

The Kremlin nevertheless tried to make the best of it. Boris Yeltsin welcomed Aliyev as an "experienced and authoritative politician," whose comeback would supposedly help improve Azerbaijani-Russian relations.[13] The new Azerbaijani leader at first acted as if he would meet the Kremlin's expectations. He renegotiated the terms of the "deal of the century" hammered out by Elchibey, allowing LUKoil to take a 10 percent stake in an international consortium led by a British-Norwegian alliance to develop the Azeri and Chirag offshore oil deposits. A $7.14-billion contract was eventually signed on 20 September 1994 between Azerbaijan's State Oil Company (SOCAR) and a consortium of nine foreign corporations,[14] the Azerbaijan International Operating Company (AIOC), after another big oil field—Güneshli—was included in the deal.

Facing huge military losses in its campaign against the ethnic Armenians of its Nagorno-Karabakh enclave, Azerbaijan was forced to call for Moscow's help in August 1993. The signing of the CIS founding documents by Aliyev one month later was another short-term victory for the Kremlin. Despite a Moscow-moderated ceasefire agreed in 1994 between Baku and Nagorno-Karabakh, Russian-Azerbaijani relations have progressively deteriorated. In particular, Baku sees in Moscow the principal initiator of several coup attempts that took place after Aliyev's comeback.

Another example of Russia's unsuccessful diplomacy is provided by the debate on the Caspian Sea's legal status. In June 1994, the Russian Foreign Ministry sent a note to the British Embassy in Baku, in which it claimed that the treaties concluded between Russia and Persia in 1921 and between the Soviet Union and Iran in 1940 were still in force. According to these documents, the Caspian Sea was, until 1991, divided into two zones, one Soviet and one Iranian. With the collapse of the USSR, the region saw the emergence of three new independent states: Kazakhstan, Azerbaijan, and Turkmenistan. Claiming that the Caspian should be considered as a lake and not as a sea, Moscow said that its resource development should be the responsibility of all riparian states and, therefore, should be developed in common. Azerbaijan, supported by Kazakhstan and Turkmenistan, objected that the earlier triaties should not be binding on states that had not signed them.

Why did Moscow wait until 1994 to raise this dispute? One possible reason is that the Russian leadership took seriously the declarations of the then Turkish prime minister Tansu Ciller, who had warned that Turkey would militarily intervene to stop the Armenian offensive in Western Azerbaijan. Another explanation is that Aliyev, suddenly aware he was sitting on a huge source of petrodollars, had chosen to negotiate with other Western oil companies to develop the Caspian reserves.[15]

Notably, arms shipments from Russia to Armenia peaked precisely in 1994. In February 1997 Russian minister for the CIS, Amangeldy Tuleyev, made the existence of a secret deal between Moscow and Yerevan public.

The arms supplies, worth between $47 million and $1.5 billion, were sent in three stages: spring–summer 1994, autumn 1995, and summer 1996.[16] The shipments coincided with the talks in Baku about the future export routes for crude oil produced by AIOC. Ironically, they also took place at a time when Russia was, along with France and the United States, co-sponsoring peace talks between Armenia and Azerbaijan under the aegis of the Organization for Security and Cooperation in Europe (OSCE).

After months of laborious negotiations, an old pipeline running from Baku to the Russian Black Sea port of Novorossiisk via the breakaway region of Chechnya and the city of Tikhoretsk, known as the northern route, was reopened on 25 October 1997. For the first time since its independence, Azerbaijan became an oil exporter. With a maximum projected capacity of five million tons a year (a hundred thousand barrels per day [bpd]), this route is meant to carry the so-called early oil produced by AIOC.[17] Claiming that the output of Güneshli, Chirag, and Azeri would reach 40 million tons a year (800,000 bpd) by 2005–2010 and pointing at the limited capacity of the only functioning line, the consortium and the United States favor multiple export routes. For the Azerbaijan leadership, the need for several pipelines is dictated by geostrategic reasons. "We do not want to depend on one single route. We want to have an alternative, so in case some problems emerge in one direction we would be able to redirect the crude in another direction," said SOCAR first deputy chairman and the Azerbaijan president's son, Ilkham Aliyev.[18]

The most favored route is a 1,730-km (1,081-mile) pipeline running from Baku to the Georgian Black Sea port of Supsa and, from there, to Ceyhan on the Turkish Mediterranean coast. Meeting in Istanbul in March 1998, foreign ministers from Georgia, Azerbaijan, Kazakhstan, Turkmenistan, and Turkey confirmed their support for this route and stressed the need "to limit Russia's influence on the regional hydrocarbons export market."[19]

Although Aliyev has repeatedly said this onshore pipeline would be the main outlet for his country's oil industry, he has left open the possibility of several export routes. One of the alternative options considered by SOCAR envisages the renovation of a 986-km (616-mile) pipeline between the Azeri capital and the Georgian port of Batumi, in the Autonomous Republic of Adzharia. The crude oil would then be shipped by tankers to an unspecified Turkish port on the Black Sea and, from there, pumped through a pipeline to Ceyhan. In August 1998, Iranian foreign minister Kamal Kharrazi suggested building a 300-km (187.5-mile) pipeline between Baku and Tabriz and connecting it to the Iranian oil transport network.

Should all or part of these projects be completed, Russia would suffer a huge loss of profits in transit fees. But first and foremost, it would be deprived of a considerable strategic weapon that would allow it to control oil flows to Western Europe and therefore exert pressure over its neighbors.

For obvious reasons, Moscow is opposed to the Baku-Ceyhan route. Despite repeated invitations from Turkey to join the project, it proposes instead to upgrade the capacity of the northern route to 17 million tons a year, in return for an investment worth $800 million. But SOCAR chairman Natig Aliyev expressed concerns that Moscow would not be able to meet its obligations.[20] Russian officials also say oil could be shipped by tankers from Supsa to Odessa in Ukraine, then pumped at lower cost to the Bulgarian town of Burgas, Alexandroupolis in Greece, Constanta in Romania, and Trieste in Italy. Moscow also claims it could build a new pipeline, roughly parallel to the Baku-Novorossiisk route, provided Azerbaijan guarantees steady oil flows.

A still unanswered question is why did Aliyev agree to the reopening of the Baku-Novorosiisk pipeline? Did he simply bow to American pressure to export crude oil as quickly as possible, or did he think that his agreement would help him gain Moscow's support on the Nagorno-Karabakh issue? It should be noted that in March 1997 Moscow unexpectedly agreed to extradite Huseinov to Baku. For years Aliyev had asked Moscow to hand over his arch-foe, but the Kremlin had always refused. The fact that the Kremlin sent Huseinov back to his native country was perhaps instrumental in getting Baku's agreement to let the Caspian oil flow across Russian territory.

FRAGILE ALLIANCES

During the years 1994–1997, Russia managed to elaborate a fragile system of tactical alliances, which secured the Kremlin the support of Armenia and, to a lesser extent, of Iran and Turkmenistan. The opposite camp comprises Azerbaijan and Georgia, supported by both Turkey and the United States. Sandwiched between Russia and China, Kazakhstan has much less room for maneuver than other regional countries of the region and therefore seems to stand in the middle.

Armenia

At war with Azerbaijan since 1988 despite the Moscow-moderated cease-fire, Armenia is the only ally on which Russia can reasonably lean. A tiny country with no oil and gas reserves, it almost entirely depends on Russia for its energy supplies—Russian and Turkmen natural gas and Russian refined oil.[21] In August 1997, the two countries decided to set up a joint venture known as ArmRosGazprom. The agenda of the new company, 45 percent of which belongs to Russian Gazprom,[22] is to provide regular gas shipments to Armenia and to export Russian fuel to other countries. A 140-km (56-mile) gas pipeline running from Kadzharan in Armenia to the Iranian town of Tabriz is currently under study. Gazprom should be part of this $100-million project, along with Western companies.

Most of the politicians in Yerevan see Moscow as a provider of energy supplies and as a bulwark against U.S. pressure to recognize the territorial integrity of Azerbaijan.[23] Bordering Turkey and Azerbaijan, Armenia is a strategic partner for Russia, which has two military bases there. Border guards from both Russia and Armenia patrol the Armenian-Turkish border. In August 1997, shortly after Aliyev had signed new oil contracts worth $10 billion in Washington, Russia and Armenia sealed a new "treaty of friendship, cooperation, and mutual assistance," which envisaged the common use of military facilities in case of aggression by a third country. This prompted a swift reaction from Baku, which saw in this "military pact" a direct threat to its national security. At the time, Yeltsin's adviser for regional conflicts and nationality affairs, Emil Pain, described this document as the only military-political union that included Russia.[24]

In late 1997, Armenian president Ter-Petrosyan unexpectedly signaled that he could agree to the proposed U.S. peace plan on Nagorno-Karabakh. This plan had been already rejected by Nagorno-Karabakh, which said it wanted direct negotiations with Baku. On 26 September 1997, Ter-Petrosyan suggested that Armenian troops should withdraw from Azerbaijan, prior to a negotiated settlement of the dispute. Led by Prime Minister Robert Kocharyan, the former president of Nagorno-Karabakh, Ter-Petrosyan's opponents accused him of pursuing a defeatist policy that endangered the security of both Armenia and Nagorno-Karabakh. Ter-Petrosyan was eventually forced to resign on 3 February 1998. A hard-liner on Armenia's territorial dispute with Azerbaijan, Kocharyan won the early presidential election called a month later.

Baku has repeatedly accused Moscow of having secretly organized Ter-Petrosyan's ousting because it feared a quick settlement of the Nagorno-Karabakh dispute would boost Western investments in the region and therefore pose a threat to its strategic interests.[25] Amid protests from the OSCE, which criticized the voting, Russian observers monitoring the election were the first to confirm its regularity.[26] Yet Moscow's participation to the political events in Armenia has not been proven. Although the new Armenian leadership advocates a balanced foreign policy toward Russia and the United States, the removal of Ter-Petrosyan and his replacement by Kocharyan could work in the Kremlin's favor. The former Armenian head of state probably saw in Aliyev's latest promises to grant a large measure of autonomy to Nagorno-Karabakh a way to end his country's economic blockade and ease its entry into the TraCECA (Transport Corridor Europe-Caucasus-Asia) project. First developed in 1993 by the former Soviet republics of Transcaucasia and central Asia, this project is sponsored by the United States and the European Union. It envisages the creation of a major route for transportation of oil and other goods from Asia to Europe, bypassing Russia.[27] Azerbaijan is also said to have expressed readiness to let the Baku-Ceyhan pipeline cross Armenia in return for a quick withdrawal of Armenian troops from its territory. Finally, with Ter-Petrosyan out, the prospects of Armenia joining the GUAM group, an informal alignment founded in October 1997 to promote energy deals between Georgia, Ukraine, Azerbaijan, and Moldova, are fading away. Created a few days before the Chisinau summit where Russia was harshly criticized by its neighbors, this group is seen as a threat by Russian policy-makers, who fear it could lead to some kind of "organized dissidence" within the CIS.[28] No wonder then that the United States would like to see Armenia join the GUAM group.[29]

Turkmenistan

Although formally opposed to Azerbaijan on the Caspian Sea dispute, Turkmenistan is not as reliable a partner for Moscow as Armenia is. Until recently, Turkmenistan seemed to support Moscow on the Caspian legal issue, but, like Azerbaijan and Kazakhstan, it considered the Caspian as a sea. It disagreed with Baku on where the dividing lines between national sectors should fall. Turkmenistan claims ownership rights over the Kyapaz oil field (Serdar in Turkmen) located 104 km (65 miles) from its coast and 184 km from Azerbaijan's littoral. The two countries are also at odds over Azeri and part of Chirag, the remainder of which Ashgabat (Turkmenistan) says is the property of Iran. In July 1997 the Turkmen Foreign Ministry said, in a diplomatic note sent to Baku, that it considered it inadmissible to undertake any practical activity on Chirag and Azeri, currently developed by AIOC, before the enactment of a full settlement on the legal status of the Caspian Sea. During a visit to Moscow a few days earlier by Aliyev, Russia's state-owned Rosneft, LUKoil, and SOCAR signed a memorandum of understanding, which gave the two Russian companies the right to develop Kyapaz-Serdar. The Russian president cancelled the deal a month later when he met with his Turkmen counterpart, Saparmurad Niyazov, in Moscow. Ashgabat said it would appeal to the United Nations to help resolve the ownership issue, and the dispute between Turkmenistan and Azerbaijan seems to have abated. After talks held in both Ashgabat and Baku in February–March 1998, the two sides were already playing down the controversy.

This rapprochement was made possible by the approval, given by Niyazov in April 1998 during his visit to Washington, to an underwater gas pipeline linking the Caspian Sea port of Turkmenbashy (formerly Krasnovodsk) to Baku, with a targeted extension to Georgia and Turkey. Promoted by the Clinton administration, which offered Turkmenistan a $750,000 grant to conduct a preliminary feasibility study, this so-called Transcaspian or East-West route would cost an estimated $2.8 billion.[30] For the

United States this project has the advantage of bypassing both Iran and Russia. For Turkmenistan, it is an additional means to diversify its export routes for natural gas, its main source of hard currency revenues. About 85 percent of the country's gas exports currently go to European markets through Russia, and Ashgabat is anxious to develop alternative routes to break free from dependence on Russian export outlets. Turkmen gas exports through Russia totaled 33 billion cubic meters (bcm) in 1995, down from an average 90 bcm a year under the Soviet regime. In 1996, Turkmenistan exported a mere 25 bcm to Europe and other CIS countries. This sharp decline is due to high transit fees imposed by Gazprom, which regularly diverts gas from European countries to insolvent former Soviet republics. On 25 March 1997, Turkmen gas exports to Ukraine through Russia came to a halt after Moscow and Ashgabat disagreed on selling price and transit fees. During his visit to Moscow in August 1997, Niyazov failed to convince Yeltsin to solve the problem rapidly. As a result, the Turkmen economy was close to paralysis.[31] Under these circumstances, one should not be surprised to see Turkmenistan looking eagerly for safer and more lucrative routes for its hydrocarbon exports.

Along with the Transcaspian gas pipeline, two major projects are currently under study. One proposes the construction, by the central Asia Gas Pipeline (CentGas) Consortium,[32] of a 1,600-km (1,000-mile) gas pipeline from the Dauletabad field in southeastern Turkmenistan to Pakistan through Afghanistan, with a possible extension to India. Ashgabat is eager to see construction of this $2.5-billion pipeline with a targeted annual capacity of 20 bcm begin soon and be completed by the year 2000. But the project is threatened by the war raging in northern Afghanistan and by the growing tension between India and Pakistan.[33]

The other giant project envisages a 3,000-km (1,875-mile) pipeline running from the Korpedzhe gas field to Turkey with an extension to Europe, via the northeastern Iranian town of Kord Kuy near the Turkmen border. The first section of this route, approximately 200 km (125 miles) long, was put into use on 29 December 1997. For the first time since its independence, Turkmenistan started directly exporting natural gas outside the CIS. Standing beside Iranian president Sayed Mohammad Khattami during the opening ceremony, Niyazov stated that, "from today on, [Turkmenistan is] a genuine independent state."[34] Under the deal Iran would receive 4 bcm of Turkmen gas in 1998 with shipments tripled in the following years.[35]

In February 1998, Niyazov and the Anglo-Dutch group Royal Dutch/Shell signed a memorandum of understanding on the second phase of the project[36] Under the deal, worth about $4 billion, Ankara is to receive annually 28–30 bcm of natural gas starting in the year 2001. Half of it will be meant for the Turkish domestic market, the other half will be exported to Europe.

Another project envisages a 1,670-km (1,040-mile) oil pipeline from the Chardzhou Turkmen deposit to Pakistan, running in a roughly parallel direction to the CentGas project.[37] Provided an agreement with Turk-menistan on the Kyapaz-Serdar dispute is reached, Azerbaijan envisages using this pipeline to export part of its crude.[38] Preliminary plans include the possibility of connecting it to another pipeline running from Western Siberia to Uzbekistan through Kazakhstan.[39]

Clearly disappointed with Russia, Turkmenistan is anxious to develop its cooperation with the West and raise its export revenues.[40] The country's leadership wants to boost oil output to 50 million tons a year in 2010 from 6 million tons in 1997. It also claims it has the industrial capacity to produce up to 60 bcm a year of natural gas. In 1997, Turkmenistan has said it will offer foreign investors eight of its thirty hydrocarbons fields (including Kyapaz-Serdar) in its own sector of the Caspian Sea with estimated reserves of 1.6 billion tons of oil and 1.3 trillion cubic meters of natural gas.[41]

Iran

At first sight Russia's alliance with Iran seems firmer than the loose ties that link Moscow and Ashgabat. But it also faces a number of challenges. Tehran sees in its cooperation with Russia a way to circumvent the embargo imposed by the U.S. Iran-Libya Sanctions Act (ILSA). This document, in force since 1996 and known as the d'Amato law, officially requires Washington to take actions against non-U.S. firms that invest more than $20 million a year in Iran's oil and gas sector. For Moscow, alliance with Tehran is a way to counter American and Turkish influence in the Caspian Sea region and the Middle East.[42] Although rapprochement between Moscow and Tehran goes back to Soviet times, the two countries openly strengthened their ties after Baku, tactically bowing to U.S. pressure, agreed not to let the National Iran-ian Oil Company (NIOC) participate in the development of offshore deposits in its sector of the Caspian Sea.[43] In 1993, Russia announced plans to help Iran complete the construction of the Bushehr nuclear power station and provide Iranian universities with small research reactors. Despite U.S. and Israeli protests that these deals would help Tehran develop a nuclear bomb,[44] the Kremlin said it would implement them. Iran is also an important market for Russian arms and military technology. Both countries are equally concerned by the situation in Afghanistan where Tehran supports the Shiite faction in the anti-Taliban coalition. Iran also fears that Baku could try to ini-tiate troubles in Iran's ethnic Azerbaijani northern territories.[45]

But the Russian-Iranian alliance is challenged by prominent U.S. politi-cians who are lobbying for a lifting of the ILSA, arguing that Washington should encourage the moderate Khattami, in power since May 1997.[46] Tehran, for its part, is interested in attracting foreign investment. In Septem-ber 1997, Total, Gazprom, and Malaysia's Petronas signed a $2 billion deal to develop the large South Pars natural gas deposit in southern Iran.

Rebuked by Russia and the European Union, the U.S. administration eventually refrained from imposing sanctions on the three companies. Tehran now wants to put into tender some of its major oil and gas deposits, both onshore and offshore, using a so-called buy-back model (i.e., repaying investment with output). Claiming that over a hundred fields could be soon opened to Western companies, Iranian officials made it clear that the national law restricting foreign operators to oil and gas development projects would be amended.[47]

Iran, which is also interested in developing some of the Turkmen deposits, is keen to become one of the main export corridors for the oil and gas produced in central Asia.[48] Turkmenistan and Kazakhstan, as well as foreign investors in the region, see Iran as the shortest and cheapest route to Europe and Asia.[49] Market analysts point out that Caspian oil and gas could be brought to those markets at one-third of the cost and in one-third of the project time of any alternative route, including a route through Russia.[50]

Voices in Russia have been warning against the risks of too close a cooperation with Iran. In December 1996, while the then foreign minister Yevgeni Primakov was paying a visit to Tehran, his Defense Ministry counterpart Igor Rodionov warned against the potential military threat represented by Iran.[51] Although Russia uses its alliance with Tehran for tactical reasons, it shares with the United States a desire not to let Iran acquire a dominant position on the international energy market.[52]

Another possible concern for Moscow is the growing Iranian-Chinese military and nuclear cooperation. In September 1997, China signed an agreement to build a pipeline from Kazakhstan and said it could also participate in the construction of an export route between Kazakhstan and Iran. The Unocal company has said that the Turkmen-Pakistani gas pipeline could eventually be extended to China.[53] Russian commentators, quoting U.S. officials, suggested that fear of a Tehran-Beijing axis could be one of the main reasons behind Washington's policy of containment toward Iran.[54] This could explain why the Clinton administration first said it would not oppose the Turkmenistan-Iran gas pipeline project then changed its mind and started lobbying against the Transcaspian route.[55]

Kazakhstan

Until recently, the Caspian Sea dispute cast a shadow on Russian-Kazakh relations.[56] Astana's stance is that Caspian resources should be developed in common, with the exception of the bottom of the sea, which should remain divided into national sectors. In 1997 Russia put into tender oil and gas deposits claimed by Kazakhstan. Nazarbayev protested the decision, arguing that his country would not "sell-off [its] economic interests."[57] Russia eventually accepted Kazakhstan's viewpoint and, in July 1998, the two countries signed a bilateral treaty dividing the seabed of the northern part of the sea into national sectors, and a "treaty of friendship and eternal alliance." Water reserves should remain undivided, the agreement read. Possible reasons for that move will be reviewed later.

Like Azerbaijan, Kazakhstan has developed successful cooperation with foreign oil companies.[58] Astana sees in Moscow a bulwark against Chinese expansion in central Asia. But, like Turkmenistan, Kazakhstan relies heavily on Russia for its oil and gas exports and is eager to develop new export routes to strengthen its economy.[59] After six years of talks over ownership rights, the Caspian Pipeline Consortium (CPC) project—in which LUKoil has a 12.5 percent stake via Lukarco, a joint venture with the U.S. Atlantic Richfield Company[60]—eventually came to life in late 1998 when Russian first deputy prime minister Yuri Kaslyukov and Kazakh prime minister Nurlan Balgimbayev agreed on the terms of the deal. This project, completion of which is scheduled for the year 2001, envisages a 1,580-km (990-mile) oil pipeline linking Tengiz to Novorossiisk with a projected initial capacity of 28 million tons a year (overall capacity is targeted at 67 million tons a year in 2013). Under the project, a new oil terminal was inaugurated in Novorossiisk in May 1999.

For a long time, shareholders and leaders of the Russian regions that the pipeline should cross have failed to agree on transit fees.[61] Clearly, further delays could conclusively jeopardize CPC, especially in view of other projects developed by the Kazakh government.

Irritated by the repeated delays suffered by this project and by Russia's claims over its deposits, Kazakhstan in September 1997 granted China National Petroleum Consortium (CNPC) exclusive rights over the giant western Uzen field with estimated reserves of 683 million tons of oil. Russian companies—among them LUKoil—were competing in the tender. Beijing also acquired a 60 percent stake in the Aktyubmunaigaz producing company in return for a $4-billion investment. At the same time, Kazakhstan and China signed an estimated $3.5-billion deal to build a 3,000-km (1,875-mile) oil pipeline running from the Kazakh city of Atyrau to Karamay, in the Xinjiang province of northwestern China, with a possible extension to Japan.[62] This giant pipeline could eventually be used to pump oil from Tengiz and Karachaganak. Such an option would undoubtedly increase the profitability of the project, which received a strong incentive when Nazarbayev told Chinese president Jiang Zemin in July 1998 that Kazakhstan would consider Beijing's claims to disputed territories.[63]

Astana and Baku are also looking at plans to build an oil pipeline under the Caspian Sea, with an onshore connection to the Baku-Ceyhan route. Also known as the Transcaspian route, this U.S. sponsored project is supported by all regional states except Russia and Iran. Kazakh oil could also be exported to Azerbaijan by tankers from the Caspian port of Aktau. Crude oil would then be shipped to European markets via the Georgian Black Sea port of Poti or pumped through the Baku-Ceyhan pipeline.

Nazarbayev pointed out that, "Of the five Economic Cooperation Organization (ECO) projects to build regional [oil] pipelines, three are in Kazakhstan's geostrategic interests."[64] According to the Kazakh leader, who said his country was also interested in building gas pipelines parallel to the oil routes, the three projects included the Transcaspian, Iranian, and Pakistani routes. He also mentioned the CPC and Chinese projects as feasible. Nazarbayev—who wants to turn Kazakhstan into one of central Asia's leading countries by the year 2030[65]—has repeatedly made clear that he would chose the solution that would get Kazakh oil and gas to international markets earliest.

Had the CPC project failed, Russia would have lost an estimated $33.9 billion revenue in transit fees and dividends. True, an alternative project to renovate and upgrade an old pipeline between Atyrau and the Russian town of Samara and eventually to Europe via Russia's Druzhba pipeline is currently being considered. But other countries, which rely heavily on Moscow for their energy supplies, are considering plans to buy oil directly from Kazakhstan. Polish president Alexander Kwasniewski used a visit by Nazarbayev to Warsaw in November 1997 to propose forging an export route for Kazakh oil, bypassing Russia, via Ukraine, to the Baltic port of Gdansk. Plans to transport AIOC-produced oil through Georgia to Ukraine—a country also caught in Moscow's energy grip—are also being discussed.[66] According to this plan, oil would be pumped from Baku to Poti and, from there, transported by tankers to Odessa.[67] Ukraine is also considering importing up to 4 million tons of Azeri oil and is buying crude from Kazakhstan.[68]

TOO MANY DIPLOMACIES

It has generally been thought, mistakenly, that Russia had worked to further the interests of its oil companies in the Caspian region, particularly its biggest group, LUKoil. But, in my view, the company owes its success in the CIS to itself, not to the Russian government. The company, with stakes in several consortia in Azerbaijan and Kazakhstan,[69] acts like its Western counterparts; in other words, it seeks profits where they are the most accessible. As early as 1994, the company's leadership announced ambitious expansion plans outside Russia.[70] Three years later, LUKoil chairman Vagit Alekperov—a native Azerbaijani—said he would prefer developing foreign oil deposits to working in the former Soviet Union.[71]

Unlike its American and European counterparts, the Russian Foreign Ministry has hardly given any support to the Russian oil and gas companies that were trying to do business around the Caspian Sea. Moreover, the Kremlin diplomacy toward the former Soviet republics has made the Caspian New Independent States (NIS) mistrust Russia and consider every possible plan to bypass Russia while pumping their hydrocarbon resources to international markets.

One is surprised, reading policy papers published by the Russian Foreign Ministry, to see how infrequently the Caspian oil is referred to as a potential source of revenues for the country's ailing economy.[72] A possible explanation is that, in the mind of its political leaders, Russia has sufficient oil reserves of its own, although new fields lie in inhospitable regions with no immediate outlet to the major export routes. Pain stated that the importance of oil in the relations between Moscow and Baku should not be exaggerated, because the volume of oil production within Russia exceeds what the country could receive from participating in the development of Azerbaijan's Caspian fields.[73]

The same could be noted about Chechnya oil—or, to be more precise, control over the Baku-Novorossiisk pipeline—which is generally seen as the main reason that pushed the Kremlin leadership to declare war on the secessionist republic. But the cost of the war far exceeds what Moscow could have expected from transit fees. Another argument against the so-called oil scenario as the main reason for the military intervention is that the Russian leadership started planning the construction of a new section of pipeline that would bypass Chechnya and cross neighboring Dagestan immediately after a peace agreement was made in 1996–97. Thus, the theory according to which the pipeline is seen by Moscow as a way to keep Chechnya within the Russian Federation is not convincing.

In today's Russia, the state is weak. As a result, each ministry, each administration, each region has its own agenda. Pain admitted that, in 1993–94, "different groups in [the Russian leadership] were pursuing diverging, even opposing policies in the [Caspian] region."[74] In 1994, the Russian Foreign Ministry raised the Caspian Sea legal issue when LUKoil, already granted a 10 percent stake in the Chirag and Azeri projects, was negotiating the right to develop Güneshli and Kyapaz. Moreover, Moscow's claim that it should have a say in all Caspian development projects came at a time when the Azeri parliament had not yet ratified the Chirag-Azeri deal. In complete disarray, LUKoil appealed to the Fuel and Energy Ministry and to the prime minister to make the diplomats see reason. Chernomyrdin could do nothing but record the "lack of coordination" between the two ministries.[75] It was not until early 1996 that the Foreign Ministry agreed to alter its position on the Caspian issue, saying that the legal dispute should be settled on a consensual basis. But this did not mark the end of LUKoil's troubles.

On 4 July 4 1997, LUKoil and Rosneft signed with Azerbaijan a memorandum of understanding, which gave the two Russian companies the right to enter into a PSA to explore and develop Kyapaz-Serdar. The document was signed during Aliyev's first state visit to Moscow. Within a month, Rosneft unexpectedly announced it would not participate in the deal and, on 5 August, the Foreign Ministry said LUKoil also withdrew from the competition. Two days later, Yeltsin annulled the deal after a meeting in Moscow with Niyazov. Here again, the move caught LUKoil unawares. According to Russian diplomats, the company supposedly promised not to start any new project in the Caspian region without prior consultations with the Foreign Ministry.[76]

Yeltsin did not elaborate on his decision to annul the Kyapaz deal. One hypothesis is that he probably expected Ashgabat, in return, to offer Gazprom a 10 percent or higher stake in the CentGas consortium to build the planned Turkmen-Pakistani gas pipeline. If so, the Russian president obviously failed. After months of fruitless negotiations, Gazprom's participation in the project was officially canceled.[77] In the meantime, the Russian gas monopoly had kept rejecting a compromise over transit fees for Turkmen gas shipments to Ukraine.[78] After a meeting with Niyazov in Ashgabat, Ukrainian president Leonid Kuchma paid a special visit to Yeltsin in late January 1998 but failed to convince him to exert pressure on Gazprom and let Turkmenistan resume gas shipments to Kiev.[79] On the eve of Niyazov's visit to Moscow, Yeltsin had a private interview with Rem Vyakhirev, then chairman of Gazprom. Immediately after the meeting he expressed his full support of Gazprom and its chairman on the Turkmen dispute.[80] Niyazov soon retaliated by promoting the Transcaspian gas pipeline route.

During his visit to Washington in April 1998, Nyazov first agreed to this U.S.-sponsored project. One of the two reasons put forward by Turkmen officials to justify the move was Gazprom's stance on transit fees.[81] If implemented, this project could threaten the so-called Blue Stream agreement sealed in December 1997 by Moscow and Ankara.[82] The Turkmenistan-Bulgaria gas pipeline project represents an additional threat to Gazprom. Half of the Turkmen gas received by Turkey at the beginning of the next century will be meant for export to Europe. In September 1997, Niyazov had a meeting with Ruhrgas's deputy chairman, Burckhardt Bergmann. The two men are said to have discussed participation in the so-called Iranian pipeline and possible Turkmen gas shipments to Germany.[83]

In 1998, Moscow further alienated Ashgabat by announcing that it had reached a framework agreement with Astana on the Caspian Sea's legal status. According to this treaty, the northern part of the seabed should be divided among the signatories, while the Caspian waters will remain under a common jurisdiction. Although the technical feasibility of this agreement was dubious, Turkmenistan and Iran refused to endorse the legitimacy of this document. The fact that Niyazov first expressed support of the Transcaspian gas pipeline in Washington only a few days after his Russian and Kazakh counterparts had announced in April 1998 that they were close to an agreement is certainly not fortuitous.

Why did Russia, in contradiction to its previous position that the issue should be solved collectively, eventually agree to meet Kazakhstan's legal arguments? Officials close to the Russian Foreign Ministry suggest that the country's leadership eventually understood that delays in making progress would further isolate Moscow in the Caspian region and in the CIS.[84]

For Moscow, which hoped the agreement would get the approval of all other Caspian states, this proposal has some advantages. First, the abolition of state borders in the middle of the sea would prevent further militarization of the water reservoir.[85] Second, the agreement could pave the way for the opening of direct communication lines between the Caspian Sea port of Olya, in the Astrakhan region, and the Iranian city of Enzeli.[86] But there is a risk that Tehran will definitely turn away from Russia. As early as April 1998, the Iranian press complained about recent changes in Moscow's regional policy. "Unfortunately influential political groups in Russia are putting economic dividends above all, sacrificing to them the steadfastness of foreign policy," wrote one of Tehran's newspapers.[87] Shortly after the Russian-Kazakh agreement was signed, Iran announced it had sealed with Turkmenistan a $25-million contract to drill four oil wells off Turkmenbashy during the following eighteen months.

NEW TRENDS VERSUS OLD REFLEXES

After years of chaotic foreign policy toward their southern neighbors, Russian decision-makers are said to have come to some kind of consensus that Moscow should now try to develop genuine economic cooperation with other CIS states.

Commentators saw a direct link between the Russian move on the Caspian issue, the nomination of financial tycoon Boris Berezovski as CIS executive secretary on 29 April 1998, and the subsequent abolition of the CIS Ministry. A supporter of economic integration among ex-Soviet republics, the former number-two man in Yeltsin's Security Council was seen as the main architect of the Russian-Kazakh agreement. After the CIS summit in Chisinau in October 1997, Moscow understood it had to change its policy toward its neighbors, lest the Commonwealth of Independent States should turn into an anti-Moscow coalition. In early 1998, Primakov acknowledged the existence of "irreversible negative tendencies" within the CIS.[88] "It is high time to undertake decisive steps to build a genuine Commonwealth of Independent States. Private capital is the only force capable of strengthening the CIS," Berezovski stated the day he was appointed.[89] Unlike Primakov, who hoped to have supreme control over Moscow's policy toward the former Soviet states, the CIS leaders welcomed this appointment. "Most important to them, Berezovski does not personify the Russian power structures. On the contrary, he represents those Russian circles with whom [our] neighbors are ready to deal," commented one Russia news-magazine at the time.[90] It was generally believed that the new CIS executive secretary not only lobbied for his own interests inside the former Soviet Union, but also stood as a spokesperson for those Russian corporate managers known as the "oligarchs." This could be particularly true in those countries that will be eventually integrated in the TraCECA project and where state property remains to be privatized.

Even those who make a distinction between the hard-line policy favored by the Kremlin during the first years of Yeltsin's regime and the recent, seemingly softer stance warn that "it does not mean that the Russian Foreign Ministry has once and for all given up its non constructive approach."[91] As an example, not all decision-makers in Moscow wanted the Russian-Kazakh Caspian agreement. Commentators noted that ministries involved in trading with Tehran were afraid it could undermine Russian-Iranian economic cooperation.[92]

Voices on the International Affairs Committee of the Duma, the lower house of Parliament in Russia, keep calling for a hardening of Moscow's policy and the creation of an anti-Western front in the CIS.[93] Experts close to the Foreign Ministry stress the need to put an end to what they call the U.S. "Drang Nach Osten."[94] Others say Russia should encourage separatist movements in Azerbaijan and Georgia to counter Western influence in the region.[95] Even Russia's insistence on implementing a $500-million deal covering the sale of anti-aircraft missiles to Cyprus's Greek government is considered as a threat to oil projects in the region. As former Greek Trade and Industry minister Andreas Andrianopoulos has pointed out, once delivered and deployed, the S-300 missiles would create new tensions between Athens and Ankara in an area only a few kilometers from Ceyhan.[96] More recently, the Georgian authorities suspected former security minister Igor Giorgadze of having masterminded an assassination attempt against Shevardnadze on 9 February 1998.[97] In an interview with an Italian newspaper, *La Republica*, the following day, Shevardnadze said it would be difficult to blame any country in particular. But he said he believed the attack had a "smell" of oil. "One thing is clear. I have disturbed powerful interests with the involvement of my country in an oil transport project . . . on a corridor from the Caucasus which circumvents Russian territory," he said.[98]

CONCLUSION

Russia still sees itself as a threatened country and has preferred to block initiatives and stall progress in the Caspian region rather than develop new projects, alone or with foreign partners. To counter the expansion of Western capital in its southern borderlands, Moscow has developed a policy of interference and built up fragile tactical alliances, in which oil is seen by its leaders not as an end but as a way to keep the former Soviet republics under their influence. Commenting on the Kremlin's support to Iraq in late 1997, one leading Russian newspaper complained that, instead of dealing with specific oil projects, Moscow was playing "the geopolitical games of a decade ago," as if it were still a superpower. "As a rule, its victories in this sphere are dubious and the losses suffered by Russian [oil] companies are considerable," the newspaper added.[99]

Oil will for a long time play the leading role in Caspian politics. But for Russia it may be already too late to get a piece of the pie. Countries of the region have already chosen to ship oil and gas resources to European and Asian markets, bypassing Russia. Recent developments in Dagestan, where part of the autonomous republic declared its sovereignty in August 1998, show that Moscow may lose control of the northern Caucasus.

NOTES

1. "Foreign Policy of Russia in 1996 and 1997," *International Affairs* (published in English by Russian Embassy in Washington, D.C.), no. 2, 1997.

2. U.S. deputy ambassador to the New Independent States Victoria Nulan, "U.S.-Russian Relations Now that the Honeymoon Is Over," lecture given at the Davis Center for Russian Studies, Harvard University, 6 February 1998.

3. Sergei Razov, "New Developments in Central Asia," *International Affairs*, no. 3, 1997.

4. In May 1992, at a summit held in the Uzbek capital, Tashkent, only seven out of twelve countries agreed to sign a collective security treaty hammered out by Moscow. Five former Soviet republics (Georgia, Azerbaijan, Turkmenistan, Ukraine, and Moldova) declined to initial a document entrusting the defense of their territories to the Russian army.

5. Russia has 25,000 soldiers and border guards in Tajikistan; 15,000 in Turkmenistan; and 15,000 in Georgia. It also keeps a naval base and a fleet in Ukraine, border guards in Uzbekistan, missile troops in Kazakhstan, a radar location in Azerbaijan, and military bases in Belarus, Armenia, and Kyrgyzstan.

6. *Xinhua English Newswire*, 17 November 1997.

7. *Nezavisimaya gazeta*, 26 March 1997.

8. Anatoli Gusher, "On Russian-Iranian Relations," *International Affairs*, no. 2, 1997.

9. A. Zaitsev, "Russia and Transcaucasia," *International Affairs*, no. 5, 1997.

10. A detailed account of the 1993 coup can be found in Elizabeth Fuller, "Azerbaijan's June Revolution," *RFE/RL Research Report*, vol. 2, no. 32, 13 August 1993. See also Yuri Fyodorov, "Kaspiiskaya politika Rossii: k konsensusu elit," *Pro et Contra*, vol. 2, no. 3 (summer 1997).

11. After a failed attempt to take power by force in 1994, Huseinov fled to Russia where he remained until 1997.

12. *Moskovskie novosti,* 21–28 June 1998. Mutalibov has always denied any links with Huseinov.

13. Elizabeth Fuller, "Azerbaijan's June Revolution."

14. AIOC now comprises SOCAR, British Petroleum, Norway's Den Norske Stats Oljeselskap (Statoil), U.S. Union Oil Company of California (Unocal), Pennzoil and Exxon, Japan's Itochu Oil Exploration, Britain's Ramco, Turkish Petroleum, and Saudi Arabia's Delta Nimir.

15. As of 31 December 1997, projected investments in oil projects in Azerbaijan totaled between $28 billion and $30 billion and involved twenty companies from twelve countries.

16. *Kommersant-Weekly,* 6 May 1997.

17. Oil produced by the consortium at Güneshli was not pumped before 1 February 1998. Prior to this date, the pipeline was used to export 64,000 tons produced by SOCAR without the help of foreign companies. Russia promised to let up to 1.5 million tons of Azeri crude cross its territory in 1998.

18. "Azerbaijan: the New Source of Energy of the 21st Century," paper presented at a seminar organized by the John F. Kennedy School of Government, Harvard University, 21 November 1997.

19. *Ekspert,* 9 March 1998.

20. "The Russian side can handle maximum volumes of 1.5–2 million tons a year, although it promised to take 5 million tons. We plan to reach this amount (in 1999) and Russia must be ready for that. If not, we'll have to keep our output or to force the western route," Aliyev said. *Ekspert,* 18 May 1998.

21. Armenia annually receives 1.5 billion cubic meters of natural gas from Russia. Because of the successive wars in Abkhazia and Chechnya, the two railway routes linking Armenia to Russia have been cut off. Russian oil products are therefore shipped to the Georgian ports of Batumi and Poti from Novorossiisk and, from there, sent by train to Armenia. As a result, Yerevan has to pay a bigger price for its energy supplies.

22. Other shareholders are the Armenian government (45 percent) and the U.S.-based Itera International Energy Corporation (10 percent), a long-standing partner of Gazprom.

23. Washington insists that Armenian troops should withdraw from western Azerbaijan. In return, it says, Baku should grant Nagorno-Karabakh greater autonomy. The proposed U.S. plan also includes the deployment of international peacekeeping forces along the Lachin corridor, which links the enclave to Armenia.

24. *RFE/RL,* 25 September 1997, quoting Azerbaijan's Turan News Agency.

25. "Russia is trying everything to make instability generated in the region by the Karabakh conflict endure," Aliyev's top foreign policy adviser, Vafa Guluzade, was quoted as saying. *Le Figaro,* 1–2 August 1998.

26. Michael Ochs, adviser to the U.S. Congress and one of the 150 OSCE electoral observers sent to Armenia, stated that members of the CIS parliamentary assembly—mainly Russian citizens—concluded that the election was fair before the vote had begun. See "Future Prospects for the Eurasian Corridor," transcript of a round-table discussion held on 23 April 1998 at the John F. Kennedy School of Government, Harvard University.

27. Armenia's foreign trade volume with former Soviet republics went down to 2.5 million tons in 1996 from 22 million tons in 1990. Trade with Russia currently hovers at about $200–250 million, compared to $300 million with Iran. Also a semi-legal provider for the Nagorno-Karabakh enclave, Tehran has let Russian arms shipments to Armenia cross its territory. See Roland Goetz, "Political Spheres of Interest in the Southern Caucasus and in Central Asia," *Aussen Politik*, vol. 48, no. 3 (1997).

28. Andrei Zagorsky, vice rector of the Moscow Institute of International Relations (IMEMO). Interview by author, 7 July 1998.

29. Nulan, "U.S.-Russian Relations."

30. The U.S. administration is looking at two possible routes: one would involve the construction of a new pipeline, the other would see the rehabilitation of an old line and its connection with a new one on part of the route.

31. Turkmenistan is the only CIS country that is not Russia's debtor. As of 1 March 1998, Moscow owed Ashgabat about $107 million.

32. Unocal—which, as a member of AIOC, controls 9.5 percent of the Azeri, Chirag, and Güneshli oil fields—has a 46.5 percent stake in the consortium. Other participants include the Turkmen government (7 percent), Saudi Arabia's Delta Nimir (15 percent), South Korea's Hyundai (5 percent), Japan's Itochu and Indonesia Petroleum Oil Company (6.5 percent each), and Pakistan's Crescent Group (3.5 percent). After Gazprom officially withdrew from the project, Unocal obtained an additional 7 percent, the remaining 3 percent being shared between the Japanese, South Korean, and Pakistani participants.

33. After the U.S. bombing raid on what were alleged to be terrorist installations in Afghanistan in August 1998, Unocal announced that it would stop work on plans to build the CentGas pipeline. The company stressed it had little invested in the project because it had found it impossible to sign an agreement with the Taliban leadership. *Wall Street Journal*, 21 August 1998.

34. *Nezavisimaya gazeta*, 27 January 1998.

35. Iran committed itself to buy Turkmen gas for twenty-five years. The pipeline was built with funds provided by Tehran. Until the year 2001, gas shipments will serve as Turkmenistan's participation in the project.

36. Gazprom has a monopoly in Bulgaria's gas market, but Sofia has made clear that it would be interested in buying gas from other countries. In September 1998, Bulgaria and Shell signed a memorandum of understanding to carry out a feasibility study on a possible gas route from Turkmenistan.

37. Unocal has been approached to run the project. The company expects to export up to 50 million tons (1 million barrels per day [bpd]) of crude oil through ports on the Arabian Sea.

38. *Nezavisimaya gazeta*, 7 April 1998.

39. This pipeline is currently used only to pump crude oil to the Chimkent refinery in southern Kazakhstan. Uzbekistan has officially stopped buying oil from Russia. *Nezavisimaya gazeta*, 16 July 1998.

40. Western investments made in the Turkmen oil and gas industry since 1991 amount to about $600 million. One possible explanation for this comparatively low level is that Ashgabat was until recently pinning its hopes on Russia. Turkmen officials claimed they expected up to $951 million in 1998 alone from Western countries, partly in the form of loans. Interfax, 23 January 1998.

41. During his April 1998 visit to Washington, Niyazov signed exploration and development deals with Mobil Corporation and the U.K.-based Monument Oil and Gas Inc., and a technical exploration deal with one of Exxon's subsidiaries. The signing of a memorandum of understanding with Mobil on Kyapaz-Serdar was postponed at the last minute.

42. "The problem of Russian-Iranian relations . . . can, and should be, regarded from a broad regional perspective, not as a purely bilateral matter," wrote one Russian diplomat. Anatoli Gusher, "Russian-Iranian Relations."

43. In May 1996, a memorandum of understanding was signed by SOCAR and Oil Industries Engineering and Construction (OIEC), a subsidiary of NIOC, to allow Iran to participate in the development of the Shah-Deniz oil and gas field along with Turkish Petroleum, Statoil, British Petroleum, and LUKoil. But the deal has still to be implemented.

44. In July 1998, Tehran tested a medium-range ballistic missile known as Shehab-3.

45. In return, the Azerbaijani leadership accuses Tehran of financing its Islamic opposition and carrying on intelligence-gathering activities in its territory.

46. See Zbigniew Brzezinski, "A Geostrategy for Eurasia," *Foreign Affairs,* vol.76, no. 5 (September–October 1997). A former assistant to U.S. president Jimmy Carter for National Security Affairs, Brzezinski is now adviser to a major U.S. oil group.

47. In May 1998, U.S. Conoco announced it remained committed to doing business in Iran despite the ILSA (under the Foreign Assistance Act, which severely limited contacts between American and Iranian companies, it was forced to give up the multimillion dollar Sirri oil and gas project in January 1995). Shell and BP recently opened negotiations in Tehran. Total is hoping to win new concessions in Iran, and France's Elf Aquitaine envisages doubling oil output at the offshore Dorood oil deposit.

48. Iranian oil export annual revenues are estimated at $16 billion. They account for 40 percent of all state revenues and 80 percent of the country's hard currency export earnings.

49. During a trip to Washington in 1997, Kazakh president Nursultan Nazarbayev said he was considering plans to export oil by pipeline to Iranian ports on the Persian Gulf. French and German companies have been commissioned by Tehran to study the technical feasibility of a Kazakhstan-Iran oil pipeline. A project to modernize the Caspian Sea port of Aktau was in 1998 being considered by the Kazakh government. If completed, it would open the way to the creation of a new export route to the Iranian port of Enzeli.

50. Mehdi Varzi, head of Energy Research at Deutsche Kleinwort. Reuters, 9 November 1997.

51. Robert O. Freedman, "Russia and Iran: A Tactical Alliance," *SAIS Review,* vol. 17, no. 2 (summer–fall 1997).

52. Moscow and Washington reportedly came to a consensus on this question in early 1998. Reuters, 21 April 1998.

53. *Ekspert,* 19 January 1998.

54. *Ekspert,* 9 March 1998.

55. Turkmenistan said it would not object to either project.

56. Another bone of contention is Russia's growing debt to Kazakhstan. As of November 1997, Moscow owed Astana (then named Akmola) an estimated $450 million for the use of the Baikonur facilities.

57. *Nezavisimaya gazeta*, 7 October 1997.

58. In 1993, a seven-member international consortium (Total, Agip, Mobil, Royal Dutch/Shell, British Gas, and British Petroleum-Statoil) signed with Kazakhstan a contract to explore a vast area in the northern part of the Caspian Sea with estimated reserves of over 800 million tons of oil. Another international consortium—made up of Agip, British Gas, Texaco, and LUKoil—has been granted exclusive rights over the Karachaganak field in northwestern Kazakhstan. A third giant project concerns the Tengiz offshore oil field with estimated reserves of 700–800 million tons, currently being developed by a Western consortium led by U.S. Chevron Corporation. LUKoil is involved in this project and also has a 50 percent stake in the Kumkol deposit with estimated reserves of 42 million tons.

59. Kazakhstan's domestic oil consumption currently stands at 13 million tons a year (260,000 bpd) and is unlikely to rise to more than 20 million tons a year (400,000 bpd) in the next future. Kazakhstan produced 27.55 million tons of crude oil (551,000 bpd) in 1997 and aims to boost its output to 120–130 million tons (2.4–2.6 million bpd).

60. Other shareholders include Russia (24 percent), Kazakhstan (19 percent), Chevron (15 percent), Mobil (7.5 percent), Rosneft-Shell (7.5 percent), Oman (7 percent), British Gas (2 percent), Agip (2 percent), U.S. Oryx Energy (1.75 percent), and U.S.-Kazakh Kazakhstan Pipeline (1.75 percent).

61. *Novoye vremya*, no. 37, 1997.

62. Chinese oil officials have warned that Beijing's decision on the feasibility of extending the pipeline beyond Karamay will depend on the productivity of the Kazakh fields. Nazarbayev said work on the pipeline would begin immediately and take five years to complete. A feasibility study is currently being carried out by CNPC and by Kazakhstan's KazTransOil pipeline company.

63. Despite a 1994 border agreement, China and Kazakhstan are at odds over part of the Tien Shan mountainous region.

64. Reuters, 11 May 1998. The ECO includes Iran, Turkey, Pakistan, Afghanistan, and six former Soviet republics: Kazakhstan, Uzbekistan, Kyrgyzstan, Tajikistan, Turkmenistan, and Azerbaijan.

65. *Nezavisimaya gazeta*, 17 October 1997.

66. U.S. policy-makers, anxious to see the Ukraine less dependent on Russia for its energy supplies, first promoted this idea.

67. Work to upgrade the capacity of the Odessa oil terminal up to 9 million tons a year has already started and should be completed by the end of the year 2000. Kiev also proposes to extend the Baku-Supsa pipeline with a section running to Gdansk via Odessa and Brody in Ukraine. Half of the proposed 667-km (416-mile) new pipeline has already been built. Another proposed route sees the construction of an oil pipeline from Baku to Ukraine through Grozny, Makhachkala, and Rostov-on-the-Don.

68. *Moskovskie novosti*, 9–16 March 1997.

69. LUKoil had already invested $145 million in Azerbaijan and was planning to flow another $90 million in 1998. Besides the deals already detailed, the company has also created a joint venture with Italy's Agip to develop the Karabakh oil field in Azerbaijan, which has recoverable reserves estimated at 85–120 million tons. It has also acquired a 10 percent stake in a consortium to develop the Shakh-Deniz

deposit. In July 1997, LUKoil and SOCAR signed an agreement on the prospecting and production-sharing development of the Azerbaijani D-222 (Yalama) structure in the Caspian Sea.

70. Reuters, 1 July 1994.

71. *Argumenty i fakty*, no. 50, December 1997.

72. The only notable exception, to my knowledge, is Feliks Kovalyov, "Caspian Oil: Russian Interests," *International Affairs*, no. 3 (1997). But the author sees Moscow's economic interests in pumping foreign oil through Russian territory, not in participating in the development of Caspian oil reserves.

73. *RFE/RL*, 25 September 1997.

74. Ibid.

75. Reuters, 12 October 1994.

76. *Ekspert*, 11 August 1997.

77. Russia claims that Turkmenistan barred Gazprom from the project. Officials in Ashgabat say that, on the contrary, Gazprom voluntarily decided not to participate, although it was promised a 10 percent stake in the project. Commentators in Ashgabat have suggested that Gazprom refused because it wanted to have the leading role in the CentGas project. Consortium members said the Russian monopoly wanted a 15 percent stake and authorization to develop Turkmen gas fields. Interfax, 30 January and 3 February 1998.

78. A close ally of Chernomyrdin, Gazprom chairman Vyakhirev had repeatedly said he would force the Turkmens and the Ukrainians to "go down on their knees" to Russia. On his way back to Moscow after a visit to Ashgabat in early 1998, Chernomyrdin reportedly admonished Gazprom's chairman: "You promised they would go down on their knees. Now you go to beg them to make an agreement." *Izvestiia*, 29 January 1998.

79. In fact, Yeltsin announced that Russia would let Turkmen gas transit through Russian territory. But he immediately added that the technical and financial aspects of the agreement would be decided by Gazprom. Yeltsin may have pretended to Kuchma satisfaction because he saw a pending Russia-Ukraine economic agreement, which would be signed three months later, as much more important for Moscow.

80. *Kommersant-Daily*, 19 August 1997.

81. The other reason is the U.S. refusal to let Turkmen gas go through Iran. *Izvestiia*, 25 April 1998.

82. This twenty-five-year deal, oficially worth $13.5 billion, sees the construction of a 1,213-km (758-mile) gas pipeline between Russia and Turkey, including a 400-km (250-mile) section on the Black Sea bed. As a result, Gazprom's supplies to Turkey are expected to rise to thirty billion cubic meters (bcm) a year in 2010, from the current 6 bcm. Construction of the pipeline has already started and is due to be completed in 2000.

83. *Ekspert*, 8 September 1997.

84. Andrei Zagorsky. Interview with the author, 7 July 1998.

85. Azerbaijan and Kazakhstan—as well as Georgia on the Black Sea—have already started building up their own border fleets. Another concern for Moscow is that NATO has started reorganizing its regional commands to protect the Caspian region.

86. *Moskovskie novosti*, 19–26 April 1998.

87. *Russkii telegraf,* 15 April 1998, quoting *Iranian News.*

88. *Nezavisimaya gazeta,* 17 March 1998.

89. Itar-Tass, 29 April 1998.

90. *Kommersant-Vlast'*, 12 May 1998.

91. Yuri Fyodorov, "Kaspiiskaya politika Rossii."

92. *Novye izvestiia,* 7 July 1998; *Nezavisimaya gazeta,* 7 July 1998.

93. See, for example, Alexei Mitrofanov, "Russia's New Geopolitics," and Alexei Podberyozkin, "Russia's New Path," both pamphlets issued by the John F. Kennedy School of Government, Harvard University, July 1998.

94. *Nezavisimaya gazeta,* 22 April 1998.

95. *Nezavisimaya gazeta,* 26 March 1997. In 1998 Moscow discreetly encouraged the creation of a left-wing opposition movement to Shevardnadze known as the Congress for the Rebirth of Adzharia.

96. *Transitions,* vol. 4, no. 1 (June 1997).

97. Giorgadze is the main suspect in a bomb attack carried out in 1995 against the Georgian president. He fled to Russia immediately after the attack.

98. Reuters, 11 February 1998. Russia has denied playing any role in the 1995 and 1998 attacks.

99. *Kommersant-Weekly,* 2 December 1997.

Index

Abkhazia, 170, 177
administrative class, and oil elites, 79
ADRs. *See* American Depositary
    Receipts
Adzharia Republic, 193
Agip, 114, 171–72, 210n58, 210n69
Agroprombank SSSR, 48
Aiatskov, Dmitrii, 156
AIK, structure of, 20
AIOC. *See* Azerbaijan International
    Operating Consortium
AKIB. *See* Commercial Innovation Bank
    for Scientific Technological
    Progress
Aktyubmunaigaz, 200
Alekperov, Vagit, 43, 56, 70, 113, 201
Alekseev, M., 66
Alfa-Bank, 49, 52, 69; financial crisis
    and, 71–72; and privatization, 35;
    ranking of, 54*t*; state monies in,
    61*t*
Alfa Group, 66
Aliyev, Heydar, 175, 191, 203
Aliyev, Ilkham, 193
Aliyev, Natig, 194
All Russia (Vsia Rossiia), 157
All-Union ministries, 5, 16
American Depositary Receipts (ADRs),
    27, 118–19
Amoco, 115, 171
Anderman-Smith oil company, 138

Andranopoulos, Andreas, 205
Angarsk Petrochemical Company,
    66–67, 119; capacity of, 120; and
    National Oil Company, 43
Anti-Monopoly Committee (GKAP),
    5–7
ARCO. *See* Atlantic Richfield Company
Armenia, 176–77, 193–96
ArmRosGazprom, 194
Asian economic crisis, 175
Astana, 200
Astarta, 31*t*, 64*t*
Astrakhan, 204
Astrakhanneft, 111–13
Astrakhannefteprodukt, 112
Atlantic Richfield Company (ARCO), 27,
    30, 114
Atroshenko, Sergei, 134, 148
Atyrau-Karamay pipeline, proposed,
    200
authoritarian statism, 15
Avars, 107
Avtovazbank, 48
Azerbaijan, 171–72, 174–77, 191–93,
    200; and GUAM axis, 182, 196;
    oil output of, 172; and Russia,
    191–92; strategy of, 175; Western
    oil companies and, 190
Azerbaijan International Operating
    Consortium (AIOC), 171–72, 192
Azeri offshore deposit, 192–93

About the Editor and Contributors

Peter Glatter is completing a Ph.D. at Wolverhampton University, Britain, on Russian regional elites with special reference to West Siberia. His publications include a Special Briefing Paper on the West Siberian Oil and Gas Province for the Royal Institute of International Affairs.

Bruce Kellison received his doctorate in government from the University of Texas, Austin, in 1998. He is currently the associate director of the Bureau of Business Research in the Graduate School of Business at the University of Texas, Austin.

Valery Kryukov is currently a head of department at the Institute of Economics and Industrial Engineering, Siberian Division of the Russian Academy of Sciences. He is a specialist in regional economic development and energy and has published studies on different aspects of the Russian energy industries. Recent works published, with Arild Moe, include: *The New Russian Corporatism? A Case Study of Gazprom: Internal Structure, Management Principles and Financial Flows* (1996); *The Changing Role of Banks in the Russian Oil Sector* (1998).

David Lane is a fellow of Emmanuel College and reader in sociology at Cambridge University. He is the recipient of a British ESRC grant to study the Russian oil industry and the banking sector. His recent books include: *The Rise and Fall of State Socialism* (1997) and, with Cameron Ross, *The Transition from Communism to Capitalism* (1998).

Arild Moe graduated from and is currently deputy director of the Fridtjof Nansen Institute, Lysaker, Norway. He is author and co-author of several books and articles on the Russian energy sector and the European gas market. His publications with Valery Kryukov are listed above.

Jean-Christophe Peuch is an associate of the Davis Center for Russian Studies, Harvard University. He has previously worked for Reuters news agency and Total Oil in Moscow and has been an analyst at the Ecole Polytechnique, Paris.

Heiko Pleines studied at the School of Slavonic and East European Studies, University of London, and the Ruhr-University Bochum. Currently he is a doctoral student at the Free University of Berlin and a researcher at the German Federal Institute for Russian, East European and International Studies (BIOst), Cologne, Germany.

Peter Rutland is a professor of government at Wesleyan University and an associate of the Davis Center for Russian Studies, Harvard University. He is the author of *The Politics of Economic Stagnation in the Soviet Union* (1993) and the editor of the EastWest Institute Annual Survey of Eastern Europe and the Former Soviet Union (1998, 1999).

Iskander Seifulmulukov is a senior research associate at IMEMO (Moscow). His specialty is the Russian oil industry.